The
Gashouse
Gang

The Gashouse Gang

by ROBERT E. HOOD

William Morrow and Company, Inc.
New York   1976

GV
875
.S3
H66
1976

Dec. 1997

Copyright © 1976 by Robert E. Hood

Grateful acknowledgment is given for permission to quote from the following sources:

"For All We Know," words by Sam M. Lewis, music by J. Fred Coots, TRO—
Copyright 1934 and renewed 1962, Cromwell Music, Inc., and Leo Feist, Inc.,
New York, N. Y.

"Ballad of Bitter Words" by John Kiernan, and "Song of Sorrows," by John
Kiernan, Copyright 1934, The New York Times Company.

American Heroes and Hero Worship by Gerald W. Johnson, published by
Harper & Row, Inc., New York, N. Y.

The St. Louis Post-Dispatch for columns and editorials from 1934.

Printed in the United States of America.

1 2 3 4 5   80 79 78 77 76

Library of Congress Cataloging in Publication Data

Hood, Robert E
  The Gashouse Gang.

  Includes index.
  1. St. Louis. Baseball club (National League)
I. Title.
GV875.S3H66   796.357'64'0977866   75-34255
ISBN 0-688-03017-3

For Ann and Sterling,
who kept me writing;
and John and Morris,
who saved my life.

Acknowledgments

THANKS to all who helped me write this book. I cannot list every name, but I am particularly indebted to those members of the 1934 St. Louis Cardinals who granted me interviews and answered questions by mail and over the telephone. I would not have finished without the strong support and help of four people. My wife, Ann, who did much of the library research and tolerated my crankiness under pressure. Bob Broeg, sports editor of the St. Louis *Post-Dispatch,* who is *the* expert on Cardinals baseball, helped by drawing on his memory and by lending moral support. Gene Karst rates a special salute for checking the manuscript and for a stream of letters full of tips and information. Special also was the help of Stan Isle of *The Sporting News,* who dug up the names and addresses of the Gashouse Gang and other players of that era.

My thanks to Bill Libby for interviewing and photographing Jack Rothrock; to Victor Orsatti for his detailed recollections of his brother, Ernie; and to Jim Brosnan for editorial help and research assistance. Special thanks and gratitude to Lillian Mussel who made valuable suggestions and who gave freely of her spare time to check this manuscript.

Several sources proved invaluable, among them the lively and colorful St. Louis *Post-Dispatch.* Three books were especially helpful and I recommend them to all: *Who's Who in Professional Baseball* by Gene Karst and Martin J. Jones, Jr.; *The St. Louis Cardinals* by Frederick Lieb; and, of course, *The Gashouse Gang and a Couple of Other Guys* by J. Roy Stockton, who covered the team in its uproarious days.

7

Contents

9

10   *Contents*

Cast of Characters

SAMUEL "LUCKY SAM" BREADON, *president*—Tight-fisted but level-headed, he never complained when his players ate high on the hog.

JAMES OTTO "TEX" CARLETON, *pitcher*—Proud and sensitive, he felt he should win twenty games every year but he melted in the heat.

JAMES ANTHONY "RIP" COLLINS, *first baseman*—A jolly fellow who slugged the ball hard and sparkled on radio shows.

CLIFFORD RANKIN "PAT" CRAWFORD, *utility man*—This great pinch hitter was a courtly Southerner who resented having to play baseball for a living.

VIRGIL LAWRENCE "SPUD" DAVIS, *catcher*—A dependable man, especially when the ducks were on the pond.

JAY HANNA "DIZZY" DEAN, *pitcher*—Baseball's ultimate braggart, and for a season its ultimate pitcher.

PAUL DEE "DAFFY" DEAN, *pitcher*—A quiet man, there was nothing daffy about him except his fast ball, which made batters look silly.

WILLIAM PINKNEY "KO" DELANCEY, *catcher*—Destined for a brilliant career, tragedy cut him down in his prime.

LEO ERNEST "LIPPY" DUROCHER, *shortstop*—You'd think he was

11

born ten thousand dollars in debt the way he hustled to make a buck.

FRANK FRANCIS "THE FORDHAM FLASH" FRISCH, *manager and second baseman*—An over-the-top leader, he sometimes looked back, and nobody was following.

CHARLES PHILLIP "CHICK" FULLIS, *outfielder*—Steady at the plate and fast in the field, his career ended on a sad note.

MIGUEL ANGEL CORDERO "MIKE" GONZALEZ, *coach*—He was "one smart dummy," this Cubano.

JESSE JOSEPH "POP" HAINES, *pitcher*—Brave men bolted when this quiet gentleman lost his temper.

WILLIAM ANTHONY "WILD BILL" HALLAHAN, *pitcher*—He was unassuming and reserved, but broken fingers couldn't keep him off the mound.

FRANCIS JEREMIAH "FATHER" HEALY, *catcher*—Serious and pious, you hardly knew he was around.

JOHN LEONARD "PEPPER" MARTIN, *infielder*—He ran the bases like an express train, and drove his manager up the wall.

JOSEPH MICHAEL "MUSCLES" MEDWICK, *outfielder*—The moody slugger swung at anything near the plate, including an occasional teammate.

JIM IRVING MOONEY, *pitcher*—He could pick a runner off first faster than you could say Kenesaw Mountain Landis.

ERNEST RALPH "SHOWBOAT" ORSATTI, *outfielder*—In Hollywood, he doubled for Buster Keaton; in St. Louis, he singled for Frankie Frisch.

WESLEY BRANCH RICKEY, *general manager and vice-president*—Pious but shrewd, he'd swap you a loaf of bread for a bakery any day.

JOHN HUSTON "JACK" ROTHROCK, *outfielder*—He played every inning of every game and was in the middle of most rallies.

CLARENCE ARTHUR "DAZZY" VANCE, *pitcher*—At age forty-three, his wit was as sharp as his curve ball.

WILLIAM HENRY "BILL" WALKER, *pitcher*—He dressed like an English gentleman and pitched like an American star.

CLYDE ELLSWORTH "BUZZY" WARES, *coach*—He pranced the coaching box and chattered about stocks and bonds—even though he didn't own a single share.

BURGESS URQUHART "WHITEY" WHITEHEAD, *infielder*—He wore a Phi Beta Kappa key and moved like a gazelle.

The Gashouse Gang and Me

IT ALL STARTED during the 1934 season when even the moon looked like a baseball hanging seamless in the sky. Sometime that year a hero slipped into my mind: Joseph Michael Medwick, called "Ducky" by the fans and "Muscles" by his friends. Good old Ducky-Wucky, the Muscular Magyar, the Hammerin' Hungarian.

I grew up in Mildred, Pennsylvania, a town of 1,000 people guarded by a dike of green hills sprinkled with laurel in the summer and flinty with snow in the winter. The remoteness of the place—Wilkes-Barre was forty-eight miles and a world away—and the lack of heroic happenings created a perfect climate for fantasy. There was the unspoken feeling that the village was dying. The railroad had stopped running when the coal mine shut down. There was no bus service. The roads were narrow and twisting. Few people owned cars or had telephones. Indoor plumbing and central heating were luxuries for those with "steady" jobs—the schoolteachers and clergymen and merchants, the postmaster and the owner of the sawmill. And, of course, the proprietors of the beer gardens, which *always* stayed in business.

During Prohibition, Mildred was a mecca for the thirsty. Once a stranger stopped a native in the street above the town. "Where can a fellow get a drink?" he whispered. The native answered in a slurred voice:

"See that building?" He pointed to the Catholic Church. "Yes."

"See the building right below and the one way over on the other hill? They're all churches. Any other house in town—you can get a drink."

The young men of the town loved to play baseball, and local fans overpraised them, believing, in their adult fantasies, that their boys were "fast" enough to play professional ball. For the most part, they were semipros at best. But sometimes professional ringers were imported from the big coal cities, from Scranton and Wilkes-Barre, Luzerne and Nanticoke, players with names like Comorosky and Witek, Sabol and Suder. On such a glorious Sunday, the old ball park would bulge and there would be a huge picnic and supper after the game, and later a dance.

The ball park stood on a hill above town, screened by a thick belt of trees from the nearby coal mine and its mounds of culm. A dirt road wound through the trees past clapboard houses. A huge old grandstand sat like a cathedral in the side of the hill, and the entire field was surrounded by a fence. It was a thing of beauty, this fence, towering with sparkling billboards: "SHOP AT HOFFMAN'S FOR SHOES AND SUITS" . . . "WEED'S BREWERY—THE BEST BEER IN TOWN" . . . "HIT THIS SIGN AND GET A FREE HAIRCUT AT TONY'S BARBER SHOP". . .

I saw myself, Muscles Medwick, standing at the plate, big brown hat cocked behind my right ear, the bases loaded, the grandstand chanting: "We want a hit, we want a hit, we want a hit." The pitch came in belt-high, the bat a blur of power, the ball soaring over second base, rising right over the letter "H" in Hoffman's . . .

The grandstand was packed on a Fourth of July. The fans overflowed onto the hillside along the right-field foul line where men in straw hats sat in the shade drinking beer iced in tin tubs. The women were in the grandstand wearing their Sunday finest and fanning themselves against the heat caused by the sun hammering against the tarpaper roof. After the game the fans walked down the hill to Connell's Park to enjoy the picnic supper. Men, women and children moved in a stream of dust that powdered the leaves of the trees that lined the road.

The ballplayers showed up later, faces reddened from the sun, hair wet from showering and slick with vaseline. They looked neat and powerful and they didn't have to stand in line. They went right into the dining hall while we waited, driven wild by the sight and smell of a country meal.

Inside you could see women and girls bustling with hot platters of meat and pitchers of steaming coffee. My mouth still waters for that fried chicken. Rusty-brown and buttery looking, it nestled on the plate next to big fluffy dumplings, snowy mashed potatoes swimming in gravy and juicy corn on the cob. Big platters of homemade bread—brown bread and white bread and raisin bread—moved up and down the long table, and hands reached out to lather it with melting butter. All this was washed down with glasses of ice-cold milk, followed by a chunk of chocolate cake or a slice of apple pie a la mode. Afterward you wandered in the shady groves among the concession stands watching adults pitch pennies for prizes, killing time until the dance started that evening.

> *"For all we know we may never meet again,*
> *Before you go make this moment sweet again."*

That tune lingers in my mind, reminding me of my uncle, Skinny, who played piano and had his own dance band. He taught me to play and hoped I'd become a concert pianist someday. But that was too prosaic a dream for a disciple of Muscles Medwick.

I was sick almost constantly from birth until the age of eight. Chicken pox, mumps, whooping cough, measles, six-day measles, English and German measles, chocolate and vanilla measles, all brands and all flavors—I caught everything. In the winter of '33 at age seven, I caught scarlet fever, which terrified my mother and father and quarantined the house. Outside, the snow drifted two feet deep and the temperatures dropped to twenty below zero. The windows frosted so solid you couldn't even see out, but once I crept to the windowpane and scratched a tiny round peephole with my fingernail to watch the wild winter.

My parents had moved my bed into their bedroom to keep an eye on me. It was a funny old bed with iron bars on one side that slid up and down. At night it was fastened tightly so I wouldn't roll out as I thrashed about feverishly. For a long, long time I was burning up and dreamed that wild animals were dragging me away from home. The nightmare stretched on and on. I lay close to death. Then, one day in February of '34, I broke out in a dreadful sweat and the fever vanished. I still can see the big grin on Dad's face as he leaned over the bed and placed his broad hand on my brow. He was a short, stocky man with forearms like Popeye's.

My mother worried that I would be "left with something," a weak heart or bad eyes. While I was recovering she wouldn't even let me read the books and magazines by my bed. Tom Swift and the Hardy Boys and Zane Grey were stacked against a pile of magazines—*The Shadow, Flying Aces,* baseball magazines and my brother's copies of *The Sporting News.* Instead she read to me, but not from my books and magazines—from books of poetry! It wasn't as awful as I thought it would be. She had a flair for dramatic reading and a special affection for Tennyson. Snatches of verse echoed in my head for years ". . . One equal temper of heroic hearts,/ Made weak by time and fate, but strong in will/ To strive, to seek, to find, and not to yield."

After recovering from scarlet fever, I wasn't sick again for many years. It was as though the fever burned away all germs in an act of purification.

That spring there was no holding me. I lit on my feet

with a whoop and started running, and ran all summer and for many a summer thereafter. I loved to see how fast I could go. I hated the thought that anybody might outrun me, even the thought that Jesse Owens was faster made me fret.

There were two major events in 1934, the first taking place in April shortly after my eighth birthday. My sister got married, and a dozen of us kids hid behind the groom's 1933 Ford V-8 to ambush the newlyweds as they tried to sneak into our house. We shouted, drummed on tin cans, blew whistles in a hideous racket known as "belling." Trapped by the childish herd, the groom had to pay ransom before he could spend that first night with his bride. My brother-in-law, Clyde, a lanky six-footer, cheerfully led us to the ice-cream parlor where we loaded up on vanilla cones, sundaes, banana splits and sodas. It must have cost him all of six dollars, a terrible price to pay for a first night with my sister, who couldn't possibly do anything worth the fee.

The other important event was the victory of the Cardinals over the Tigers in the World Series: the Dean brothers winning four of the seven games; Ducky Medwick being escorted from the field by police; the Cardinals' sharp needling of Schoolboy Rowe and Mickey Cochrane; the savage base running of both teams.

The major events of '34 left me untouched: the birth of the Dionne quintuplets in Canada, the burning of the *Morro Castle* off the Jersey coast, the assassination of Chancellor Dollfuss of Austria. I do remember my grandfather lecturing on the evils of Dr. Townsend's old-age pension plan, which would "bust" the country. My mother and sister, Doris, went to see *It Happened One Night,* and chattered on about how *wonderful* Claudette Colbert was, and wasn't Clark Gable the handsome dog. Gooey! They also *whispered* a good deal about the capture of Bruno Richard Hauptmann, the kidnapper and killer of the Lindbergh baby. They shut up in midsentence when I entered the room. It was enough to make a boy believe there was a *Something* that women didn't want you to hear because it might stunt your growth.

That June in 1934 we gathered in the living room to listen to the Heavyweight Championship of the World, fought between Max Baer and Primo Carnera. How could any man beat Carnera, a giant of six feet six and a half inches, weighing 260 pounds? Baer knocked him out in the eleventh round and collected $40,000 for winning. Carnera got $112,000 for losing. How could a loser get more than a winner? The whole business seemed unfair. Why should either fighter make so much money? What could they possibly do with it? How could they carry it home? It wasn't right when our entire family was living on $15 a week. Anyway, who were Baer and Carnera compared to Ducky Medwick? Why, I bet my father, Medwick could beat both of them in the same ring. Wasn't he the Hammerin' Hungarian; also, the *Bellwether* of the Cards as well as being a *Stormy Petrel*. What was a bellwether? A stormy petrel? I wondered.

The walls of my bedroom were papered with baseball photographs, big glossy prints—mostly of Medwick—kneeling in the on-deck circle, standing at the plate, following through on a vicious swing; sliding into third; a big close-up of his smiling face with an autograph scrawled, "Joe Medwick." One fall day I wrote an essay for a class assignment, "The Man I Admire Most—Joseph Michael Medwick." The teacher was a powerful six-footer who doubled as coach of all school sports. He was dumbfounded by the essay and his reaction stunned me. Evidently, I had picked an improper hero. The class assignment obviously demanded Lincoln, Jefferson or Franklin D. Roosevelt.

"Medwick!" The teacher was red in the face, and sputtered as he pointed at me. "Medwick? Why, his arms are bigger than your legs!"

His arms are bigger than your legs. The sentence rang

in my ears. What a crazy thing to say, I can remember thinking. It also was a crushing thing, puzzling to me, perhaps even an expression of bewilderment on the teacher's part —but it was exactly right!

His arms were bigger than my legs. I was a skinny, freckle-faced runt longing to be a famous slugger. Me. Muscles Hood, five feet ten, 180 pounds, iron-hard body with arms thick as fence posts, flicking the big brown bat like a fly-swatter. Crouching slightly, teeth clenched, glaring at the pitcher pale on the mound, powerful hands grinding sawdust from the bat.

My infatuation with Medwick led me to adopt his team, the Gashouse Gang, a lean, tough and hard-nosed bunch. I aped their style as a teen-ager, strutting around with a chew of tobacco in my cheek.

During World War II, I expended a good deal of my energy playing center field and managing a baseball team. Afterward, in the spring of 1947, I found myself in Troy, Alabama. A sleepy litle town of 8,000 people, it was the training site for the Williamsport Tigers of the Class A Eastern League—a league noted for its fast brand of baseball, a "pitcher's league."

The team had left Williamsport one day in March in a bus loaded with players and baggage and equipment. My photograph appeared in the local newspaper, grinning out the bus window, head to head with a pitcher named Rankin Johnson, an "old" man of thirty who was viewed with awe by the players. He had pitched for the Philadephia Athletics in 1941 (seven games, 1–0 record). Also aboard was a tiny shortstop named Clem Koshorek, who later played for the Pirates in 1952–53. Koshorek made me feel powerful; he was about a half inch shorter than I. The sight of him at short and me at third base in practice must have made the manager shudder.

I had switched from center field to third base the year before, in the mistaken notion that you didn't have to hit so hard to play third as you did as an outfielder. Unfortunately, there were three other third basemen in camp, each larger, stronger and a heavier hitter than I. No amount of chatter or hustle could conceal my mediocrity from the steady eye of George Francis Detore, the manager. A stocky, balding man, he had once played for Cleveland, and—just my luck!—had been a third baseman.

My recollections of the brief stint as a near-pro are like quick flashbacks in a Bergman movie—a race from the right-field foul line to the center-field fence in which I tied for second . . . hitting line drive after line drive, an unbelievable performance in the batting cage . . . college girls sitting in the bleachers during a workout . . . That evening my friend, an outfielder, gave me the word: "Skipper wants to see you."

I can still see George Detore sitting in his hotel room, his eyes sad and gentle, his voice kind. After the preliminaries—"You hit the ball pretty good, but—" he leaned toward me: "Do you have any money to get home?"

"I have plenty." I blushed. He frowned and reached into his pocket for his wallet. "Don't be embarrassed. I'll let you have some money." He started to remove some twenty-dollar bills.

I was flustered. "No, George, honest. I have money."

"Let's see it," he said, not believing me.

I had to show this kindly "oldster" my book of traveler's checks. I haven't seen manager Detore since that mournful day when I didn't thank him enough for a kindness that kindles memory.

In 1974, I wrote George asking his recollection of my performance that spring in Alabama. It must have puzzled the old manager to hear from an obscure infielder after all those years. Weeks went by. Finally, he replied, his letter a manly effort to be kind.

"I regret to say," he wrote, "that I don't remember much

of you at all. No matter how I racked my brains, I always end up with only your name."

And Detore concluded, "I am sorry I can't give you anything definite on your ability, because if I do, I would only be lying . . ."

Couldn't you tell just one little lie, George?

My pro baseball career lasted two weeks, two days and twelve hours, followed by an eternal train ride from Birmingham to Atlanta, from Charlotte to Raleigh to Richmond, an endless tunnel through the old Confederacy, where I dearly longed to linger as a tiny star in Alabama (Lord, was that asking too much?).

This and other experiences did not dampen my enthusiasm for baseball. I continued to play: four years in college, another tryout with a Class A team, a summer in an industrial league and back home in Mildred, Pa.

To this day I sometimes find myself in front of a mirror and, instead of shaving, I fall into a new batting stance, holding an imaginary Louisville Slugger and glaring at a phantom pitcher. This is not as silly as it sounds. There are literally thousands of middle-aged almost-pros in our land, American Baseball Addicts (ABAs). They wear warm-up jackets and little-league caps. You can spot them in the supermarkets wheeling their wife's grocery cart as though they were slouching in from the bullpen or strutting up to pinch hit.

Baseball is the only American game that can sustain such a lifetime fantasy. I think this is so because it is the only team sport that is suitable for an individualist. During a long interview in his home in North Carolina, Pat Crawford discussed that theory at length. A great pinch hitter for the Gashouse Gang and a sharp student of baseball, Crawford declared:

"Baseball is a game of records. Each man is involved in making just as good a record as possible. If each member plays well the team should be a winner. As far as helping the other guy when he goes to the plate—well, he's on his own. It's not like a backfield man carrying the ball—he's got to have blockers. But a batter's on his own. Baseball's less of a team game than either football or basketball. About the only way you can say it is a team effort is getting together-ness, encouraging players to pull for each other."

Togetherness? That's a sugary word to describe the Gas-house Gang. Yet they certainly had that feeling in 1934. There were fistfights, players complained about the manager, the Dean brothers went on strike—through it all, on the field, they played as a single unit to edge out a strong New York Giants team for the National League pennant. Then they beat Detroit in one of the roughest World Series ever.

Although they weren't the greatest team ever to take the field, six of the Gashouse Gang made baseball's Hall of Fame. The first was manager Frankie Frisch. A dynamic second baseman and switch-hitter, the Fordham Flash was picked in 1947. Next came Dizzy Dean in 1953. Dizzy won only 150 games in his big-league career, but at his peak he was a sensational player. Dazzy Vance, who had won his first major-league game at age thirty-one, was elected in 1955. Nearly all his 197 victories had come while toiling for the ragtag Brooklyn Dodgers. In 1968, after years of waiting, Joe "Muscles" Medwick won his place in Cooperstown. He had collected nearly 2,500 hits, many of them off pitches most batters couldn't reach, let alone sock. Jesse "Pop" Haines was elected in 1970. In eighteen years with the Cardinals, Haines had won 210 games. The sixth "member" of the old gang made the Hall of Fame in 1967, when Branch Rickey was voted in. Imaginative and innovative, Rickey had re-shaped the game of hard ball by perfecting the farm system and breaking the color line by signing the great Jackie Robinson. He also had forced Major League expansion through his work with the Continental League.

Baseball was a lot different then. It hadn't evolved to the

pure business status of today, with its spastic scoreboards and synthetic grass. There were no major-league games played under the lights in '34. Baseball was played in the sun on real grass. Although this was a grim decade, the players had fun and so did the fans who were closer to the field than they ever get today. It was an intimate sport, not the TV spectacle the game has now become. That era is gone, and we shall never see those days again.

This book is about the days of the Gashouse Gang, about the players and coaches and top management, and about baseball as played in the Depression.

Nineteen thirty-four began on a happy note. Prohibition had been repealed the previous year and the people ratified it with glasses on high to the tune of "Sweet Adeline." There was optimism in the air, a sense of recovery as the new year began and, Depression or not, it was time to whoop it up. It was the year of the Gashouse Gang, the perfect team to lighten gloomy days.

Nothing changes more constantly than the past; for the past that influences our lives does not consist of what actually happened but of what men believe happened.

—GERALD W. JOHNSON,
*American Heroes and
Hero Worship*

PART ONE

THE GATHERING
OF THE GANG

1

Stormy Weather

THE MAN CAME UP the stairs so rapidly he sounded as though he were taking them two at a time. One of the clerks looked up from his desk and grinned: That *had* to be Sam Breadon. Nobody else ran that fast. The old man was probably in better shape than most ballplayers, especially at this time of year, February 1934. The clerk glanced at his watch: 10:15 A.M., the normal time for President Breadon to start work.

Sam Breadon walked brisky through the outside hall, opened the office door, and waved as he passed secretary Mary Murphy. He stopped to talk to Bill DeWitt, the treasurer of the Cardinals, then turned and disappeared into his office, closing the door behind him. He hung up his coat and moved toward his desk, which was neat and tidy, exactly the way he liked it. Silver-haired, with blue eyes, ruddy skin and regular features, Sam Breadon was a handsome man, trim and youthful looking at age fifty-seven.

Breadon had begun a typical day at 7:30 A.M., with breakfast at his comfortable but modest home on the west side of St. Louis. Then he had walked two blocks to his automobile agency where he spent an hour or so, then drove to Sportsman's Park. Now, he paused at the window, looking down on Dodier Street where an occasional car moved at a snail's pace through the slush. The sidewalk lay under a blanket of snow whose whiteness was marred only by the black smears of footprints.

Six inches of snow had fallen on St. Louis, piling up drifts and making driving hazardous. It was the largest snow-fall in four years, and children and adults were coasting and skiing on the slopes of the city parks. The editorial writer for the *Post-Dispatch* fell into a poetic trance, comparing the snowflakes to "tiny pellets which the wind dashed from the building tops and along the sidewalks."

The snow was part of a general storm that had enveloped the Midwest, disrupting train, bus and airplane travel. Only two airplanes had reached the Lambert-St. Louis airport, and through flights to New York were grounded, for the East was buried under its second blizzard in a week.

The news was as dreary as the weather. The stock market went into a three-day spin, with steels and motors the hardest hit. General Motors and Chrysler were down more than $1 each and U. S. Steel was down from fractions to $2 . . . John J. McGraw, former manager of the New York Giants, died at age sixty of uremic poisoning and cancer of the prostate gland . . . Abroad, Austrian Fascists threatened to march on Vienna and seize the government . . . In London, 15,000 police were standing by to handle an unemployment demonstration of 2,000 "hunger marchers" in Hyde Park.

About the only light news on this February morning was a bulletin out of the capital concerning President Roosevelt's newest dog. Wings, a setter pup, invaded the breakfast room of the servants' quarters and cleaned up every plate of food before being discovered. The President remarked that "the only reason the dog didn't drink the coffee was because it hadn't been poured."

In St. Louis, the temperature was falling and the *Post-Dispatch* "Weatherbird" predicted four degree above zero for the night. Sam Breadon turned from the window. Linking both hands behind his head, he leaned back in his chair, looking relaxed but thoughtful.

The year 1933 had been a poor one with the Cards wind-ing up in fifth place. They had finished seventh the pre-vious year after winning pennants in 1930 and 1931. Attendance had been poor throughout the National League, and St. Louis closed the year in the red. At a meeting of the board of directors in January, Breadon had called 1933 one of the worst seasons since those dismal days when the Cardinals could only dream of placing in the first division. No dividend was declared. This year would be different. The Cardinals should be in contention. Breadon had fired manager Gabby Street in the middle of the '33 season, replacing him with Frankie Frisch, one of his favorite players. But the move had come too late. In 1934, Frisch would start fresh, and the aggressive "Dutchman" had some exciting players to work with—Tex Carleton, Dizzy Dean, Leo Durocher, Rip Collins and Ducky Medwick *and* Pepper Martin. They were the kind of ballplayers that could win a pennant, and if they did the Cardinals would get back into black ink.

Breadon moved across the room, stopping to study a photograph on the wall. Of all the framed pictures—and there were photos of baseball stars, managers, friends—he was most proud of one. It was a group shot of a football team, circa 1891, with young Sam looking tiny in his big shoulder pads. He had been the smallest member of the team when he played for the YMCA of New York City. Now, at five feet nine inches tall, sturdy and successful, it pleased him to look back on those days when he was just beginning to fight his way up the ladder.

Breadon opened his office door and called to Bill DeWitt: "Would you ask Miss Murphy to come in, please?" Even thirty years or more in St. Louis hadn't completely erased Breadon's New York accent, and the name came out "Moiphy."

Born July 26, 1876, Samuel Breadon was the son of an Irish emigrant who worked as a drayman on New York's West Side and eventually died from overwork while only in his forties. Young Sam had had an insecure childhood, with the family moving around a good deal as the father changed jobs. Early in his youth Breadon made up his mind he was going to make something out of himself.

He moved to St. Louis around the turn of the century to work in an automobile agency, for he felt that automobiles were the wave of the future. Working for $75 a month, anxious to get ahead and start his own agency, he talked about his dream with the customers. Breadon was too bold to suit his boss, who got word of the young man's ambitions —and fired him. Suddenly, he had to scramble to survive.

Sam Breadon's savings soon disappeared. He was forced to sleep in a garage and to live on a food budget of fifteen cents a day. But he was tough and determined—and lucky. St. Louis was holding a huge parade to kick off the World's Fair of 1904. Sam Breadon had an idea he could make money by selling popcorn to the spectators. He wangled some credit and acquired 3,000 packages of popcorn, hired boys to peddle them and wound up with $35 profit. Years later he said that this was the turning point in his life. He was on his way up. Later that year he became a partner in an auto agency and made $20,000 the first year of operation.

Sam Breadon turned into a supersalesman. In one year alone he sold 280 Pierce-Arrows at a minimum of $5,000 each. By 1906, he owned the agency. As a prominent business man and baseball fan, he involved himself in a civic effort to keep the Cardinals in town. The club was down on its heels and the owner, Mrs. Helen Hathaway Britton, wanted to find some buyers. A St. Louis attorney, James C. Jones, came up with a stunt to sell shares. He called it the "Knothole Gang." Anybody who bought a share of stock for $25 could give a youngster a season's pass so he could watch from the bleachers instead of through a hole in the fence.

Within a few years the Knothole Gang was handled through schools, churches, the YMCA and other youth agencies with no money involved. A boy would be handed an identification card to present to his teacher, coach or leader, who in turn gave him passes which the youngster then presented at the ticket gate. In the beginning, to get a pass, a boy had to achieve something or to demonstrate good conduct. Later, the identification pass alone was sufficient to gain him entry into the left-field bleachers. In the long run, of course, the knothole scheme would build attendance when boys grew into manhood and became ticket buyers.

Sam Breadon bought $200 worth of stock and then $1,800 more and, before he knew it, he had lent the club an additional $18,000—just to keep the team in town. He was named to the board of directors and in 1920 was elected president. He teamed up with Branch Rickey, who had been president and field manager of the Cardinals the year before.

Wesley Branch Rickey, vice-president and general manager of the Cardinals, was a remarkable man. A former big-league catcher and manager, ex-college coach and school-teacher, trained lawyer and skilled orator, he was the highest paid executive in baseball next to Commissioner Kenesaw Mountain Landis. His salary for 1934 was over $40,000 with a bonus clause based on attendance. In addition, in the years when the club showed an annual profit he received a 10 percent cut on the sales price of each player. His annual income was over $75,000, more than the salary of the President of the United States. He was worth every cent of what he got—or Sam Breadon wouldn't have agreed to such a contract.

Rickey directed the St. Louis Cardinals' major-league team and the farm teams. He did all the hiring and firing for the Cardinals, signed all the players (unless unusual sums were involved), and supervised the movement of players throughout the minors. No player was transferred within the system or traded to another organization without his approval.

Sam Breadon and Branch Rickey were an unbeatable combination. They were also as different as whiskey and lemonade.

Breadon was a Democrat and a Scotch drinker who loved Irish ballads, which he would sing anywhere—in a locker room, a hotel or in the compartment of a train. A self-made millionaire with only a grammar school education, he was direct and honest.

Like Breadon, Branch Rickey had scrambled up the

ladder. He too had known poverty. Born in rural Ohio in 1881, Rickey, the son of a farmer, had worked hard to acquire an education. He was a Republican, a teetotaler and psalm-singing Methodist. He had promised his mother he would not go to the ball park on Sunday and, a conscientious man, he kept his promise. His idea of fun was to lecture at the YMCA or before a church group.

Sam Breadon loved to play golf, to swim and to ride horseback. He dressed neatly and was in excellent physical condition. Rickey's idea of exercise was to put in eighteen hours at his desk. He took poor care of himself and was indifferent to his appearance. Rickey could make an expensive suit look like a flour sack minutes after he put it on his back. He would walk into a hotel room, drop down on the bed fully clothed—and forget to remove his hat. He ate enormous quantities of food at odd hours, starting with a dish of ice cream!

Only the year before, in May 1933, Rickey had summoned reporters to his room to announce an important trade. He had been on the telephone most of the night and greeted the press from his bed, where he was dining. There was a big steak, a mountain of potatoes, buttered rolls, coffee and apple pie—all to be consumed before going to sleep. He interrupted his feast long enough to make a dramatic announcement:

The St. Louis Cardinals had acquired a superb shortstop, Leo Durocher. They hadn't had a good one since Charley Gelbert accidentally shot himself in the leg while hunting.

Sam Breadon considered Rickey a "blue-nose," but had enormous confidence in his general manager. It was Rickey who devised the system that turned St. Louis into a winner. To compete with the wealthy teams in Chicago, Detroit and New York, he developed a farm system—minor-league clubs in various classifications, from Class D to Double A, which would be owned by the Cardinals. The minors would be training grounds, feeding the big team with talented youngsters who could not be raided by other major-league teams with fat wallets. Breadon instantly saw the sense of the scheme and gave Rickey the kind of financial backing he needed.

Sam Breadon promoted the Sunday doubleheader as a means to stimulate attendance and keep the team prosperous. On the day of a double bill, he would stand at the window studying a coal-black, stormy sky and say: "I see some blue up there. We'll get the games in." The office staff would grin behind their hands, for there wasn't a smidgen of blue to be seen. Suddenly it had turned a little lighter. By God, it *was* clearing.

In addition to luck, he had good judgment and the rare ability to make a tough decision and stick with it. His hardest decisions involved two of baseball's greatest figures, Branch Rickey and Rogers Hornsby, the finest right-hand hitter of all time.

By 1925, the Cards had a solid baseball team; the farm system was paying off with young stars like Chick Hafey and Jim Bottomley and Flint Rhem, coming up from Fort Smith and Houston and Syracuse. The great Hornsby was at his peak with a batting average of .400 in a four-year span. Yet the team had not won a pennant. And the problem was the manager, one Branch Rickey. A genius at spotting talent, a brilliant strategist, he could not lead players to victory. Too smart, they said. Talks way over the head of the team. After the 1924 season when the team finished in sixth place, Breadon knew what must be done. He tried to get Rickey to step down, voluntarily and peacefully, but Branch just didn't want to let go. He was evasive and elusive.

In late May 1925, Sam Breadon took a train to Pittsburgh where the Cardinals were wallowing in the cellar of the National League. He summoned Rickey to his hotel room and told him he was through as a manager.

Branch Rickey protested. "You can't do this to me, Sam. You're ruining me."

Sam Breadon shook his head and replied: "I'm doing you

the greatest favor one man ever did for another." Branch Rickey was kicked upstairs to the front office where his talents could flower. Rogers Hornsby became the new manager.

In 1926, Hornsby led the Cardinals to their first pennant and a World Series victory over the New York Yankees. Breadon and Rickey and Hornsby and all the players—Jesse Haines and Bottomley, O'Farrell and old Pete Alexander —were the toast of St. Louis. Temporarily. Until Sam Breadon had to make his second tough decision, which involved the cantankerous Hornsby.

Late in the '26 season when the Cardinals were fighting for the pennant, Sam Breadon went to the clubhouse to work out a problem with Hornsby. The manager wanted Breadon to cancel an exhibition game so his tired players could have a day of rest. Breadon refused. An honorable man, he would not break his contract to play the exhibition. Hornsby began to curse Breadon.

"Get the hell out of here," he yelled at the red-faced, retreating president.

Then, after winning the World Series, Hornsby had demanded a salary of $50,000. Breadon was willing to give him a one-year contract at that figure, but Hornsby demanded a three-year agreement. So Sam Breadon traded the greatest hitter in the National League and the manager of the Cardinals' first winning team to New York for second-baseman Frank Frisch and pitcher Jimmy Ring.

The city of St. Louis erupted. The Chamber of Commerce denounced Breadon. The newspapers attacked him with savage editorials. He was abused in person and on the telephone. Irate citizens hung crepe on the doors of his auto agency and even on the front door of his home. Fans threatened to boycott the ball park. Then along came Frankie Frisch. Playing like a madman, the spectacular "Fordham Flash" made St. Louis forget Hornsby.

Frisch could do everything on a baseball field. He could

run like a streak and steal a base with a swooping slide. He could hit from either side of the plate, and do so with power. He was an agile bulldog of a fielder, knocking down hot grounders and pouncing on them like an angry tomcat. An electrifying player, he batted .337 in 1927, collected 208 hits, stole forty-eight bases and hit ten home runs. Running, fielding and hitting, he captivated the fans of St. Louis, who flocked to Sportsman's Park.

The Cardinals lost the pennant on the last day of the season, but the fans forgave Sam Breadon. "I'll always be thankful to Frankie Frisch for saving me in St. Louis," Breadon said.

Breadon learned a lot from the Hornsby-Frisch episode: Never again would he be afraid to trade a star or fire a manager. When Bob O'Farrell didn't work out as a manager, he replaced him with Bill McKechnie. When McKechnie didn't deliver the Series victory in 1928, Breadon brought in Billy Southworth, who gave way to McKechnie (who returned in 1929). McKechnie didn't stay long the second time. The Boston Braves offered him a better deal, a long-term contract at more money. He took it, partly to erase the humiliation of his first dismissal, which Breadon had admitted was a mistake.

Gabby Street succeeded McKechnie. The "Old Sarge," as he was called, survived until late July 1933. Street had alienated his key players—Frisch, Jimmy Wilson and Pepper Martin—by taking the credit for winning the two pennants. When they rebelled, he wasn't strong enough to crack the whip over their heads. Frankie Frisch was the kind of firebrand the Cardinals needed. At least, Sam Breadon was convinced of that and he had final say on the choice of managers.

By 1934, Breadon owned about 75 percent of the stock in the club. Widely respected as a businessman, he was considered a penny pincher by many people. Outsiders thought he was flinty and miserly. Insiders knew that this was not so. Breadon had struggled to get ahead, to escape hunger and poverty, but money could not erase his insecurity. It went too deep. He was always afraid of losing all his money and possessions. This fear caused him to shake a tight fist at the world.

Early in the Depression, he walked into the office of the traveling secretary, Clarence Lloyd, and pointed at an electric clock. "How much current does that use?" he asked. Lloyd didn't even bother to answer. He simply disconnected the clock. Several years later it remained unplugged. During the early years of the Depression, Breadon cut the salaries of his office force, his managers and his players, earning the label of "Cut-Rate Sam." Yet the salaries of the Cardinals were above average for the league. And Breadon never quibbled about the players' meal money when they were on the road. Even when some of the boys ate more than a trencherman could consume, he approved payment without protest, that is, as long as they didn't get frivolous and try to slip in a bottle of booze.

Still, Breadon kept a careful eye on the cash register. He had to restrain Branch Rickey because the dynamic general manager was inclined to spend money faster than Breadon wanted to. With all their differences, outsiders wondered how Breadon and Rickey could work so well together. By 1934, they had brought four pennants and two world titles to town. They had a strong common bond: They both were winners who would shuffle managers and players to bring a pennant to St. Louis. And they were determined to have another championship team in the coming year.

While Sam Breadon was working quietly in his office and Branch Rickey was working not so quietly in his, several of their players were popping up on the sports page. Dizzy Dean was a "professor" of pitching at a baseball school in Hot Springs. From his podium in Arkansas, Professor Dean predicted he would win twenty-three games in the coming season.

Outfielder Joe Medwick had been around for two weeks,

taking daily treatments for a charley horse from the club physician, Dr. Robert Hyland. Medwick, who lived in New Jersey, had fled the bitter Eastern weather for the dubious sanctuary of Missouri. "I almost froze to death during that last cold spell," he said.

Leo Durocher came to town the week before the blizzard for an exhibition match of pocket billiards. His opponent, Frank Taberski, the former world champion, outclassed the shortstop 100–64. But Durocher, with runs of 23 and 21, proved again that he was the best pool shot in the big leagues.

John Leonard "Pepper" Martin drove to St. Louis to sign his contract. The hero of the 1931 World Series, the "Wild Horse of the Osage," wasn't prepared for the cold weather. He was decked out in a summer suit and a light topcoat. Pepper had had a busy winter as a hunter and public speaker. He told an interviewer that he had attended fifty "literaries" to preach the gospel of the great American game of baseball. The literary life was risky, he declared, particularly in Oklahoma where folks still drank "battery acid" and strummed "gitars" late into the night. A "literary" such as Martin was a source of mirth to a hooched-up Okie.

Pepper was scheduled to drive to spring training with a teammate. One year he had arrived in camp aboard a freight train. Another he had driven into town in an old car carrying two bird dogs and a shotgun. En route he had stopped at a small hotel where, dressed in overalls and carrying the gun, he had signed the register: "Pretty Boy Floyd." Minutes later an armed posse arrived at his door led by the town's sheriff who, frustrated at not finding the notorious bandit, shook his fist under Martin's nose.

Within a month, St. Louis would take thirty-four players to Bradenton, Florida. Eleven would have to be cut from the roster before May 15. Manager Frankie Frisch faced some tough decisions as spring training drew near.

2

Spring Training

IT DIDN'T MATTER where you were or what the weather was like. When March rolled in, winter was over—if you were a big-league ballplayer. You packed up and headed for Bradenton, the Florida training base of the St. Louis Cardinals. Young Paul Dean was already there because Bradenton had become his winter home. So was veteran pitcher Bill Hallahan, who lived in Binghamton, New York. Hallahan had left Binghamton ten days ahead of the rising waters of the Chenango and Susquehanna rivers, which threatened to flood the city in early March.

Catcher-coach Mike Gonzalez flew in from Havana. Outfielder Ernie Orsatti drove from California, even though he was officially a holdout. Veteran right-hand pitcher Jesse Haines motored from Hot Springs and rookie catcher Bill DeLancey was en route from Greensboro, North Carolina.

In Lewiston, N.C., 160 miles to the east, infielder Burgess Whitehead was about to leave. Accompanying him was his younger brother, Lewis, a speedy, hard-hitting outfielder slated for minor-league duty with Mobile. For his part, Burgess "Whitey" Whitehead, was sure he would make the majors this year. In 1933, he played twelve games with the Cards before being sent to Columbus to help win the pennant in the American Association. A brilliant second baseman, Whitey hit .346 as one of the stars of the Columbus team that captured the "Little World Series."

Outfielder Jack Rothrock remained in Columbus for the winter to work as a tie salesman in a department store. He, too, was anxious to get to Bradenton. The twenty-eight-year-old had spent eight years with the Boston Red Sox and Chicago White Sox before dropping back to the minors in '33. A switch-hitter and all-around player, he hoped to be back in the big leagues with a strong team.

In Fort Worth, Tex Carleton finished packing. His black Hupmobile stood in front of his mother's house where the Carletons had been visiting for several weeks. His vivacious wife, Fanny, came down the steps looking lovely in a white dress that reached nearly to her ankles. The Carletons were on their way to New Orleans where Fanny would stay with her parents while Tex was in training. He would leave the car in New Orleans and take a train to Florida, a trip of some twenty hours, a lot of time to think about the coming season. Carleton had won seventeen games in 1933: this year he wanted to win twenty. He could do it, too, if he didn't wilt in the blistering heat. Most ballplayers reported in at ten pounds overweight, much to the displeasure of their managers. Tall and slim, Carleton was checking in at 176 pounds, which left no fat to be boiled off in the heat of a pennant race. His thinness was a source of worry to the front office in St. Louis.

Frankie Frisch arrived in St. Louis on March 1 after attending the funeral of John McGraw, his old mentor. The newspapers also reported that on the same day Eleanor Roosevelt spoke to a group of 3,000 women, urging them "to aid in reforms under the New Deal," so that the "lessons of the Depression shouldn't be forgotten." Gloria Swanson denied the rumors that she and Michael Farmer were heading for the divorce courts. Warden Frank Whipp of Joliet, Illinois, sent gangster Roger Touhy to the new state penitentiary to serve his ninety-nine-year sentence for the kidnapping of John (Jake the Barber) Factor. From the nation's capital came the report of a "sharp drop in federal spending during February—decline from $980,000,000 in January to $635,000,000 last month."

In St. Louis, Mayor "Barney" Dickmann proclaimed March 3 and 4 to be the "First Anniversary of National Recovery in St. Louis." Local merchants supported the mayor's proclamation with a salvo of sales, celebrating the success of the New Deal.

At Scruggs-Vandervoort-Barney, ladies could buy a bouclé dress and suit for $10. Wolff-Wilson's announced a weekend sale of drugs and toiletries: cod-liver oil for seventy-nine cents a quart, a bottle of bay rum for seventy-nine cents and a pint of Lone Tree whiskey for eighty-nine cents. As a special treat, customers could get a fried chicken dinner with potatoes, string beans, corn bread and butter—all for twenty-five cents. A local Ford agency advertised a V-8 coupe for $615. At Hellrung & Grimm, a furniture and appliance store, electric refrigerators were on sale for $97.50, gas ranges for $59.75 and electric washers for $29.95.

The weather in St. Louis was cloudy on March 1, with "fair and warmer" predicted for the following day. In his office at Sportsman's Park, Branch Rickey signed the last letter on his desk, added it to a foot-high stack of correspondence, and rose heavily from his chair. The team's general manager was ready for the long ride to Florida, as a passenger in the comfortable Cadillac of a local businessman and friend, Walter Weisenburger, president of the National Association of Manufacturers. Gene Karst, director of information, planned to leave later in the day, driving down in Rickey's Buick. Sam Breadon would depart the next afternoon by car.

Manager Frisch sat in Breadon's office, conferring with the president about the coming season. Frisch was to leave St. Louis on Saturday with a small party of players and officials. As spring training drew near, the pressure mounted. He had managed the Cardinals from late July in 1933 to the end of the season, but this would be the first time he would lead a team into training. There were fundamentals to be taught—sliding, bunting, tagging out opponents in a rundown, showing a pitcher how to hold a runner on base.

He also had to find a suitable style of managing, natural to him, while avoiding the ways of John McGraw, the old martinet. The year before, Frisch had taken over from the easygoing Gabby Street, and some of his players had bristled at the strictness of his discipline. There was to be no heavy drinking or gambling and everybody had to be in his hotel bed by midnight. In his first speech to the troops, Manager Frisch had spoken like a Prussian general.

"There'll be no loafing out there on the field" he shouted. "Look at that big crowd. Give them their money's worth. No clowning, mind you, or it's going to be just too bad. Bear down from start to finish!"

The speech had to be made. The players had been taking advantage of Gabby. Frisch's toughness didn't win many friends, but then managing wasn't meant to be a personality contest. He did not believe in complimenting a man who made a good play. Professionals shouldn't expect praise for doing what they were paid good money to do. However, as spring training got under way, Frankie Frisch knew he had to modify his stern tactics.

"All I ask of any of my players is to do his best," Frisch told a sportswriter from the *Post-Dispatch*. "That's all any of us can ask. We will have only the usual sound rules in effect that are in effect on other teams. There will be a time for the players to go to bed and another time for them to get up. But that's only common sense."

Frisch was intelligent and educated, with a variety of interests other than baseball. He liked books, plays and classical music. He was an amateur gardener, he collected pipes, he was a world traveler who knew how to handle a wine list. He also was a fierce competitor, a proud and determined man. Managing was another great challenge in his dynamic career.

His first test had come in 1919 when he joined the New York Giants after graduating from Fordham where he had starred in football, basketball and baseball. The Giants had offered him a $400-a-month contract plus a bonus of $200. Frisch accepted over the objection of his German-born father, a wealthy linen importer, who considered baseball a profession for lowbrows. But Frisch wouldn't play in the minors. He insisted on playing in the big leagues, and his flashy play and high spirits won the respect of John McGraw, who enjoyed needling the youngster by calling him "College Boy." Frisch had some great years under McGraw, playing on four straight pennant winners from 1921 through 1924, with respective batting averages of .341, .327, .348 and .328. He also led the National League in stolen bases in 1921, and McGraw paid him high tribute by naming him captain of the Giants.

Frisch was McGraw's "boy," destined to be the next manager of the team, until he fell out with the old master in 1926. He did the unthinkable. He talked back to the old man. Then on a road trip, the angry Frisch jumped the club and went home to New Rochelle. After cooling off, he returned to play out the season, but that was the end of his career with the Giants. He was traded to St. Louis for Hornsby, which angered him. "There's no way I'll go to St. Louis," Frisch said. Like George M. Cohan, he considered that "anything west of Broadway is Hoboken." Eventually, he relented and prepared himself for the move.

In the winter of 1926, Frisch and his wife went to Saranac Lake where he would train like a prizefighter to be ready for the challenge waiting in Missouri. This was one of the reasons he had such a spectacular season, winning the gratitude of Sam Breadon: "In all the years I have had the Cardinals," Sam said, "no player ever played ball for me as Frank Frisch did in 1927."

Frisch continued his fine play in 1928, and the Cards won the pennant but lost the Series to the Yankees. In 1930, Frisch again had a fine year, the Cards won the pennant but lost the Series to Connie Mack's Athletics. In 1931, Frisch hit .311, the Cards won again, and Frankie and Pepper Martin ran like wild ponies as the Cards racked up the Philadelphia Athletics. From 1927 through 1931, Frisch helped the Cardinals capture three pennants and one World Championship. He led the league in stolen bases in '27 and '31, when he was named the most valuable player in the National League. (He had demonstrated that he could replace Rogers Hornsby.) It was the second great success of his career.

When Frankie Frisch took over as manager of the Cardinals, he had ranked as one of baseball's great second basemen, in a class with Eddie Collins, Napolean Lajoie and Rogers Hornsby. By 1934, his fielding had slowed down but he was still one of the game's great money players, and an excellent switch-hitter. In his day, he had remarkable physical ability. He could easily go from first to third base on a hit to left field; he once scored from second on a routine fly ball. As a second baseman, he handled 1,037 fielding chances in 1927 to establish a major-league record. A sports reporter once asked manager Joe McCarthy about the perfect baseball player, one who could hit like a Cobb, play the outfield like Speaker, throw like a Hafey.

Manager McCarthy did not hesitate to answer. "What are you going to all that trouble for? What *couldn't* Frankie Frisch do?"

On March 5 Frankie Frisch arrived in Bradenton at 12:30 P.M. and immediately put the players through their first workout. The schedule called for two practices each day, one in the morning and one in the afternoon. But since his train was three hours late, manager Frisch could only squeeze in one session. Of the players signed to contracts and scheduled to report, only second-baseman Whitehead, first-baseman Rip Collins and catcher Virgil Davis were missing. Pitchers Flint Rhem and Paul Dean and outfielders George Watkins and Ernie Orsatti were holdouts. The youngest player on the roster, Paul Dean, had come to camp to confer with Branch Rickey. Paul was asking $1,500 more than the $3,000 the Cardinals were willing to pay.

"There is nothing to say about the case," Branch Rickey announced from the Dixie Grande Hotel, headquarters of the club. "We have offered Dean a contract and it is up to him to sign it or reject it. I fear he is being advised badly. We will not conduct any negotiations with him. We have made our final offer."

Coach Mike Gonzalez was bubbling with optimism, telling everybody how great Paul Dean and Jack Rothrock had been with Columbus and how they would help the Cards win the pennant. "We have to win," the veteran catcher said. "If everybody she hustle, we win. Good year to win, too. I tell you, my friend, *we* win and St. Louis forget we had what you call him a Depression."

Frisch had his squad on the run. Literally. "There will be more running each day and more hard work as we go along," he told his men. He was a great believer in running as the best and fastest way to get in shape. And time was precious. The Cardinals would play their first exhibition game on March 14, just nine days away, against the New York Giants. From then until April 8 they would play twenty-one exhibition games before moving north for the annual five-game spring series with the rival St. Louis Browns. They had to make the training pay off. It was costly to take a team south. The total bill for the sixteen big-league teams ran to $350,000, about $20,000 per team!

Other major-league teams were hard at work, too. At St. Petersburg, Vernon "Lefty" Gomez arrived in camp roaring that he wouldn't sign until he got a better deal. Up in Orlando the Brooklyn Dodgers went through their opening drill under the direction of manager Casey Stengel. Veteran players such as Joe Stripp, Van Lingle Mungo and Hack Wilson were delighted that their manager had done away with calisthenics as a means of getting in shape. At Fort Myers Connie Mack was said to be searching for a first baseman. If Jimmy Foxx refused to sign, Mack announced he would use Lou Finney at first, and if third-baseman Pinky Higgins didn't sign his contract, George Detore would take over at the hot corner. In California, the Chicago Cubs were training on Catalina Island. Citizens of the town of Avalon turned out in large numbers to welcome such stars as Chuck Klein, Lon Warneke, Guy Bush, Gabby Hartnett, Kiki Cuyler and Billy Jurges. Woody English was absent, remaining in Los Angeles for treatment of an inflamed eye. Babe Herman was on his way after signing his contract. But two other stars, Charlie Root and Billy Herman, were holding out.

The Chicago Cubs, Pittsburgh Pirates and New York Giants were pennant contenders. The Pirates, who finished second in 1933, boasted some top hitters in outfielders Paul and Lloyd Waner and Fred Lindstrom; infielders Arky Vaughan, Pie Traynor and Gus Suhr. They had pretty good pitching, too, in Waite Hoyt, Heinie Meine, Larry French and Red Lucas.

But the real powerhouse of the National League was the Giants, led by manager and first-baseman Bill Terry. Terry and Mel Ott, Jo-Jo Moore and Lefty O'Doul gave New York batting punch. And Carl Hubbell, Hal Schumacher, Freddie Fitzsimmons and Roy Parmelee were first-rate pitchers. Pitching was about 85 percent of a winning team, as Connie Mack had proclaimed. And with Gus Mancuso catching, Hughie Critz at second base and Travis Jackson at short —they were "strong up the middle."

Now baseball people have always been addicted to axioms, which they worship like ancient tablets fetched from a far-off mountain. One axiom was that a winning team must be strong up the middle—that is in catching and pitching, with a classy double-play combination and a swift, sure-handed center fielder. As the St. Louis Cardinals went through their paces in Bradenton, there were some "iffy" ingredients in their up-the-middle department.

First, the catching. Virgil Davis was a powerful hitter who

had averaged well over .300 in his major-league career. In Bradenton, he hit the ball as everyone knew he would, day after day, lining baseballs against the fences and over the palm trees. But he was a very slow runner and as Rickey studied him, he began to have doubts that Davis was up to the standards of a pennant winner. *If* young Bill DeLancey proved as great as Gonzalez said (another Bill Dickey?), the problem would vanish. However, DeLancey was a rookie, untested by major-league play.

The pitching staff looked good, led by two right-handers, Dizzy Dean and Tex Carleton. The left-handers, Bill Hallahan and Bill Walker, would have to pitch strongly for the Cards to win. Backing them up were two forty-year-olds, Jesse "Pop" Haines, and Burleigh Grimes. Jim Mooney, a talented left-hander, had won only two games the previous year, but he had shown great promise while with the Giants in 1931 and 1932. If he could come back after his illness in '33, he would prove a big help.

Of the rookie pitchers, the most promising were Jim Winford and Paul Dean. After Paul signed his contract on March 12, his brother Dizzy, "The Great," announced: "I don't see how anybody can beat us now, with two Deans on the ball club. We'll be sure to win forty-five games between us and if we have six other pitchers they ought to account for about fifty more games on the right side of the ledger and that should put us in the World Series. It ought to be a breeze from now on."

As March drew to a close the pitching looked impressive. Walker and Bill Hallahan were firing the ball as they had in the past. The Dean brothers were blazing away. Tex Carleton had gained six pounds, and only needed a few more to be ready for the summer grind. And Flint Rhem signed his contract. Rhem had been a good pitcher in the 1920s, but he was a problem for any manager. A heavy drinker, he was capable of disappearing from the team, returning red-eyed and rumpled, with a wild alibi as to his whereabouts. He had been a drinking companion of Grover Cleveland "Pete" Alexander, one of baseball's great tipplers. Still, he was only thirty-one years old and possessed a strong right arm. He convinced Branch Rickey he could still pitch in the majors and the general manager signed him to a contract. With or without Flint Rhem, the Cardinal pitching staff looked solid.

Their infield was set with Rip Collins at first, Frisch at second, Leo Durocher at shortstop and Pepper Martin at third. Martin wasn't the fanciest third baseman in the game. He tended to field a grounder with his chest rather than his glove. But he could gun down runners in their tracks—if he didn't throw the ball into the stands. The infield reserves included hard-hitting Pat Crawford, who was primarily a first baseman but could fill in at second or third; Burgess Whitehead, who could play second, short or third; and Lew Riggs, a third baseman.

Leo Durocher was a great shortsop who knew how to play the hitters. His arm was good, his throw accurate. He could go deep to his right with the best of them, scooping up a grounder and getting off the throw in a hurry. On a double play he fed the ball to the second baseman quickly with a chest-high throw that seemed to float softly into the glove of a teammate. When he was the middleman in a double play, he could line the ball to first base while leaping high in the air. There wasn't a more acrobatic shortstop in baseball than Lippy Leo.

He was a brassy competitor, this Durocher. A former pool shark and factory worker in Springfield, Massachusetts, he had caught fire as shortstop with Hartford in the Eastern League, where his aggressiveness attracted the attention of the New York Yankees. With the Yankees he continued his fancy fielding but his weak hitting earned him the nickname of "All-American Out." He collected plenty of enemies, because he could peel the bark from a tree with his raspy tongue. With the Yankees he had been a big spender, a lover of fine clothes, whose tastes outstripped his wallet. After the 1929 season, he was $10,000 in debt. He needed a salary of $7,000 ($1,000 in advance) for 1930. In negotiations with the general manager of the Yankees, Durocher thought that he and Ed Barrow were in agreement. But when it came to signing, Barrow reneged.

Leo Durocher told Ed Barrow where he could go. In an earthy way. And general manager Barrow told his shortstop where *he* could go. In a cold way. Durocher was traded to the last-place Cincinnati Reds where he played brilliantly in the field for three years until traded to St. Louis in May 1933. He didn't want to move to the Cardinals, convinced they were a bunch of cheapskates, and he told Branch Rickey so to his face.

Lippy Leo had burst into Rickey's hotel room while the general manager was lying in bed with a cold. Durocher poured out a torrent of insults about the Cardinal organization. General manager Rickey just lay there, chewing on an unlighted cigar, listening and waiting for the storm to subside. When Durocher ran out of breath, Rickey started to talk, admitting that perhaps some of what the shortstop said was true, even some of his remarks about the general manager. Of course, Rickey had also heard things about Durocher, not that they worried him one little bit, no sir; the important thing was the way Durocher could play shortstop. Finally, the general manager had leaned over, pointing the cigar at Durocher, and said; "I made this trade because I think we can win a lot of pennants with you at shortstop. You can do it for us, you can be the spark. You can help us win pennants."

Leo Durocher had met his match. He retreated to the playing field, which was where he was needed. And where Rickey wanted him.

Lippy Leo and the Fordham Flash—now that was a winning combination. Branch Rickey wasn't so sure as he watched Frisch during spring training. One day early in

April the general manager got to thinking out loud, rambling on to Gene Karst.

"You know, Gene," he said, "Frisch has really slowed down in the field. I'm afraid he's going to play himself at second too often. I don't think we can win the pennant with him playing second base. We ought to trade Frankie to Boston. We could get Al Spohrer for him." Spohrer was a good fielding catcher, but a weaker hitter. "I really ought to fly to St. Louis and convince Sam Breadon to make a trade," Rickey said. Breadon was back in the home office overseeing the final preparations for the opening of the season. Rickey would have to make a dramatic flight north and an even *more* dramatic presentation to get the owner to agree to such a deal. Branch Rickey knew full well how tough it would be. Frankie Frisch was a very special player in the eyes of Sam Breadon, and it would take exceptional persuasion to get the owner to trade him away.

To Rickey's young associate, Gene Karst, the very thought of trading Frisch was shocking. He knew what a storm such a deal would cause, yet he also understood Rickey's thinking. Rickey had a high regard for Burgess Whitehead, the young second baseman they called the "Gazelle." Whitey Whitehead was young, fast and skillful. But he was unproven as a major-league hitter and he didn't have Frisch's power. He might never even hit for such a high average as had the old Fordham Flash. It would be a risk to trade Frankie Frisch and depend on a youngster.

If Frisch were to be traded, the Cards would need a new manager. That would present no problem, at least not in the mind of Branch Rickey. He believed that players made the manager and that with proper material, various managers could handle a team. There were several around who would please Rickey. Unfortunately, they all could be classified as "Rickey men," and Sam Breadon might resist giving any of them the job. No, it would be a sticky thing to trade Frisch, replace him with Whitehead and hire a new manager, too.

Branch Rickey decided not to act. Besides, there were other problems.

There was the outfield. Left field was settled; Joe Medwick was a fixture, and the Cards expected him to drive in a lot of runs. And Jack Rothrock looked like he could do the job in right field. But center field was unstable. Ernie Orsatti was a capable fielder and a good, left-hand hitter who averaged .300 or better year after year. He had been with the team since 1927. He was well conditioned and fast on his feet. The only problem—in all his years with the team he never played a full season. He seemed to get hurt a lot, making tumbling catches. Rickey thought George Davis of the Giants might do the job. He was a right-hand hitter, just what the team needed. So Rickey traded George Watkins, a left-hand hitter, for Davis. Watkins was a good player, a hustler, but he was holding out for more money and he didn't hit left-handers too well. It seemed like an appropriate trade. Now, with Davis, Orsatti and two rookies, the team had four center fielders.

Manager Frisch was pleased by the trade for Davis. "This deal makes our club," he said. "He'll be our center fielder against left-hand pitchers. The people in St. Louis are going to like George Davis. He can really perform in that center field. He'll make some spectacular catches."

Two of Frisch's colorful cast injected a little comedy relief into spring training. Pepper Martin and Dizzy Dean were a source of merriment to their teammates and to visiting sportswriters. Writer Frank Graham came into town for an exhibition game between the Cards and the Giants. Passing the barbershop of the Dixie Grande Hotel, Graham did a double take: The barber in the first chair looked like Pepper Martin. It was indeed Pepper, decked out in a green smock.

The customer of "barber" Pepper turned out to be Dizzy Dean, whose boyish face was being assaulted with a shiny straight razor. Dean, calm and peaceful beneath a coat of lather, grinned when he spotted the sportswriter.

"Hi," Dizzy said.

"What's the gag?" Graham asked.

"Aw, nothing," Dean replied. "Old Pepper here had a new razor he wanted to try out, so I said he could try it on me. Boy, he is some barber!"

Martin finished the shave with a flourish, slapping Dean with a hot towel. He massaged the pitcher's face, dusted him off with talcum powder and sat him up in the chair. Martin ran a comb through Dean's hair, flicked him again with the towel, and bowed him out of the chair.

"Next!" he cried, grinning at Frank Graham, but the sportswriter declined the offer.

Leo Durocher tangled with a pool hustler. The shortstop won several games and then decided to hang up his cue. Before he could do so, the stranger snarled:

"You ain't quitting now. What's a matter—you yellow?"

Durocher charged the hustler, stick in hand.

"Nobody could call Leo yellow," Medwick recalled afterward. "He chased that pool shark right down the middle of the street."

Frankie Frisch was in high spirits as he faced the opening of his first full season as a manager. The team seemed to be in condition and had looked impressive in exhibition games. And during the training, he had won the confidence of his players with his knowledge of baseball and with his style of coaching and teaching. J. Roy Stockton, sportswriter for the St. Louis *Post-Dispatch,* praised the manager:

"Frisch seemed in control of the situation. He was a tough hombre last year when he took over the reins. He had to be. He was moving up from the ranks and the club was out of hand. The club was demoralized. Drastic measures were necessary and he took them. He gained the nickname of 'John McGraw, Jr.' and there was grumbling and muttering. But Frisch has 'softened up,' in the language of the dugout. He is closer to his players, kinder to them, more sociable. And while he makes it plain that he is boss, he is not unreasonable and if there is any dissension or discord in camp, this observer, with many friends in the ranks, has failed to see or hear of it."

Before the Cardinals broke camp, manager Frisch gave a fire-eating speech: *Don't let anybody push you around. You've got to win games, especially the close ones. Your nights are your own, but your bodies belong to the Cardinals in the daylight.*

He ended his talk on this note:

"Now, if you'd rather go back to the mines and dig coal or ride around the country in Pullmans and live in the best hotels at the expense of the club, speak right up. We haven't any room for softies, no holds are barred. That's the way we're going to play ball."

"You said more'n a mouthful, Frank." Dizzy Dean spoke for the whole team.

PART TWO

THE CHAMPIONSHIP RACE

3

Opening Daze

"Any team with nine players like ole Diz wouldn't need no manager."
— *Jay Hanna Dean to a friend*

"Any team with nine Dizzy Deans would trigger another St. Valentine's Day Massacre."
— *An unfriendly critic*

THE SEASON BEGAN on Tuesday, April 17, with Sportsman's Park adorned for the occasion. The front of the stands gleamed with fresh paint as did the metal girders and frames, and the railings of the box seats. Three fresh billboard ads appeared on the outfield fences. And the grounds keeper, Bill Stocksick, reported that the field was in excellent shape, although a discerning fan could detect the faint signs of last season's football play.

During fielding practice, the Cardinal Boys Band, consisting of thirty boys in their teens, won loud applause from the fans with their rendition of "Take Me Out to the Ball Game." The weather was sunny with temperatures in the 60s, but in the shady parts of the stands a topcoat was needed to ward off the chill.

A few minutes before game time, the teams marched out to the flagpole and stood at attention for the raising of the colors and the playing of the national anthem. Then the Cardinals, dressed in their new white uniforms trimmed in red, took their positions as Mayor Barney Dickmann threw out the first ball to catcher Spud Davis.

The Cardinals lined up with Rip Collins on first, manager Frisch at second, Durocher at shortstop and Pepper Martin at third base. Jack Rothrock was in left field, Gene Moore, a rookie, in center and Joe Medwick, normally a left fielder, was in right field. Before the game, Frisch had named Durocher captain of the team, a move that puzzled some observers, who couldn't understand why a team needed a captain at short with a manager playing second. (Actually, Rickey had maneuvered the nomination, seeking to give Durocher more responsibility by making him a field leader.)

If Durocher was a captain, then clearly the man on the mound should have the rank of colonel, perhaps even general. Because pitching for St. Louis was the one and only Dizzy Dean, the world's greatest pitcher. If you didn't believe that, all you had to do was ask him. He would tell you.

Dizzy Dean had arrived on the major-league scene at a most appropriate time. Baseball's biggest hit at the box office, George Herman "Babe" Ruth, was winding down his extraordinary career. With a little help from the Cardinal front office, Dean could become the new Ruth. Dizzy was colorful, vain, tough and shrewd. He knew his value as a pitcher and as a gate attraction, and he wasn't going to let the opportunity for money and fame pass him by.

Dizzy Dean had flair, even to the extent of flashing a cavalier creativity about his biography. He told three New York sportswriters three different stories during the course of a single day. He was born, he told the first man, in Lucas, Arkansas, on January 16, 1911. For the second writer he supplied the town of Bond, Mississippi, and the date of February 22 ("to give old George Washington a break"). To the third, he declared his birthplace was Holdenville, Oklahoma, on August 22. His given name was Jerome Herman Dean, he said—or maybe it was Jay Hanna Dean. At any rate, he was consistent as to the year of his birth, which he always gave as

1911. This consistency, so out of keeping with Dean's tongue-in-cheek autobiographical blatherings, made some skeptics suspect that he just might be somewhat older. Baseball players often subtracted at least two years from their age to prolong their careers.

The third son of a poor sharecropper, Jay Hanna Dean *was* born in Lucas, Arkansas. His childhood was hard. Depending on his mood of the moment, Dean either went "clean through the second grade"—or the third, maybe into the fourth. No matter. At an age when most youngsters were building model airplanes, he was working in the cotton fields, long, grueling hours for fifty cents a day. To escape this drudgery, he joined the army as a teen-ager and served for three years. Then his father sold his cotton crop for $100 and turned the money over to the U. S. government in exchange for his son's freedom. (At that time, you could buy a discharge from any of the Services.)

While with the army, Dizzy had shown spectacular ability as a pitcher. After his discharge, he starred in semipro baseball, and scout Don Curtis signed him to a contract with Houston, which sent him in 1930 to St. Joseph in the Western Association. Before his first game, he shook hands with the opposing players, asking each what pitch he would like to hit. Then Dean beat them, 4–3. He had a 17–8 record with St. Joseph, and was moved up to Houston where he won eight and lost two.

At the end of the 1930 season, Dean was called up by the Cardinals. The day he was scheduled to pitch he came down with a bellyache caused, he claimed, by eating a bad hot dog in a local beanery. His debut had to be postponed.

The next day, Dean was in the Cardinal office chatting with a scout when Sam Breadon came by.

"How do you feel today, Mr. Dean?" the Cardinal owner asked.

"Fine," Dean said.

"Well, you'd better be," Breadon warned the pitcher.

"You're going to pitch today and that Pittsburgh team is pretty tough—the Waner brothers and Pie Traynor. Good hitters."

Dean looked up with a grin. "You might think they're tough. But they won't look so tough when they have to face old Diz."

That afternoon the brash rookie pitched a three-hitter, going the full nine innings, striking out five and beating the Pirates 3–1. In his first year in pro ball, he had won twenty-six games and lost ten, without a single dent in his cockiness. He was nineteen years old.

Later that year in the winter, Dean confronted Branch Rickey in his private office in Sportsman's Park. For two hours he bombarded the general manager with reasons why his salary should be higher than the customary $3,000 a year given to a rookie. After the long, wearing session, a rumpled Branch Rickey emerged, coatless, his shirt wrinkled, his tie askew.

"Judas Priest!" he exclaimed. "If there was another player like Dean in baseball, as God is my judge, I would most certainly get out of this game."

After Dean's fine performance in 1930, it was obvious that he was great and could even make the majors after just one season of professional experience. Only one thing stood in his way—Dizzy Dean himself. He was constantly popping off, to the distaste of veteran Cardinals who wanted him put in his place. In 1931, he was a nuisance to manager Gabby Street. Dean slept through one morning of training. When scolded he simply replied that he didn't need the practice. He could win games without working out. Let those other bums practice.

Dizzy Dean wasn't mean, nor was he a drunk or a playboy. But he had little sense of money, signing IOUs at cafés, clothiers and drugstores, and expecting the Cardinals to pick up the paper. At the end of 1930 he was in debt to the organization, and in spring training the management warned the merchants of Bradenton not to take checks or chits from one

Jay Hanna Dean. The Cardinal front office put Dean on a daily allowance, a humiliating arrangement that the pitcher resented. Every morning, he had to report to Clarence Lloyd, traveling secretary, who gave him a single dollar bill, for which Dean had to sign a receipt.

When Rickey decided to send Dean to Houston for the 1931 season, Dizzy was downcast. Why, he could pitch as good as any of those bums. But the Cards had strong pitching that year with Hallahan and Haines, Paul Derringer and Burleigh Grimes. They simply did not need a twenty-year-old wise guy.

Rickey was convinced that Dean would not be essential in St. Louis that season, so he deliberately kept him in Houston. The general manager wanted his farm club to win a pennant, too. Of course, if the Cards required Dean in their stretch drive in 1931, Rickey would have recalled him. But he hated to do so because it would cause bad will among the Houston fans.

Dizzy Dean had a great year with Houston, winning twenty-six and losing ten, striking out 303 batters and posting a 1.57 ERA. He couldn't be kept back now. In 1932, he won eighteen and lost fifteen for the Cardinals and led the league in strikeouts. In 1933, he was a twenty-game winner and again had the best strikeout record.

In July 1933, shortly after Frisch took over as manager, Dizzy Dean set a major-league record by striking out seventeen of the Chicago Cubs. He poured the ball by the likes of Cuyler and Demaree and Koenig, and fanned Babe Herman three times. The infuriated Cubs were standing up in their dugout screaming at him.

"You lucky son of a bitch," one of them yelled. "You got a horseshoe in your pocket." He didn't, though; it was just one of those superlative days that a great pitcher has. "Hell," he said later, "if I'd a knowed I was near a record I could of struck out twenty easy. Why I just toyed with Billy Jurges a couple times. He couldn't hit nothin' anyhow."

Dizzy Dean's madcap style was the talk of baseball. Once

he wandered into the Dodger clubhouse the day he was due to pitch. The Brooklyn manager, Max Carey, was going over the Cardinal hitters. Dizzy sat down and listened quietly to every word. When Carey finished he turned to Dean.

"Was I right about how to pitch to you fellows?" he asked.

"Yep," said Dean. "Now I'm going to tell you how I'm going to pitch to you bums." He went right down the Dodger batting order, man after man, pinpointing the weakness of each. The Dodgers were astounded at his accuracy. Then Dizzy Dean got up, grabbed his glove, and said:

"I've told you how I was going to pitch. Come on out now and see if you can hit."

He shut the Dodgers out that day.

He was formidable, this Jay Dean, the kind of pitcher to open—or to close—a season or to pitch any vital game. He would rear back and kick that long leg in a batter's face, and flash his fast ball or bend a curve over a corner. He was intimidating. A rawboned country boy (over six feet three, and weighing 200 pounds), he soon became the mythical pitcher of a Ring Lardner epic of his own weaving, carrying in his sleeve an arm with the velocity of a .30–30 Winchester. Loud and unlettered, swaggering and arrogant, he had been a success from that instant his right foot toed the rubber of a pitching mound. Anything he claimed he could do, he did.

At 3:00 P.M. on that April 17, Dizzy Dean stood on the mound watching umpire George Magerkurth dust off home plate. Dean waited coolly with the supreme confidence of the natural pitcher. As a twenty-year-old in his first spring training, he had fanned eighteen members of the Chicago White Sox, the players retreating to the bench cowed by his fast ball, their third-base coach chasing them with a yell: "What's the matter with you guys? You're supposed to be big-leaguers! You're letting a *dizzy* kid make a fool out of you."

Since Dean had been called "Dizzy" from the beginning of his career, the coach's epithet didn't bother him at all. He continued to burn the ball by the Chicago hitters until *they* were dizzy.

"Play ball!" Umpire Magerkurth roared and Lloyd Waner, the "Little Poison" of Pittsburgh, stepped in to start the 1934 season. Dean got the younger Waner on a line drive to Moore in center. After Fred Lindstrom, batting second, lined out to Durocher, Paul Waner advanced to the plate.

"Big Poison," as Paul Waner was called, was one of baseball's premier hitters, having averaged well over .300 for his first eight years in the majors. He also was one of the game's more dedicated imbibers who, it was reputed, could hit a line drive while dead drunk. At a game in Chicago he once smashed a ball off the fence and, as it bounded between the fielders, he steamed around second heading for third. Unfortunately, he was still woozy from a long, strenuous evening on the town, so when he made a long, swooping slide he wound up in the left-field bullpen, yards away from third base.

In the Cardinal dugout, Tex Carleton shook his head when he heard Waner's name announced. Carleton remembered all too well a day in 1932 when "Big Poison" wobbled up to him before a game.

"Hey, Tex," Waner said in a slurred voice. "You pitching today?"

"Yep," Carleton said.

"Well," Waner said, "don't you hit me, old buddy, cause Heinie Meine and me was out all night. Haven't been to bed yet."

During the course of that game, Waner sneaked a drink or two in the dugout. And at one point, umpire Bill Klem, who did not look unkindly upon the grape, held up the game to wait for Waner to appear at the plate. This was the afternoon that Paul Waner tied the National League record for most doubles in a game. He hit four doubles off Tex Carleton—and did a handspring at second base after each one!

Even the great Diz was wary before the batting stroke of Paul Waner, for he too had felt its swift sting. "I wouldn't let nobody hit *me* that way," he had told Carleton in that game of '32. "I'd knock him on his ass."

He would, too. And like all pitchers, he hated to see a batter digging a hole with his spikes to anchor his back foot. "Go ahead," he'd shout. "Dig it real deep. Because that's where they're going to bury you!" Then he'd shoot in an explosive fast one that would turn a hitter's cap around if he didn't fall to the ground.

On opening day, Dizzy Dean wasn't about to be embarrassed by *any* hitter. He pitched carefully to Paul Waner, moving the ball up and down and in and out, until he got the tough little guy to hit a foul near the Cardinals' dugout. After Martin made the catch, Dean strutted from the mound to a round of applause.

It wasn't a large crowd for opening day, certainly not a crowd that would light up the face of Sam Breadon, who sat in his box behind the third-base dugout. The bleachers were full, but there were large patches of vacant seats in the pavillion and grandstands. One observer estimated the total attendance at 10,000 which included the knothole boys who were admitted free of charge. Back east in Brooklyn, the Dodgers entertained the Braves before a crowd of nearly 35,000. In Cincinnati, the Redlegs opened before 30,247 fans, a figure which puzzled a reporter for the *Post-Dispatch*. How could Cincinnati, with only half a million population to draw on and with a second-division team, outpull St. Louis with more than a million in the area and with two top teams "battling and with the sun shining brightly"?

Branch Rickey saw nothing puzzling about it. "The Cincinnati crowd is easily explained," he said. "Attending the opening game in Redland is a rite with the fans. For years this game has been a sellout. All reservations are gone weeks before opening day. Fans even make Christmas presents of a pair of opening-day tickets."

The general manager took the unlighted cigar from his

mouth and, with a wave of his hand, declined a match offered him. "As a consequence," he went on, "the club always shows capacity attendance on that day. In St. Louis no such condition exists. In fact, spring series games—" the games between the Cards and the Browns—"in the past have taken the edge off the season's opening, to some extent. Overcoat weather hurt us this year. The opening day crowd here is no criterion of what to expect during the current season. Our attendance will be commensurate with our performance just as it always has been."

Rickey's comment was well thought out. Unlike Cincinnati, St. Louis had never been a great opening-day city. It was a summer city, a Sunday city, as far as baseball crowds were concerned. On a weekday it was a working town and people didn't flock to the ball park. If the Cardinals played winning ball, they should pull fans into the park during the pennant race. At any rate, 10,000 wasn't a bad showing for those Depression days. More important, St. Louis performed in a style that brought smiles to the faces of both Rickey and Breadon. Breadon sat in his box behind the Cardinal dugout, and Rickey was in the Cardinal box behind first base not far from the business offices.

Dizzy Dean went on to beat the Pirates 7–1, pitching a six-hitter and striking out five. His colorful "podner," Pepper Martin, came up in the first inning with two out and hit a drive into center field. As he roared down the first-base line his teammates surged to the top of the dugout, led by Jesse "Pop" Haines. The old knuckle-ball specialist always stood up when Martin batted.

"I'd pay my way in just to watch Pepper," Haines often said.

Martin went into second with a headfirst slide that brought the fans to their feet. It was a typical double for Pepper. As the crowd exploded with cheers, a delighted grin spread over his square, open face. It was an innocent, country-boy face, with a wide mouth and a hawk nose set between high cheekbones.

An exciting, aggressive player, Pepper Martin had become one of the most popular men ever to wear a Cardinal uniform. On any all-time, all-competitors' team, he would rank alongside Ty Cobb, not for playing ability but for fury and flair. He was not a large man, standing five feet eight in his baseball stockings and weighing about 170 pounds, but he was muscular and strong. He ran the bases like Bronco Nagurski hitting the line, barreling from home plate with a charge that made first basemen give him *all* the bag. He had a peculiar way of stopping. Rather than running over first and down the foul line as most players did, Martin came to a dead stop after a sprint! Ballplayers shook their heads, wondering how he didn't break both legs.

Born in Temple, Oklahoma, on February 29, 1904 (it was a leap year), John Leonard Martin was a farm boy who loved to ride motorcycles and midget automobiles. Mostly, he loved baseball, which he started playing professionally in 1924 for Greenville in the East Texas League as an outfielder and pitcher. (Of his pitching, teammate Tex Carleton said: "You weren't safe anywhere in the ball park when he let the ball go!")

Martin's forte was his running. He was fast and daring from the beginning. After playing for Greenville, he went to Fort Smith, Syracuse and Houston, before joining the Cardinals who used him mostly as a pinch runner in 1928. In 1929, he was back in the minors and had a big year at Rochester in 1930.

In the spring of 1931, Pepper Martin charged into the office of Branch Rickey. Furious at riding the bench, weary of minor-league play, the twenty-seven-year-old stormed at Rickey.

"Play me or trade me! I wasn't born to sit on anybody's bench."

Branch Rickey liked "hungry" ballplayers and Pepper Martin was one of the hungriest he had ever seen. Besides, the Cardinals' regular center fielder, Taylor Douthit, was beginning to slow down and also was drawing a fancy salary of $14,000. Who needed a high-priced outfielder who had begun to grow a trifle ripe? Rickey traded Douthit to Cincinnati and Pepper Martin took over in center field, and in the World Series of '31 drove the Philadelphia Athletics wild with his hitting and base running.

Leading the Cardinals to a victory in the seven-game series, Pepper had a batting average of .500. His twelve hits (including four doubles and a homer) set a record for total hits in a World Series. He stole five bases, scored five runs and drove in another five.

His wild style earned him the nickname of "The Wild Horse of the Osage." A national hero, he made $10,000 for stage appearances before tiring of the phony performances. After his brief "acting" career, he showed up in the business offices of the Cardinals. When Branch Rickey asked him what he'd done with the $10,000, Martin patted his bulging pockets. "I got it all here, Mr. Rickey." Each of his pockets was stuffed with hundred-dollar bills.

"Judas Priest!" Rickey was appalled. "Somebody will rob you."

"No, they won't." Martin grinned as he strolled out of the office.

Martin loved pranks and practical jokes. He and Diz were like Keystone Cops, staging mock fights in hotel lobbies, horrifying the guests and infuriating the management. The fight would be a careful setup with each player filling his mouth with popcorn before entering the lobby. When Dean swung at Martin, Pepper would spit out white kernels, which onlookers mistook for teeth! With Martin around, it just wasn't safe to concentrate too carefully while reading a newspaper. He would sneak up and set fire to it—or give you a hotfoot if you dozed off in a hotel lobby. Or he would sprinkle sneezing powder in a lobby or locker room. Some of his stunts were dangerous. Like the time he threw chunks of ice out of a New York hotel window. They exploded like grenades on the street far below.

A nature boy in the crudest sense, Pepper wore *nothing*

under his uniform—no sliding pads, no underwear, no jock-strap and no protective cup. Now, playing third base with-out a protective cup is like—well, it's like buying a round-trip ticket on the *Titanic*. Unless you are fearless (which Pepper was), or supremely gifted at grabbing line drives or sucking up grounders (which he wasn't).

In 1933, Martin had his best year in the National League, batting .316 and leading the league in stolen bases with 26. He was a skillful bunter and a dangerous, unorthodox hitter who could slice an *inside* pitch to right field for a game-winning hit.

In the third inning of the opening game of the 1934 season, he came to bat with one out and socked another double, this time to left field. After Jack Rothrock flied out to Lindstrom, the action seemed over for the Cardinals.

But in the first-base coaching box, coach Buzzy Wares went into his famous cheerleading and rally-provoking act. Tiptoeing down the line and clowning to get the attention of the fans, he pleaded and pranced in the hope of igniting a rally.

At third base, Mike Gonzalez watched carefully as the next batter approached the plate. There was a stirring of expectation in the stands.

"Now batting for the Cardinals," the announcement came over the PA system, "Joe Medwick, number seven, right field."

Medwick approached the plate in the duck-like waddle that had earned him the nickname, "Ducky-Wucky," while he was playing for Houston in the Texas League. It was a nickname that brought a scowl to his face, for he preferred to be called "Muscles."

Muscular, he was. A compact 180 pounds with arms bronzed from the Florida sun, biceps rippling and threaten-ing to sever his sleeves—a handsome devil, the women thought. With his jet-black full head of hair and his dark, flashing Magyar eyes, he was a menacing figure. A savage line-drive hitter, he attacked a baseball viciously and didn't particularly care whether a pitch was low or high or whether it was in or out of the strike zone. It was a baseball, round and available, and he had a bat and was paid to swat it.

When the pitcher seemed to be stalling, Medwick backed out of the box and took a resin bag from his pocket. Unlike most players, who used the bag near home plate, Muscles Medwick carried his own resin. Stepping back into the batter's box, he glanced at third-base coach Gonzalez.

Miguel Angel Cordero "Mike" Gonzalez had come to the major leagues in 1912 as a slick-fielding catcher, and had gained a measure of fame while playing for John McGraw. Sent by McGraw to scout a young player, Gonzalez had reported with a telegram: "GOOD FIELD, NO HIT." He was an astute judge of talent, a skillful sign stealer—and he spoke a marvelously comical English. His highest compliment to a player was, "He one smart dummy."

Gonzalez clapped his hands and shouted to Medwick.

"Come on, Yoe. Ba-bie. You can do, Yoe. Keed. You can do. He easy, Yoe. He easy."

The Pirate pitcher was Henry William "Heinie" Meine (pronounced "my-knee"), St. Louis-born and a resident of Luxemburg, Missouri. Meine, sometimes called "The Prince of Luxemburg," went into the stretch position, checking Martin at second base. He wheeled the ball plate-ward: a fast ball, obviously out of the strike zone, head-high to make an eager young hitter "fish" and foul it up. It was an "impossible" pitch to hit with authority.

Medwick jumped at the ball, lashing it on a rising line over the shortstop. Left-fielder Lindstrom turned his back on the infield and raced back, pausing at the fence in left center and watching, hands on hips, as the ball sailed into the seats.

As Ducky circled the bases, Heinie Meine stood in dejection. Over in a box were several members of his family, watching their prince so rudely treated.

The Cardinals hammered out thirteen hits to overwhelm the Pirates. Medwick wound up with three hits, Martin,

Durocher and Frisch had two each; everybody had at least one, except Dizzy. Starting a season with a win before home-town fans was a heady thing, particularly for the manager, whose position always hinges on the record column.

The editorial writer of the *Post-Dispatch* was ecstatic. "Dizzy Dean has already awarded the pennant to the Cardinals," he wrote. "He himself plans to win 30 games, while his brother Paul will deposit 15 victories in the Breadon-Rickey basket. That, as we understand it, is about half of the pitching obligations devolving upon a championship team. Can the other pitchers deliver the remaining half? Look at them! There is Hallahan of cyclonic velocity, the venerable Haines, wise as a serpent, and that battle-scarred warrior, home again from the foreign legions, the Tamer-lane of the diamond, Burleigh Grimes himself."

After their promising opening-day victory over Pitts-burgh, the Cardinals went into a tailspin. Young Paul Dean was knocked out of the box by the Pirates as was Wild Bill Hallahan. The Cubs came to town and took a 2–1 game, even though Tex Carleton struck out eleven and gave up only five hits. The next day, Dizzy Dean and three others were bombed for fifteen runs as Chicago's Lon Warneke pitched his second one-hitter, having hurled the first against Cincinnati in the season's opener.

The Cardinals reeled out of town and into Pittsburgh where they suffered their fifth straight defeat. Frisch had used four center fielders and seventeen pitchers in six games; the team's batting average was .200; and only Medwick was listed among the league's top hitters.

By the end of April, the Cardinals, with a record of 4–7, were deep in the second division. Dizzy Dean had been knocked out of the box three times and brother Paul hadn't won a single game. A sarcastic tone had crept into the speech of Frankie Frisch, and Branch Rickey was beginning to frown.

4

Dusty Trail to the Top

IN MAY, the American earth started to blow away as violent winds triggered dust storms in the Great Plains. The dust crept into automobile engines, causing short circuits, and into clocks and refrigerators. It blocked roads and railbeds, grounded airplanes and blackened everything in its path.

Blinded by dust, a South Dakota woman was killed in a car accident. Another woman died in North Dakota when a high wind pinned her beneath a flying chicken coop. The cloud of dust moved eastward, blotting out the view of Chicago's skyscrapers. New Yorkers licked their dry lips, spitting out particles of fine dirt. The Empire State Building looked like a yellow spike in the sky. Airplane pilots reported dust reaching as high as 15,000 feet in parts of the country.

In St. Louis, on May 10, the sun was nearly hidden from view. The cars on the streets were coated with gray particles and inside the office buildings desk tops were gritty and dirty. At Sportsman's Park the Cardinals were entertaining the New York Giants, with Wild Bill Hallahan opposing "Prince" Hal Schumacher. There was a brisk wind blowing and the air was full of dust, making it difficult for the batters to pick up Hallahan's fast ball.

In the fourth inning the wind blew Durocher's pop fly away from catcher Gus Mancuso, the ball falling in fair ground for a single. The Cardinals went on to score a run, breaking a tie to gain a lead, which they held the rest of the way. It was their second straight triumph over New York and their eighth victory in their last ten games.

That night the weather became fair and cooler. It had been unusually hot, with the thermometer at a high of 91 degrees two days before. And dry. Throughout Missouri the spring rainfall was almost 60 percent below normal.

On May 11 there was a hint of showers in the air as Colonel and Mrs. Charles A. Lindbergh flew into the Lambert-St. Louis airport. It had been an eight-hour trip from New York, in "favorable" weather, with fuel stops at Pittsburgh and Indianapolis.

"Lindy" and his wife, Anne Morrow Lindbergh, touched down at shortly after 1:00 P.M., and the famous visitor taxied his canary-yellow monoplane to the hangar. Bareheaded, dressed in a dark gray suit and wearing a blue shirt and tie, Colonel Lindbergh grinned at the small crowd waiting to greet him. Mrs. Lindbergh waved and smiled. She looked chic and lovely in her blue suit and yellow shirtwaist. The Lone Eagle, relaxed and genial, answered questions from a circle of reporters.

Yes, he was in town to visit friends and to do some business. He didn't know how long he'd stay, though. No, he did *not* intend to move the Lindbergh trophies from the Jefferson Memorial, for he "knew of no better place for them to be." Mr. and Mrs. Lindbergh got in a friend's car and waved good-bye to the well-wishers and reporters.

May 11 was a Friday and Ladies Day (admission: twenty-five cents for taxes and service charges) at Sportsman's Park where 5,000 fans had turned out to see the third game of the four-game series with New York. The Giants were considered the team to beat, even though they currently were tied for third place with the Cardinals. They had won the 1933 pennant and became world champions by beating the Washington Senators in the World Series. Although some people felt the Cubs might take the '34 pennant, most experts picked the Giants, believing that the crown had to be lifted from the head of the champs. The Cardinals felt they could do it, too, having beaten the Giants when the two teams played in 1933.

A hero of the 1933 Series, King Carl Hubbell was scheduled to pitch for New York. When the New York manager needed to win a game he sent this star left-hander to the mound. A master of the screwball (which broke into left-hand hitters), Hubbell had won over a hundred games since joining New York in 1928. His current record was four wins and only one defeat.

With Hubbell on the mound and Mancuso, a smart catcher, behind the plate, the Giants were nearly unbeatable. Their first baseman was manager Bill Terry, a great player and brilliant student of baseball. Terry was a superb hitter. "Memphis Bill," as he was called, had won the batting title in 1930 with an average of .401, and no National Leaguer had reached that level since.

A fine manager too, Bill Terry was respected by his players for his knowledge of the game. Blunt and caustic, he was unpopular with the press. When he did speak out, he could make headlines, as he had the previous winter. Asked about the Dodgers as a pennant contender, Terry had wisecracked: "Brooklyn? Are they still in the league?"

That was not the kind of quip most managers cared to make, for it went against an ancient maxim, to wit, let sleeping dogs, or baseball teams, stay asleep.

At second base that May afternoon was Blondy Ryan, whose claim to fame was a telegram. Injured in the '33 pennant race, lying in a hospital bed, he had wired his teammates: "WE CAN'T LOSE. I'M ON MY WAY."

The Giant shortstop was Travis Calvin "Stonewall" Jackson, one of the league's best infielders. He had been with the team since 1922 and was a clutch hitter who had batted over .300 in five of his eleven seasons.

At third base was Johnny Vergez, a journeyman who had been with the club several years. Jo-Jo Moore, an all-round ballplayer, played left field. In center field, the hitting star of the 1933 World Series was Melvin Thomas Ott, who normally appeared in right field. One of the top batters in baseball, Mel Ott had been a protégé of John McGraw, who refused to send the sixteen-year-old to the minors when he first joined the team. McGraw didn't want young Ott's unique batting stroke ruined by any stupid minor-league manager. He kept the boy on the bench most of two seasons before sending him into full-time action. Once he became a regular in the lineup, Mel Ott began hitting home runs like a miniature Babe Ruth. A left-hand batter, he had an unusual way of cocking his right leg high as he swung the bat.

Frank Joseph "Lefty" O'Doul, a left-hand hitter, played right field. Going into the 1934 season, O'Doul had a batting average of around .350. Though slowing down at age thirty-seven, he was still a dangerous hitter.

Against this powerhouse the Cardinals sent twenty-year-old Paul Dean, who had been hit hard in his previous three experiences. Fans and sportswriters were getting skeptical about young Dean's ability. The newspapers in Columbus were predicting he would soon be back in town to help their team win another pennant. Even Diz's influence and Rickey's yearning for a brother act could not keep the younger Dean with the Cards if he didn't soon pitch a strong ball game. Paul knew this when he took the mound; he had talked it over with his big brother only minutes before. But if he was worried he certainly did not show it.

Also born in Lucas, Arkansas, in 1913, Paul Dee Dean was the youngest of the Dean boys. Like brother Dizzy, Paul had worked hard as a boy, but as long as he could remember he had played baseball, usually as a shortstop to back up his big brother on the mound. At age seventeen he was pitching in an industrial league in Texas when he was spotted by

Don Curtis, who also launched Dizzy's professional career. Curtis signed Paul to a Houston contract in 1931, but he stayed there only briefly, moving on to Columbus and to Springfield in the Western Association. He was with Springfield that year, and in 1932 had a 7–16 record with Columbus. In 1933, he was the best pitcher in the American Association with a record of 22–7.

At six feet and 180 pounds, Paul Dean wasn't as big as Dizzy, but he could throw as hard—and some players claimed, even harder. Unlike Dizzy, who had a good curve and a change-up, Paul was strictly a fast-ball pitcher, using a three-quarter and, sometimes, side-arm motion. In contrast to his talkative brother, Paul was quiet and unassuming. But he was fiercely loyal to Dizzy, always ready to take his part in a fight.

On May 11, 1934, Paul Dean and Carl Hubbell hooked up in a "blistering pitching duel," as a *New York Times* reporter said. Young Dean got into trouble in the very first inning by walking lead-off man, Joe Moore. But then he struck out O'Doul and Terry with fast balls. When Ott singled to center sending Moore to third, there was a worried hum from the Ladies Day crowd. But Dean got the tough Travis Jackson on a fly to center for the third out.

In the Cardinals' first, Pepper Martin pranced up to the plate accompanied by shrieks from the ladies. He grinned like a schoolboy at the chorus of feminine encouragement. "Come on, Pepper. Get a hit. We want a hit."

Martin slashed Hubbell's first pitch down the left-field line and slid hard into second. There was a cloud of dust. As the umpire gave the "safe" sign, Pepper jumped to his feet, slapping dirt from his uniform. You could see his look of delight from the upper stands.

After Rothrock grounded out, a familiar stocky figure emerged from the dugout as the voice of Jim Kelley, the announcer, came over the PA system.

"Now batting for St. Louis, number three . . ."

The ladies cheered Frankie Frisch in the on-deck circle. Many of them remembered his dashing play in 1927. He used to run the bases so hard and play second with such fury his cap would fly over the field. Fans sitting close to the diamond could see the gleam of black polish on his baseball shoes, which were perfectly shined before the start of each game. Waiting his turn at bat, Frisch had a habit of shining his shoes by rubbing them against the calves of his legs.

The switch-hitting manager stepped in to bat right-handed against Hubbell. Like most switch-hitters, he was a better left-handed batter than a right-handed one. As a south-paw, he could line the ball to the opposite field for extra bases or pull an inside pitch to right.

Now he crouched, batting from the right side against the southpaw Hubbell.

"What a stance!" Bill DeLancey snorted in the dugout.

"Very unorthodox," Rip Collins observed.

"Strictly a high-ball hitter," Tex Carleton drawled.

On the mound, Hubbell stretched and checked Martin edging off second. Coach Wares tiptoed down the base line, clapping his hands for a rally. Mike Gonzalez shouted from third base. "Come on, Frahnk. He easy. You can do, Frahnk."

Frisch took the first pitch, a knee-high strike on the inside corner.

"We wanna hit, we wanna hit, we wanna hit," the knot-hole gang chanted.

Hubbell's next delivery was a screwball, designed to break down and away from the right-hand batter. Ideally, it would have nicked the outside corner of the plate at the knees. But the ball was belt-high and Frisch hit it on a line to right center field. As the manager rounded first base, his hat flew off, but he never broke stride.

The Cardinals were on the dugout steps. "Look at that old Dutchman go!" young DeLancey exclaimed.

Manager Frisch raced around second base and slid headfirst into third with a triple. All the fans stood and cheered.

St. Louis scored another run before Hubbell got the side out. The Giants scored once in the second and again in the sixth to tie the game 2–2.

That was all the scoring for three innings as King Carl and young Paul staged a tense duel. In the tenth, Leo Durocher doubled to left field with one out. Then Paul Dean lifted an easy little pop fly to short right field. Second-baseman Blondy Ryan drifted back confidently. Then suddenly he wavered, lunged—and the ball popped out of his glove. Ryan had seemed to flinch at the sound of right-fielder O'Doul's pounding feet. Hubbell walked Martin to fill the bases, but Jack Rothrock drove the ball deep to left center and Moore didn't even bother chasing it. The game went to the Cardinals, 3–2, their third straight over the Giants.

It was an important victory for Paul Dean and the Cardinals. St. Louis lost the next game to New York, split a pair with Brooklyn, and then left town on May 15 for a long road trip. As they piled on the train at Union Station, their record for May was eleven wins and three losses. The pitching had been sharp, the fielding good, and the hitters were producing. Their getaway loss to the Dodgers on May 15 was a disappointment; they might have won the game with a little luck. But Jack Rothrock's spectacular hitting had pleased manager Frisch, for the right fielder had gone five for five with three singles, a double and a home run.

On that day, the team left town in third place with fifteen wins and ten losses. Dizzy Dean had three wins and three complete games, Carleton and Hallahan were in mid-season form and lefty Bill Walker had looked strong until his accident. While pitching batting practice, he was hit by a line drive off the bat of Joe Medwick. The drive broke his left arm above the wrist, putting Walker out of action for six weeks.

A week later, Medwick was involved in an episode at the batting cage. He and Tex Carleton exchanged words and punches before they could be parted. According to observers, each player got in two blows, neither doing much damage, and they shook hands a few minutes later.

Riding eastward that night of May 15, the Cardinals were in a festive mood as card games got under way and players needled each other across the aisles. Pepper Martin, dressed in a brand new suit that soon would look like a dusty sack, started to sing "Birmingham Jail," and was quickly joined by Dizzy Dean and the mischievous Rip Collins. Collins coaxed Martin to sing louder and louder, going from song to song, finally reaching a crescendo of noise with a chorus of "The Wabash Cannonball," Dizzy's tune. A loud growl was heard from manager Frisch. Seated at a window seat, the manager was listening to coach Mike Gonzalez deliver a soliloquy in broken English:

"Mike, she tole you, Frahnk . . . We can do . . . She one smart dummy, Frahnk . . . Mang hit three-fifty cinch, you see, Mike, she tole you . . . Maybe he dong hit so many home rung . . . He not humpy-dumpy . . . I, Mike, dong care . . . We gotta win, you see, best club in league, Frahnk . . . You watch Mike, Frahnk."

Several of the Cardinals were sitting quietly reading newspapers and magazines. Bill DeLancey was staring into the night, chain-smoking cigarettes. In the club car, coach Buzzy Wares was involved in a serious discussion of the stock market. Dressed in a conservative double-breasted suit, puffing on a cigar, he impressed the stranger who sat listening to his wise words. Wares laid down the financial section of the newspaper, removed his gold-rimmed glasses, and delivered a pronunciamento:

"The market is sluggish, but I sense an upward turn soon. Don't you agree?" The stranger leaned forward and nodded his agreement.

"Note that wheat is up three cents a bushel," Wares said. "Cotton is better, rubber is making a comeback and silver is steady."

Yes, indeed, the stranger thought, this man does *know* the market. The stranger hesitated, wondering if he dare ask for an opinion on General Motors, which at 32½ was up a point. Certainly, the thoughtful, distinguished-looking man with the cigar and gold-rimmed glasses could offer sensible advice.

Of course, the stranger would have been astonished if he had known Coach Clyde E. "Buzzy" Wares didn't own a single stock. Nor was he likely to purchase any on his salary of $3,000 a year. Now, should the Cardinals win the pennant, then just maybe Buzzy Wares would invest in the market . . .

On May 17 at Braves Field in Boston, Paul Dean won his third straight game, going all the way and giving up nine hits. It was the Cards' fourteenth win in their last seventeen games. But the Braves came back the next afternoon and bombarded Jim Winford and Flint Rhem to win 6–2. The Cardinals won the last of the series behind the three-hit pitching of Tex Carleton. It was the finest game pitched by any Cardinal so far in the season, and sportswriter J. Roy Stockton called it a "masterpiece." It might easily have been a two-hit shutout, for the Braves scored their only run on a pop-fly double that fell between shortstop Durocher and left-fielder Medwick.

Streaking through the East, the Cards won five out of seven games and found themselves in first place. After the Philadelphia series, manager Frisch spoke to his team in the clubhouse in Huntington, West Virginia, where St. Louis was to play an exhibition game against their farm team.

"Don't let this first place thing get you excited," Frisch cautioned. "It doesn't mean a thing except that we won a few games in the month of May. They don't pay off this month, or next month or the month after that. But if we keep on winning 'today's' game it will mean something when September sags into October. If we keep this up you'll get some nice letters and *enclosures* from Commissioner Landis that will make a very pleasant winter for you."

With visions of a very green winter in their mind, the Cardinals put on a spirited exhibition for the folks of Huntington. Before going to the park, Diz and Pepper entertained the local townsmen. Dean walked down one side of a main street and Pepper the other. They shouted across at each other.

"You pitching today, Diz?"

"Sure am. You gonna play, Pepper?"

"You bet I am," Martin called out.

The Cardinals moved to Cincinnati where they swept a three-game series, ending the month with six straight victories, which was only fitting, since they had also opened May with a winning streak. Their record for May was twenty-one wins and only six losses; the Deans now had eleven games in the winning column (only thirty-four more to reach the prediction of forty-five): Tex Carleton had pitched strongly; and Bill Hallahan had looked good when shutting out the Phillies to put St. Louis in first place.

Joe Medwick was hitting the ball with a ferocity that frightened opposing pitchers. In the thirteen-game road trip, he had collected twenty-six hits, including four doubles, four triples and a home run. Pitchers couldn't find his weakness: pitched inside, he'd line the ball off the left-field wall; outside pitches he sent zooming to right field. High or low, fast or slow—it made no difference where they threw.

"I just smell the lettuce," he told a reporter. "I have two good friends in this world. The *buckerinos* and the base hits. If I get the base hits, I will get the buckerinos. I smell World Series lettuce and I'll be getting two or three [hits] a day."

Another strong player, young Bill DeLancey, broke into the starting lineup on Memorial Day and banged out four hits, a homer, a triple and two singles. And Rip Collins was hitting the ball hard and far, batting in runs almost as furiously as Medwick.

Hard hitting and fine pitching—May ended like a sunny melody, with only one sour note to mar it. During the series in Boston, Jay Hanna Dean had grumbled that he might lead a two-man strike ("Me and Paul") to get more money for the brothers Dean. Manager Frisch had talked with Dizzy and, while he didn't discount a possible revolt, Frisch couldn't believe that any pitcher—or any catcher, for that matter—would quit during a pennant race. Nor did the players take the matter seriously, figuring the team was a winner and nobody in his right mind would jeopardize a World Series check.

When a reporter questioned Dizzy about the strike, the big pitcher said: "Let's forget it. Everything is going to be all right."

Branch Rickey's response puzzled those close to him. Instead of a thunderous, "Judas Priest! What next?" the general manager had sat quietly, his bushy eyebrows raised in thought. Then he smiled enigmatically. The thought of a strike didn't seem to alarm him. On the contrary, he appeared pleased at the prospect! What was the old fox up to now?

5

Trouble in June

Frankie Frisch was worried. Hurrying through the lobby, he paid little attention to Mike Gonzalez, who was chattering at his side. "Dong worry, Frahnk. Dissy and Pablo not craysey. They not strike. You see, like Mike tole you."

The coach continued talking on the elevator, smiling broadly in an effort to erase the sour look from the face of his boss.

It was June 1. The Cardinals were in Pittsburgh. The night before, in Cincinnati, Dizzy had told his manager he wouldn't throw another ball until his brother got a raise of $2,000 and a new contract at $5,000 per year. Throughout the road trip, which had begun in May, Frisch had spent hours trying to placate Dizzy, who was convinced Paul was being exploited.

Frisch and Gonzalez were on their way to a meeting in the manager's room with Dizzy, Jesse Haines, Buzzy Wares and traveling secretary Clarence Lloyd. The session was long and loud.

"It's no use arguing, Frank," Diz said. "I told you I ain't pitching until Paul gets a raise."

"You'd better pitch," Frisch growled. "If you know what's good for you."

"The hell you say!" Dean shouted.

At this point, Mike Gonzalez rose heavily from his chair,

and muttered, "Mike, she can do." The tall coach walked out of the room and returned in a few minutes with Paul Dean in tow. Gonzalez flashed a large smile that revealed a silver tooth in the side of his mouth.

"Pablo," he said, "you tole them what you say to Mike in your roong."

Paul said he couldn't understand all the fuss. He didn't have any intention of going on strike, because he didn't have anything to complain about. Hearing this, Dizzy suspended the strike. If Paul was happy, podner, then old Diz was too.

As the meeting broke up, Frisch motioned Gonzalez to stay. "You and I, pal, we're going to have a couple brews." Frank winked at his coach. "Sometimes, you know, Mike. *You* can do."

The next day, June 2, J. Roy Stockton reported in the *Post-Dispatch* that Dizzy was ready to "throw this arm off to win for Old Frank and the boys." He had been scheduled to pitch the day before but "union" business prevented him from doing so. Bill Hallahan was rushed in with only three days' rest, not enough, for he faltered in the ninth and the Pirates scored three runs to win 4–3.

Ole Diz would take care of the Pirates today, though, because "Gee," he told Stockton, "those Cardinals are swell fellows and there never was a man quite the fellow that Frisch is. Isn't he a pip, though? You know there must be something wrong with anybody who wouldn't pitch their arm off for Old Frank."

Dean didn't need to throw hard, for the Cardinals easily won the first game of the doubleheader, 13–4. Playing in his 2,000th major-league game, Frankie Frisch had three hits and turned in a sparkling play to end a Pittsburgh rally. But the leader of the June 2 attack was Rip Collins, the happy-go-lucky first baseman. One of three switch-hitters in the lineup, Collins drove in seven runs with two homers and a triple.

A small man for a first baseman (under five feet ten and weighing 165 pounds), Collins had surprising power for his size. He was just coming into his own after years of waiting in the wings for Sunny Jim Bottomley, a superb hitter, to step aside. Collins had joined the team in 1931 and for the next two years played first base and the outfield.

Born in 1905, in Altoona, Pa., James Anthony Collins had gone to work at age fourteen in the coal mines in Nanty Glo, not far from Altoona. That same year, he started playing semipro ball in the outfield, alongside his father. He learned to switch-hit and to throw with either hand, because his father was a switch-hitter and ambidextrous. He acquired the nickname "Ripper" when a line drive from his bat stuck on a nail in the right-field fence.

Like many youngsters in the coal fields, Rip Collins matured early, marrying at seventeen and playing his first game of professional baseball in 1923 for York in the New York-Pennsylvania League. He spent the next two seasons at Johnstown in the Middle Atlantic League. Next he moved to Savannah, Georgia, and Danville, Virginia. In 1930 at Rochester, he led the International League in hitting with .376. He was ready for the big leagues, a chunky, powerful man who hit long home runs even though he choked up on the bat.

Rip Collins was clever. Although he had little formal education, he started out the 1934 season writing daily news stories for the East St. Louis *Journal* and the Rochester *Times Union*. Part way through the season, he suspended his writing career when, after he struck out one day, manager Frisch shouted at him, "Next time, swing your typewriter."

Collins was the resident statistician on the Cardinal bench, carrying in his head batting averages, doubles, home runs and the strikeouts of each of his teammates. "That's Medwick's seventh homer, fellows," Collins would announce, "and it's his forty-eighth run batted in. Joe's now leading the league with an average of three sixty-nine."

Collins enjoyed appearing on radio shows and he loved to sing. In 1933, he and Dazzy Vance, Martin and Dizzy formed a quartet and performed over station KMOX in St. Louis. He was a pixie and a prankster, this Collins; with his baby face and innocent eyes, he could model for a choirboy, but he was behind many of Pepper Martin's pranks.

Wouldn't it be fun, he might suggest, to take some sneezing powder and put it in the lobby fan in the hotel? Why, that way, you could spray the lobby and the cocktail lounge. While the drinkers and lobby-sitters were having a sneezing fit, Rip Collins would be doubled up with laughter—and Pepper would be on the carpet.

It wasn't true, though, that he thought up the idea of dropping water bags from hotel windows. Nor was he responsible for getting Pepper and Dizzy and Leo thrown out of the Hotel Benjamin Franklin in Philadelphia, after they nearly decapitated a policeman with a water bag dropped from a window high above the street. Not that Collins wasn't capable of masterminding such a stunt.

Quick-witted, lively and spontaneous, he served as master of ceremonies when the players staged their exhibition "pepper" game. The squad was made up of Collins, Martin, Ernie Orsatti and Jack Rothrock, who usually handled the bat. Collins would have them line up in foul territory, behind home plate or near first or third base.

It started like a "normal" pepper game, with a batter hitting a ball to three players standing about twenty feet away. The fielders would pick up grounders or catch line drives and toss the ball back to the hitter. It was good practice —the normal pepper game, that is.

The Gashouse version was show business. Rothrock would hit the ball to Martin, who would fake a return but instead flip it to Collins, who might throw it behind his back to Orsatti. Orsatti might bounce it off his biceps to Martin. Round and round went the ball, behind a back, over a shoulder, between a player's legs. Meanwhile, Rothrock would stand ready with the bat not knowing when or where or from whom the ball might be delivered.

Fans loved it and roared their approval. And as the cheers mounted, Pepper Martin would end the game with a strutting demonstration of bat control by prancing along the foul line and bouncing the baseball off the end of the bat. He made it look so easy he would bring down the house.

Sometimes, after infield practice, Martin and Frisch would stay on the field and stage a "burn out." Frisch would throw the ball hard to Martin, who would shake his gloved hand. Then Frisch would move a step or two closer and make another hard throw. Martin would back off third and retreat toward the stands as Frisch kept advancing and throwing. Until, finally, Frisch would heave the ball like a bullet at Martin—who climbed into the stands to end the byplay.

The fun stopped when the game started. From then on, it was no-nonsense baseball played by men hungry for a share of World Series money.

The Cardinals lost the second game of the doubleheader on June 2, they lost the final game of the series on June 3 and they headed home griping about the Pirates. But they were still in first place, despite losing three out of four in Pittsburgh.

Back in St. Louis, the Cardinals landed in second by losing two out of three to the Chicago Cubs. The pitching staff, though, was stretched thin. The Deans and Carleton were overworked, hurling in rotation and in relief. And Bill Hallahan didn't look at all like the "Sweet William" of his glory years. Jim Mooney should be a winner, Frisch argued, but wasn't, even though he had as much stuff as any left-hander in baseball. His control was shaky. Bill Walker was still out with a broken arm, Flint Rhem and Jim Winford had been sent to the minors. (Rhem refused to report.) That left only Jesse Haines and Jim Lindsey, who had been picked up from St. Paul. The fans of St. Louis had hoped their team would make a deal for a pitcher before the June 15 trading deadline, but instead the front office had traded George Davis to Philadelphia for Chick Fullis, an outfielder who had hit

.309 in 1933. Fullis was a speedy outfielder and a solid player, but certainly no substitute for another pitcher.

The team was hitting *and* fielding in superior style. Medwick was leading the league, and Collins was among the top hitters; Martin, Frisch and DeLancey were batting over .300; and Rothrock and Davis were near the .300 mark. The fielding of Durocher, Frisch and Collins was superb and young Burgess Whitehead was worth coming to the park to watch play the infield. He could cover second, third or shortstop gracefully and skillfully.

Catcher Bill DeLancey began to look like another Bill Dickey. A powerful left-hand batter with a strong and accurate arm, he was a tough customer. After one minor-league game, a gambler accused him and his teammates of dumping a game. DeLancey spit in the man's eye. The gambler complained to the team's owner, who telephoned a protest to Branch Rickey. After hearing the entire story, Rickey replied: "Tell DeLancey to spit in that fellow's other eye."

DeLancey took no nonsense from lazy pitchers, not even from Dizzy Dean. He would charge out to the mound and shake his fist at Diz. "Don't jake on me, you dumb son of a bitch." Dean would laugh. He loved the tough talk of the young catcher.

By late June, the pitching staff was in such a sorry state that the Cardinals went out and obtained Arthur C. "Dazzy" Vance. *Again.* They had got him from Brooklyn in 1932, traded him to Cincinnati in February of '34 and now picked him up on waivers. They felt he might be helpful, even though he was now forty-three, well past his pitching prime.

"The Dazzler" had had an unusual career, not having won a major-league game until he was thirty-one. In 1922, he played his first full year in the major leagues for the Dodgers, winning eighteen games. He won eighteen games the following year, and in 1924 had his biggest season, for which he received the most valuable player award. That year he was the strikeout king, obtained the best earned run average, and the best record, 28–6. In 1925, he pitched a no-hit game; he led the league in strikeouts from 1922 through 1928, relying on a fast ball and a big, tantalizing curve.

A tall, florid-faced man, Dazzy Vance also was a wit who could keep a clubhouse relaxed with quips and homespun philosophy.

Never much of a hitter, Vance had once collected three hits off Wee Willie Sherdel, a pitcher who threw a change-of-pace that seemed to inch its way to the plate. After the game, relaxing with a cool drink, Dazzy had explained his feat. "You know, I sure feel sorry for Willie, cause he didn't know I was a slow-ball hitter. But I found that out years ago when I was a boy on a farm. We were plagued with rats, so we got a ferret and shoved him down a hole. I stood at another hole with a baseball bat. When a rat ran out I swung and missed. Another came and I swung and missed. I must of missed half a dozen. Then out came this fellow nice and slow and I clouted him good. Unfortunately, it was the ferret. From then on I knew I was a slow-ball hitter."

With Vance aboard, the Cardinals now had twenty-three players. St. Louis was carrying three catchers, nine pitchers, six infielders and five outfielders. They all would have to start producing if the team was to get out of third place, where it was on June 26, the day of a key game.

The first-place Giants were in town and had already beaten St. Louis in two of a four-game series, dropping the Cardinals four games back and percentage points behind the second-place Cubs. The games were wild, hardly the kind you'd expect when the league's two best pitching staffs faced each other. The Giants won the first 9–7, as New York pitchers outlasted as many Cardinal hurlers.

Dizzy Dean had been scheduled to pitch the second game on June 25 but had developed an upset stomach. Fifteen thousand fans had turned out, many of them lured by the advertisement: "Dizzy Dean—in person—versus the Giants today." Farmers came from Arkansas, Illinois, western Tennessee and Kentucky—even northern Mississippi and western Indiana. Traveling salesmen arranged their schedules to catch the great Dean in action. Local fans rushed to the park. Everybody loved to see Dizzy perform. On the mound or off, the eccentric Dean could be depended upon for an unpredictable and colorful show, such as the one he staged one hot summer day.

The temperature had been over 100 degrees when Diz set the stands humming. He and Pepper emerged from the dugout carrying sticks of wood and scraps of paper. They built a fire in front of the dugout, wrapped themselves in blankets, and squatted on their heels, twin Indians around a fire. Then Dizzy jumped up and began an Indian war dance, slapping himself on the mouth and yipping like a warrior. The stands rocked with laughter and applause.

Naturally, when Diz failed to pitch on June 25, the fans were angry. Between the fifth and sixth innings, the Cardinals' front office did an unusual thing. It sent its PA announcer, Jim Kelley, *onto* the field with a megaphone. Walking up and down in front of the stands and bleachers, he explained why Dizzy couldn't pitch, and extended the club's apology. His announcement was greeted by jeers from the crowd, whose mood wasn't improved when the home team lost, 10–7. The Giants knocked out Bill Hallahan in the second and collected a total of fifteen hits off him, Mooney, Lindsey and Walker. Hubbell won his eleventh game of the season, struggling to survive in the steaming weather.

June 26, the third game of the series, was the annual Tuberculosis Day game and thousands of fans poured into Sportsman's Park. As they entered, they were greeted by over two hundred young women selling souvenir scorecards.

Despite the 100-degree temperature, the spectators were good-natured, laughing and applauding the pregame entertainment of "horse and bicycle exhibition, tumblers and boxers, demonstrations by drum and bugle corps and the third annual three-mile road race." An intriguing addition to the scheduled program was a motion picture crew shooting background scenes for the film, *Death on the Diamond,* starring Robert Young and Madge Evans. The Cards' own Ernie Orsatti, who sometimes doubled for Buster Keaton, was helping with the baseball scenes.

The game began in a weird way, at least it seemed so to anyone who arrived at the last moment. It started with two Cardinals on base and Orsatti at bat. Orsatti slammed a long drive into left center where it was kicked around by the fielder, who then threw wildly past third. Sprinting toward the plate, Orsatti suddenly collapsed in a heap. The New York catcher rushed out, retrieved the ball, tagged Orsatti, and umpire Bill Klem signaled him out with a grand and sweeping gesture.

The Cardinals rushed out of their dugout and surrounded their fallen comrade. Then a movie director appeared on the field, shouting, "Cut!" It hadn't been the real game at all, but was a scene from the movie. The crowd enjoyed the make-believe episode and then settled back to watch the beginning of the actual game.

They saw another slugfest, but this time St. Louis won 13–7, as twenty-year-old Paul Dean went all the way to wear down three Giant pitchers. It was an impressive display of stamina in the heat.

The final game of the series was the wildest of the lot. Dizzy Dean was on the mound opposing Hal Schumacher. The Cardinals scored four times in the first; it looked like an easy day for Diz, but the Giants came back with two runs in the second and four in the third—and Frankie Frisch blew his top.

After Ott was called out at home by Bill Stewart, the Giants charged the plate and claimed that catcher DeLancey had fumbled the ball. Stewart conferred with second-base umpire George Barr, who said, yes, DeLancey had indeed fumbled. Whereupon plate umpire Stewart reversed his decision and ruled the runner safe. Frankie Frisch told Barr what he thought of an umpire who could see all the way from second through a cloud of dust. Furthermore, Frisch called Barr a variety of names. Barr scowled and shook his head. Frankie Frisch slammed his glove to the ground and, as the crowd roared, threw his hat on top of it.

Umpire Barr then ordered Frisch from the game and the Fordham Flash, whose neck was fiery red, detoured by home plate to tell Bill Stewart what he thought of umpires who reversed their decisions. He stood toe-to-toe with Stewart, shouting in the umpire's face and waving his arms wildly. The crowd jeered when the umpire pointed toward the dugout. Frisch left the field, shouting insults over his shoulder as the fans stood and cheered.

The Cardinals scored single runs in the third, sixth and seventh to lead 7–6 going into the ninth. The Giants tied the score with two out, and Jim Mooney came in to relieve Dizzy. Mooney got the last out on a Mel Ott grounder which he caught in self-defense and then tossed to Collins at first.

In the last of the ninth, reliefer Dolf Luque retired Collins on a pop fly. But young DeLancey hit the first pitch for a tremendous home run on top of the pavillion roof in right center. St. Louis won 8–7, splitting the series and cutting the Giants' lead to two games.

That evening, Jay Hanna Dean took his wife, Pat, dancing. They went to a little amusement park high above the city. A full moon sprinkled the trees with silver, and the light bulbs on the pavilion glowed like fireflies.

Dizzy wore a white polo shirt open at the throat, and a soft wind ruffled his hair. When the orchestra began playing a waltz, he sang to Pat, his lips close to her ear. There was a look of contentment on his handsome face.

Understandable. Dizzy had just won his twelfth game, brother Paul had ten to his credit, and the Deans were about halfway to Dizzy's spring prediction of forty-five victories. And the team had only completed its sixty-third game. There was a world of time and chances for many more victories.

6

Death Valley

DEATH AND DROUGHT, dust and murderous heat—the entire nation was like Death Valley. Hundreds of people and thousands of animals collapsed under a burning sun. July 1934 was a dreadful month for most Americans.

St. Louis was a cauldron. On July 25, seventy-three people died from heat prostration in a twenty-four-hour period, bringing the monthly total to 217 deaths. It was the eighth consecutive day with temperatures over 100 degrees. Hundreds of people flocked to the parks to sleep on the ground or upon cots they carried with them.

Baseball players shuddered at the thought of playing in Sportsman's Park. Noting the temperatures of St. Louis, Carl Hubbell moaned: "Into the valley of death." Dizzy Dean estimated that, by mid-July, the Cards had lost a ton of weight in their home park where the field thermometer registered at 112 to 116 degrees.

"It's not uncommon for the team to drop up to sixty pounds per game," Dean said. "I bet there's been at least thirty games when we've dropped that much. By the end of the season we'll melt away two tons of weight."

Diz claimed to have lost seventeen pounds in one game, perhaps boasting to establish all-time weight loss for pitchers. Tex Carleton, who could ill afford to lose much weight, actually did lose eleven pounds in a game against Brooklyn and, in another game, southpaw Bill Walker dropped eight pounds in seven innings.

As the torrid month of July began, the standings of the National League teams were:

	WON	LOST
New York	42	25
Chicago	41	26
St. Louis	38	27
Pittsburgh	34	29
Boston	35	30
Brooklyn	27	40
Philadelphia	24	42
Cincinnati	21	43

The top three—the Giants, the Cubs and the Cardinals—wheeled through the month like racers at Indianapolis: holding their positions lap after lap. Neither the Cubs nor the Cards could gain on the Giants, led by the great pitching of Hubbell, Schumacher, Parmelee and Fitzsimmons and supported by the hitting of manager Terry, Mel Ott and Joe Moore. The Giants won nineteen and lost eleven; the Cubs were 17–12; and the Cardinals had a seventeen and thirteen record for the month.

Frisch's men played in-and-out baseball, with occasional bursts of brilliance followed by dumb and spiritless play. Dizzy Dean pitched superbly. Carleton and Hallahan pitched well. Bill Walker was spotty after the long layoff with a broken wrist, but showed flashes of his old talent. Dazzy Vance pitched a strong game in Boston during the Cardinals' seven-game winning streak. Five of the regulars were batting over .300: Medwick, Collins, DeLancey, Frisch and Orsatti; and Pat Crawford was delivering clutch pinch hits. But the team sometimes looked like Class C professionals. In one game in Brooklyn, two Cardinal base runners were picked off base. Burgess Whitehead wandered off second and was tagged by Lonnie Frey to end an inning. Umpire Bill Klem gleefully shouted, *"You're out!"*

Manager Frankie Frisch stormed toward the Cardinal dugout. As he reached the bench he gave a mighty kick with one spiked shoe, sending bats flying in various directions. The old Fordham Flash was suffering from a triple case of frustration. First, it was galling to have his runner picked off in a close game (the Cards were then leading, 1–0). Second, Frisch was out of action due to injured legs and had to station himself on the first-base coaching line. Third, he was still smarting over a disputed decision by umpire Klem in a game played early in the month.

In that earlier game, the Cards were at Chicago, trailing 5–1 in the seventh inning, with the bases full of Cubs and one out. Chicago's Chuck Klein hit a high, twisting pop fly between first and home, the wind first blowing the ball foul and then back into fair ground where it eluded the lunge of catcher Bill DeLancey. The Cub runner scored from third base, the next hitter singled in two more runs and the Cubs won the game 7–4.

Meanwhile, Frisch was protesting, officially, unofficially and profanely, as were Dizzy Dean and Mike Gonzalez, all of whom were bounced from the game. Frisch and Gonzalez were fined $100 and $25 respectively. Frisch *knew* he was right on the protest, which he based on the Infield Fly rule, which stated: A batter is out if, with first and second occupied or the bases loaded with less than two out, he hits a fair ball other than a line drive that can be handled by an infielder. Umpire Bill Klem ruled that the fielder, DeLancey, wasn't in position to "handle" the ball. And Bill Klem, the old arbiter, was never wrong. At least according to Bill Klem, and he was a majestic, imperial man who tolerated no criticism. But he could be fair. If he initiated the needling of a player—as he sometimes did with Frisch—then Klem would tolerate a retaliatory insult. But he would not tolerate the nickname "Catfish," which threw him into a fury, because he looked a little like a catfish.

That day in Brooklyn, Frisch and Klem had been "discussing" the disputed play in Chicago as well as each other's ancestry. So when Klem called Whitehead out, Frisch blew up. That one play wasn't bad enough. Three innings later, Bill DeLancey, another sleepy Cardinal, was picked off third base, the victim of the ancient hidden-ball trick. It had happened while Mike Gonzalez, the third-base Cardinal coach, was exhorting Leo Durocher—"Come on, Leo, you can do, you can do." With the coach's attention turned elsewhere, Joe Stripp, the Brooklyn third baseman, tagged DeLancey. Umpire Klem again let loose a majestic bellow, *"You're out!"*

Frankie Frisch jumped up and down, waving his arms and swearing in fury.

In the Brooklyn dugout, Casey Stengel was shaking with laughter at the tantrum of Frankie Frisch. Stengel had known the rival manager since 1921 when they were teammates on the New York Giants. Casey had been an "ancient" thirty-two-year-old and the young second baseman used to wave him off pop flies into short center field. "I'll take it, Pop!" Frisch would shout. He was a brash kid, but Stengel enjoyed his wit and style.

The Brooklyn manager needed humorous moments in order to contend with the characters on his roster. Hack Wilson, his right fielder, often was so hung over he could barely hold up his head. At five foot six inches and 200 pounds, he was built like a beer barrel and had a drinking capacity equal to his size. He had been a powerful hitter, the holder of the National League record for most homers (56) and most RBIs (190) in a season. But now he was well past his prime.

Walter "Boom Boom" Beck, one of Stengel's pitchers, was having an atrocious season. It seemed that every time the manager looked up some opponent was rattling the fence with a line drive. This forced him to walk out to the mound and signal for a relief pitcher. And when Casey did this, he met with furious resistance from Beck who, like most hurlers, wanted to throw to just one more batter.

A source of humorous solace was Nicholas "Mickey Mouse" Tremark, a five-foot three-inch outfielder who had played baseball for Manhattan College. With Tremark at bat, Casey Stengel put on a lively show from his station in the third-base coaching box. The manager would crouch and squint toward the plate, shaping his hands into imaginary binoculars, acting as though he could not locate Tremark. The fans would roar their appreciation.

Frankie Frisch had the last laugh that afternoon in July in Brooklyn. Dizzy Dean shut out the Dodgers 2–0 and added a home run for extra measure. And, joy of joys, the very next day the President of the National League overruled umpire Bill Klem's Chicago decision, declaring that the game must be replayed from the point of dispute.

President Heydler's decision was greeted with mirthful "poetry" by sportswriters in St. Louis and New York. In the *Post-Dispatch*, L. C. Davis penned a poem called "Flys." The first and final verse:

> Bill Klem for 30 years an ump,
> The guy with eagle vision,
> Received a goshalmighty bump,
> And lost his first decision.

> Bill knows the game at every turn,
> And offers no apology,
> But still he has a lot to learn
> Regarding entomology.

In *The New York Times,* John Kieran dashed off a "Song of Sorrow." (First and last stanzas follow.)

> Come gather, ye mourners; bow down to the ground
> And grieve for a dream that is o'er

Bill Klem in an error of judgment was found:
It never had happened before . . .

So let's get together and jump off a cliff
As soon as I've finished this song;
For the end of the world can't be far away if
Bill Klem can be found in the wrong!

A measure of mirth and a mixture of trouble and problems. July had been a typical month for a struggling player-manager. Frisch was named by the fans to the National League All-Star Team, polling 120,141 votes, the third highest in both leagues (Bill Terry was first with 121,110 and Charley Gehringer of Detroit was second with 120,181). Medwick, Dizzy Dean and Pepper Martin also played in the contest. Although the National League lost to the American League, Frisch and Medwick played like stars. They had the only two homers in the game, and Frisch had another hit and scored three runs.

En route to the game, Frisch had talked to Roy Stockton. "I'll tell you something, Roy," he said. "If Lefty Gomez starts the game and gives me a good pitch, I'll hit it out of there." Frisch came up in the first inning and took the first pitch for a ball. The next was shoulder-high and he hammered it into the second tier in right field. The fans stood and roared as Frisch circled the bases. Gomez stood on the mound making faces at the Fordham Flash.

Medwick hit his home run with two men on, a towering blast in the upper left-field stands of the Polo Grounds. Of course, the most exciting performance was the pitching of Carl Hubbell, whom sportswriter John Kieran called "the best pitcher in either league!" The great left-hander had struck out six American Leaguers in two innings, fanning five great hitters in a row: Ruth, Gehrig, Foxx, Simmons and Cronin.

Before the All-Star game, Frisch had been praised by a *Post-Dispatch* writer for the "fine spirit" of his Cardinals.

"The inspiration undoubtedly is Manager Frisch who is the real surprise of the year both from a playing and a managerial standpoint. Frisch was all over the lot, making wonderful stops and going after forlorn hopes just as if they were at his fingertips. Once he ploughed up the dirt with his nose when he missed knocking down a base hit to right field."

The writer continued to praise Frisch as a leader:

"Frisch really has the world popeyed. It was freely predicted last fall and early this season that he would be a flop, because he was not temperamentally suited to the job of manager and also because his players were not in sympathy with him. Both charges have been completely disproved."

At the All-Star break, the Cards were carrying only twenty-one players on their roster, two less than the National League limit. Buster Mills had been assigned to Rochester in the International League and pitcher Jim Lindsey released to Atlanta in the Southern Association. On July 13, the team looked like a squad of walking wounded: Frisch, Orsatti, Whitehead, Hallahan and Paul Dean were injured, leaving only sixteen players fit to play. The "fine spirit" of the team was beginning to sag. They were moving from elation to dejection and back again. Sportswriter J. Roy Stockton wrote on the thirteenth that "Frisch was disgusted with the showing of his team . . . The base running alone was enough to make the Cardinals look like a team fighting for the cellar, and there was little of the snap and dash that characterized the play of the Redbirds earlier in the year."

The key to the trouble seemed to be the undermanned squad, as Stockton pointed out: "Everybody would feel better if the team were strengthened in the pitching department. The team is traveling two under the mid-season player limit and could profitably add another pitcher and a good pinch hitter." Since nobody in the Cardinal front office seemed to be listening, Stockton attacked the matter with another column on the following day, pointing out that "the crippled Cardinal team . . . has been staggering in the pennant race because of an inadequate pitching staff. The front office tried to help. It sent Flint Rhem and Jim Winford away after they had lost a few games and now has disposed of Jim Lindsey, perhaps on the theory that if you get rid of losing pitchers you will have only winning pitchers remaining; but the Cardinals have been going nowhere for the last month."

In Cincinnati, Frankie Frisch decided to run a bed check, placing his first call to the room of Ernie Orsatti. Unbeknownst to the manager, his handsome center fielder had an arrangement whereby the telephone operator switched his calls to the night club in the hotel. When Frisch called, Orsatti picked up the phone and answered in a sleepy voice.

"Yeah, who is it?"

"It's Frisch."

"Jesus, Frank. You woke me out of a sound sleep."

"What the hell's that noise in the background, Ernie?"

"Aw, I forgot and left the radio on."

"Turn it off," Frisch said, "and get some sleep."

Orsatti hung up, smiled and ordered another round of drinks. Although not a big drinker, Ernie loved a good time. Nicknamed "Hollywood," he was a dashing fellow with black, slicked-down hair. A natty dresser, he could not resist the latest styles, even though they put a crimp in his budget. "He is a Beau Brummell," his sister Estelle said, "and a real charmer with the ladies." Only Leo Durocher rivaled him as a clotheshorse.

Ernie Orsatti never graduated from high school, but he had excellent taste. He had grown up in a large affectionate Italian-American family. From his father, who had been a vice-president in a bank, Ernie acquired a love of classical music. He collected opera records, particularly the works of Enrico Caruso. He had a flair for interior decorating, and he was the gourmet cook of the St. Louis Cardinals. He liked to stage little dinner parties in his suite at the Coronado Hotel in St. Louis, where he would entertain teammates Joe Medwick, Leo Durocher, Jack Rothrock and Bill Walker

"Ernie could cook anything," his brother Victor said. "His roast beef was excellent and his quail and pheasant were superb. But his specialty was Italian dishes, spaghetti and meat balls, lasagna, chicken cacciatore, pastas, a delicious antipasto and, of course, minestrone soup."

The night Orsatti played the trick on Frisch, two other Cardinals went wandering around town into the wee hours of the morning in search of liquid refreshments. Unfortunately for the wandering duet, manager Frisch was checking that night, stationing himself in the lobby of the hotel to catch the boys as they returned after visiting various water holes. At 12:20 A.M., he called the absent players' roommates and learned they had not yet tucked themselves in. At 2:05 A.M., one of the absentees called manager Frisch to enquire as to what the skipper wanted. Now, this was an honest, albeit innocent, thing to do. It also proved costly, for Frisch fined the culprit $100 and also fined his playmate the same sum of money The names of the two players were not revealed to the press, but an astute observer could tell who they were by looking into their reddened eyes.

Then the team went on a seven-game winning streak and the mood of all went from depression to elation. In Boston the Cards swept a five-game series and on July 23, as the train left the terminal there was laughter, singing and shouting: "We can win the pennant. We can win the pennant." Because of the winning streak, the Cards were only four games back of the Giants, and if they could sweep the series in New York they would be tied for the lead.

Winning the series proved to be a large order, although Dizzy Dean acted as though they could do it. The next day in the Polo Grounds Dizzy won his tenth game in a row, 6–5, and his eighteenth victory of the season. Rip Collins smashed out five hits, including a home run, and Ernie Orsatti collected four hits. But the seventh win was marred by an injury to Joe Medwick, who fell on his right shoulder trying for a tumbling catch. And Pepper Martin was also on the sidelines with a swollen, stiff elbow, said to be filled with bone chips.

New York ended the Cardinals' victory streak the next afternoon as Leroy "Tarzan" Parmelee pitched a four-hit shutout and the Giants collected eleven hits and five runs off Tex Carleton. The next day the two teams split a double-header and the Cardinals left town as they arrived, four games out of first place. A split of the four-game series might be considered a moral victory, except some of the Cards didn't take it that way. According to J. Roy Stockton:

"There is an alarming tendency in the ranks of Frankie Frisch's men to let defeat knock them into an 'I don't think we can win' frame of mind . . . 'This club can't win,' one Cardinal moaned.

" 'Don't I know it,' replied another. 'I'd sell my World Series chances for $600.'

" 'You want too much,' ventured another. 'I'll let you have mine for $400.' "

One Cardinal spoke out sharply against such pessimism. "You boys quit too easy," Dazzy Vance protested. "Don't let yesterday's defeat or today's defeat get you down. The thing to do is go out and get the next one."

The Cards moved into Pittsburgh for a three-game series. Before the first one, Pepper skipped batting practice, not showing up until near game time. "Where the hell have you been?" Frisch asked. Martin looked as though he had just climbed out of a grease pit. His face was streaked with mud, his clothes grimy and black.

"Aw, some damn fool bet me I couldn't beat him in a two-mile street race," Pepper said.

"That's sweet!" Frisch exploded. "We're trying to win a pennant and you're out driving a race car through the streets. You must be out of your Goddamned head."

A hurt look appeared on Martin's square face and he smiled ruefully. "Anyway, I won the race, Frank."

"What were the stakes in the famous race?" The manager asked.

"Two gallons of ice cream." Pepper grinned.

The Cardinals lost the first two games, Haines getting the first loss and Dizzy the second. For the final game of the series, a delegation of 275 fans journeyed from Nanty Glo, Pa., to honor their hometown hero, Rip Collins. They had been planning the excursion for weeks, saving up hard-earned nickels and dimes to make the day possible. They brought little stickers bearing the phrase, "Greetings to Collins," and carried a big banner with a Lions Club insignia painted on it. They hung the banner on the grandstand. A local brass band made the trip to the park and played before the game. Then the fans of Nanty Glo sat back and waited for their boy Collins, whom they called "Lefty," to do his stuff.

Rip went to the plate three times, popping up in the second, grounding out in the third and popping up in the fifth. He was disappointed and so were his fans. Until the eighth inning. Then, with the score tied at 5–5 and one man on, Collins lined a home run into the stands. The Cardinals finally won the game 9–5, and everybody was happy—except the fans from Pittsburgh.

The Cards took a train from Pittsburgh to Detroit where they beat the Tigers in an exhibition game the next afternoon. On July 31, St. Louis was in Chicago for the final series of the month. The first game was the replay of Bill Klem's "only mistake," and began in the seventh inning with the Cubs at bat, two men on base and two out. The Cardinals lost the game "again" to Lon Warneke and also lost the regulary scheduled game, also pitched by Warneke.

So the Cardinals finished July with four losses in their last five games. With a record of 55–40, they were in third place, five games back of the league-leading Giants. With fifty-nine games remaining on the schedule, they still were in good position in the pennant race. Bill Hallahan was ready to pitch again, Bill Walker was throwing hard, and Paul Dean was about to get back into the starting rotation. Ducky Joe Medwick had recovered from his shoulder injury and Pepper Martin was just about ready to return to third base.

As coach Mike Gonzalez said, again and again, in the dugouts and in clubhouses, aboard trains and in hotel lobbies: "We can do. You believe Mike, she told you. We can do."

7

Revolt in August

ON TUESDAY, AUGUST 14, the weather report for St. Louis was "possible showers with little change of temperatures." Shortly after lunch, the temperature was 94 degrees. At Sportsman's Park, the Cardinals opened a four-game series with the Philadelphia Phillies. The atmosphere in the Cardinal clubhouse was tense, angry and, in the case of at least one man, nearly volcanic.

Earlier in the day, Dizzy Dean had torn up his two uniforms, the first one out of rage, the second for the benefit of a press photographer. The reason for the furious performances were fines imposed on Dizzy ($100) and Paul ($50) for their failure to appear at an exhibition game in Detroit on August 13, following a doubleheader the previous day, a Sunday.

That had been a long, tough day for all the Cardinals, especially the Deans. Before a crowd of over 36,000, the largest in St. Louis since 1931, the Cards lost two games to the Cubs, Paul losing the first and Dizzy the second. The Cardinals had played sloppy baseball, giving the Deans little support in the field. They played so poorly that J. Roy Stockton virtually wrote them out of the pennant race:

"The Cardinals don't quite measure up to pennant-winning specifications. They make too many of those breaks at critical times. Infielders go after grounders with one hand when they could make surer stops with two. Throws for base runners are not as accurate as they must be to help win pennants. Outfielders don't back up plays the way they should. And leading hitters on the team fail too frequently in the pinches." Stockton conceded that "a mathematical chance" remained for the team to win but "only a certain kind of optimist" would wager on the team.

They were seven and one-half games behind the Giants after their double defeat. After the second game Sunday, they had to shower and dress in a rush to catch a train for Detroit and the exhibition game the next day. Dizzy's locker was next to that of Pat Crawford, utility infielder and pinch hitter. "I'm not going to make the trip," he told Crawford. And he didn't. Instead, he went to visit a friend near the ball park. An official of the Cardinals spotted him sitting in his friend's backyard.

Later, Dizzy claimed he had left his suitcases at his hotel and didn't have time to gather his luggage and still catch the train. He also said he was tired and that his arm was so sore he couldn't possibly pitch. But he wasn't expected to pitch in the exhibition game; all he had to do was make an appearance on the field so the fans could see him.

Paul claimed to be ailing.

"I don't see how the Cardinals could expect me to pitch in Detroit," Paul said. "My ankle, which I hurt in Philadelphia last month, was bothering me to such an extent that I could hardly walk at the finish of that game I pitched Sunday."

Manager Frisch refused to accept any excuses and fined the Deans. "There must be discipline on a ball club," Frisch said. "I played eighteen innings in the doubleheaders with the Cubs Sunday, and so did the other regulars. Paul pitched five innings and Dizzy seven and two-thirds rounds. So they didn't do as much work as lots of others. You can't fine one player for missing a train and let others go. So I had to fine both pitchers. The Deans are no better than the others."

The fines led to the confrontation on Tuesday, August 14, in the clubhouse. Before getting into uniform and taking the field for practice, Dizzy Dean had braced Frankie Frisch.

"Do those fines still stand, Frank?" he asked.

"Yes, they do," the manager replied.

"You can't fine me," Dizzy shouted.

"Oh, can't I?" Frisch shouted back. "You're fined. You and Paul, and the fine is going to stick."

"If that fine sticks," Dizzy shouted again, "then me and Paul are through with the Cardinals. I'll show you what I think of this organization."

Frisch then ordered the Deans to get on the field. When they refused, the manager suspended them. Then Diz ripped up his uniform and said he wouldn't play until Frisch apologized for "popping off like that in the clubhouse." Brother Paul said, "I don't care if I ever play baseball again." Dizzy and Paul stalked out of the clubhouse, declaring that they would go fishing in Florida if the fines weren't canceled.

The Dean brothers and Mrs. Jay Hanna Dean spent most of the afternoon in the press box at Sportsman's Park watching as the Cardinals, led by two oldsters, Dazzy Vance and Jesse Haines, and by young Bill DeLancey, trimmed the Phillies 5–1. The three Deans seemed to be in a festive mood considering the circumstances. At one point Mrs. Dean suggested they might as well leave for Florida since they "weren't being paid anyway."

"Better be careful with the groceries," Dizzy said with a grin. "Don't know when we'll get more grocery money."

"We might as well go to Florida," Mrs. Dean said. "Is that OK with you, Paul?"

"It sure is," Paul said.

"All right," Mrs. Dean said. "Why wait? Let's go right now."

"No, we can't do that!" both of the brothers exclaimed. "Tomorrow is payday and we gotta wait and get our checks, or what's left of them, from Bill DeWitt."

The next day the jocular mood of the Deans changed dramatically when the brothers reported at the business office for their paychecks. Dizzy was shocked to find out that not only had he been fined $100, but he had been docked an additional $36 for ripping his uniforms.

"I don't think that was nice," he said. "I was mad and lost my temper when I tore my uniforms but they weren't destroyed. They could have been mended."

That very day, August 15, Frankie Frisch and Sam Breadon agreed that the fines and suspensions should be upheld. The Deans were sidelined for ten days. Hearing this, the brothers postponed their departure for Florida, confident that the ban would be lifted. After all, how could the Cardinals hope to finish in the money without them? Dizzy had a record of twenty-one wins and five losses and Paul had won twelve and lost six.

Dizzy and Paul failed to reckon with several facts of life. They were locked in a power struggle with a stubborn, determined man, Frankie Frisch, whose managerial career was threatened by their behavior. If he capitulated to their prima-donna conduct, he would lose control of the team. Furthermore, Sam Breadon was backing Frankie Frisch. Breadon was not the kind of man who could be blackmailed by a loud-mouthed cotton picker from Arkansas. In addition, Breadon was being urged by Rickey to take a firm stand against the Deans who, Rickey insisted, had to be put in their place. The fourth fact was the attitude of the team. Dizzy Dean, with all his pitching greatness, was not loved by his teammates, who disliked his boasting, his high-handedness and his flaunting of rules. If other players had to obey the rules and pay a fine when they misbehaved, Dizzy and Paul should do the same.

All eighteen players rallied behind Frisch, the old Fordham Flash, the skipper and regular second baseman. They would carry on without the Deans. Even Pepper Martin volunteered to pitch, telling everyone about the velocity of his fast ball, the sharpness of his curves and the befuddling action of his dancing knuckle ball.

The Cardinals were rained out on August 15. On August 16, before the start of the doubleheader, Dizzy Dean was ready to make peace with the management.

"I don't want to lose any more money," Dizzy said. "How about it, Paul? I'll pay part of the money you've lost."

Paul, a quiet man, stubbornly shook his head. This time little brother wouldn't listen to big brother; Paul insisted the club rescind his $50 fine. The Cardinals refused and without the Deans the team swept a doubleheader from the Phillies, winning the first game in eleven innings as Leo Durocher doubled to score Rip Collins. The team was beginning to call Durocher "Captain Slug," rather than "the All-American Out." Old Jesse "Pop" Haines was the winning pitcher, relieving Tex Carleton in the tenth inning with one out. The Cardinals went on a hitting spree to take the second game 7–2. The team's victory, coupled with a loss by the Giants, put the Cardinals five and a half games out of first place.

On the next day, Paul Dean declared a truce, perhaps impressed by the team's three straight wins without him and his brother. Every day of mutiny cost Paul a day's pay. He paid his $50 fine, repented and apologized in a signed statement released by Sam Breadon, president of the club.

"I know I was in the wrong when I refused to go to Detroit," Paul said, "and again when I refused to go on the field when asked to do so by manager Frisch."

The Cardinals won their fourth straight game for a clean sweep of the series with Philadelphia. With the score 4–2, Paul came in to relieve Mooney and Vance, who were being hit hard. The young Dean pitched the final seven innings, allowing no runs and only four hits as the team went on to win 12–2, lashing out seventeen hits including four by Rip Collins.

Meanwhile, the pot boiled. Dizzy Dean went to Chicago

to take his case directly to the commissioner of baseball, Judge Kenesaw Mountain Landis. Back in St. Louis, the Cardinal front office declared it was backing Frankie Frisch "100 percent in his controversy with the Deans." However, general manager Branch Rickey said no announcement would be made during the season as to who might manage the team in 1935.

"That does not mean," Rickey said, "that Frisch will be replaced and it does not mean that he will be reappointed. It merely means the club has adopted a policy to make no more announcements about managers during a season."

Although the statement didn't sound like a complete vote of confidence, the wily Rickey had something in mind. Privately he was delighted by the rebellion of the Deans, as he confessed to his associate, Gene Karst.

"Football coaches pray for an incident such as this," Rickey said. "They want something, some development, which can change the direction of the team, fire it up to superhuman effort." Prior to the revolt the team had been playing erratically, going on winning streaks and then lapsing into sloppy and indifferent play. They were a formidable club but seemed to lack the fire of a pennant winner. Rickey, a master of sports psychology, figured the team would rally to prove they didn't need the Deans and to help save Frisch's job. It was a matter of self-respect for the players to demonstrate their professional skill and courage while showing up the Deans as publicity hogs.

On Saturday, August 18, Dizzy Dean was still on the sidelines, but it didn't seem to make much difference. The Cards buried the Boston Braves with twenty hits. Wild Bill Hallahan, who had been undependable early in the season, allowed only five hits as he won his fifth straight game, 15–0. The next day the Cards split a doubleheader with the Braves.

Pepper Martin, the Wild Horse of the Osage, pitched two innings in the first game, relieving Jim Mooney in the fourth inning. Pepper allowed only one hit. Between the the fourth and fifth innings, pitcher Pepper went to the bullpen to loosen up his arm, because he had come into the game with little warm-up. He then went on to pitch the fifth inning, and set the Braves down in order, using a mixture of fast balls, knucklers and a side-arm change of pace.

The Cardinals had won six out of seven games without the great Dizzy Dean, who was due to state his case the next day before Judge Landis. The commissioner had journeyed to St. Louis for the hearing.

The hearing was held on an off-day, Monday, August 20, at the Park Plaza Hotel. It began at 10 A.M. and was long, loud and occasionally ugly, filled with charges and counter-charges. Although the session was conducted behind closed doors, the wrangling could be heard in the hotel corridors. In attendance were the Dean brothers; Breadon and Rickey; Frisch, Durocher and Jesse Haines; trainer Harrison "Doc" Weaver and traveling secretary Clarence Lloyd; coaches Mike Gonzalez and Buzzy Wares. Judge Landis questioned each witness separately, but often was interrupted by noisy exchanges, including one between Breadon and Dizzy in which each called the other a liar.

Branch Rickey also questioned each witness, acting as cross-examiner for the management. The hearing droned on, covering everything from Dizzy's sore arm to Paul's sprained ankle, and even included the subject of Elmer Dean, who Dizzy charged had been brought to St. Louis for a job, then had been offered the humiliating position of peanut vendor. Under questioning by Rickey, Dizzy admitted requesting employment at Sportsman's Park for Elmer. But, Dizzy said, "I didn't think Mr. Rickey would try to bring Elmer up here and then make a peanut peddler out of him."

Dizzy objected when repeatedly cross-examined on the same points in the case.

"For crimminy sakes," Dizzy would say. "You all know I missed the train. I missed it and I was sorry and I took my fine and suspension and paid for the uniforms I damaged and wanted to get back and pitch again. What I want to know is why didn't you let me come back Thursday when I wanted to? Why did you tell me I had to bring Paul back? I didn't have no shackles on him."

Commissioner Landis devoted half an hour to the questioning of witnesses as to what happened in the office of Sam Breadon when the Cardinals' president refused to allow Dizzy to return unless he brought Paul along, too. Breadon admitted he had made such a statement, but with the qualification that the whole matter was in the hands of Frisch, and the manager would have "to approve or disapprove anything that was done."

After four hours and five minutes of testimony and acrimony and cross-examination, Judge Kenesaw Mountain Landis decreed that the punishment meted out to the Deans was just, that the Club had been within its rights to fine and suspend the players, and that there was no cause for the baseball commissioner to interfere in the case.

"My mind is so constituted," the crusty judge declared, "that I cannot accept the stories told by these players about how they missed the train. I also find it difficult to accept the stories of the two boys that they missed the train independently without either knowing that the other had not made the trip." Commissioner Landis shook his head. "I will dismiss the disputed question of what President Breadon said in regard to whether Dizzy could or could not come back into the fold without Paul. My opinion is that it was up to the manager, in this case Frank Frisch, to decide when the suspension was to be terminated."

Near the close of the hearing, Sam Breadon made a conciliatory speech, praising the greatness of Dizzy as a pitcher, but chided him for "hurting your own game" by telling people "the Cardinals are cheap and that I'm cheap and that Branch Rickey is cheap."

Throughout the long trial, Paul Dean had very little to say. But when it was over, he turned to his brother and said: "Why didn't you pop that Dutchman on the nose, Diz?"

Dizzy Dean accepted his public rebuke without further

protest and the suspension was lifted. The revolt had cost him $486, including the fine, the price of two uniforms and the loss of seven days' pay. He also sent a telegram to the Detroit Tigers, apologizing for his failure to appear at the exhibition game. "Believe me," Diz wrote, "when I say I deeply regret not being there for the game."

Dizzy was back in uniform on Tuesday as the Cards beat the Braves 6–2, behind the steady pitching of Tex Carleton. The team was idle on Wednesday, but the league-leading Giants came to town on Thursday for a three-game series. New York won the opener 5–3, on a three-run homer by Joe Moore off Paul Dean in the ninth inning. The Giants' victory kept the Cards in third place, seven games out of the lead. Dizzy came out of exile the next day and threw a five-hitter, beating New York 5–0, for his twenty-second win. Rothrock hit a homer and Rip Collins hit his thirtieth of the season.

The Giants won the third game of the series 7–6. It was another cliff-hanger decided by a single by Travis Jackson with the bases loaded in the eighth inning. The victim of the hit was Dizzy Dean, who had volunteered to relieve a faltering Bill Walker in the seventh inning. It was New York's first win over Dizzy in his six games against them.

The Cardinals were to close their home stand against the Dodgers. After one of the losses in that series, Frisch left the clubhouse steaming mad. He walked through the streets with a thunderous look on his face. Casey Stengel, the Brooklyn manager, caught up to him in his cab and shouted, "Come on, Dutchman, hop in and ride along."

"Piss on you, Pop," Frisch called over his shoulder. He continued his furious pace with Stengel cruising alongside and calling: "Forget it, Squarehead. Come on. We'll go have a couple drinks."

This went on for blocks, Stengel imploring and cajoling, offering various drinks and dinner, and the Cardinal manager refusing profanely. Finally, the Fordham Flash could not resist. His face broke into a smile.

"OK. Goddamn it! But you're paying for everything."
And he climbed into the cab.

St. Louis took three out of five from Brooklyn. Paul Dean
shut out the Dodgers 2–0 in the fourth game for his fourteenth victory of the season; and Bill Walker pitched a
strong five-hitter to win the fifth 4–1. As they hopped a train
to begin a road trip, they were accompanied by a rumor:
Paul Dean would be sold to Brooklyn for $50,000 for de-
livery in the spring of '35. Sam Breadon laughed at such a
notion, declaring that "neither of the Deans will be disposed of."

The next afternoon, on August 31, Dizzy Dean added an
exclamation point to Breadon's statement by beating the
Chicago Cubs 3–1, for his twenty-third victory. This tied him
with Lefty Gomez of the Yankees for most wins in the majors.

The Cardinals closed out August with a record of 19–11;
they finished the month five and a half games behind the
Giants—and the Deans led the nation in strikes.

In Houston, Texas, Elmer Dean, the champion of all
peanut and soda salesmen, walked off the job.

"He's out on strike," reported Walter Benson, the concession director. "He called me on the telephone. 'I want
more money,' Elmer demanded, 'or I'll let your goobers go
stale.' "

When the concession director had refused to meet the
salary demand, Elmer Dean said: "I quit."

Even the August weather was erratic. Areas of the North-
west and Rocky Mountains that had suffered 100-degree
temperatures were struck by a cold wave. Fields in Wis-
consin, Iowa, North Dakota and Minnesota glistened with
frost, and flurries of snow grounded airplanes in Billings,
Montana. New England suffered its coldest month in thirty-
one years, with freezing temperatures. Yet for the entire
nation at large, the summer of '34 was the hottest and driest
in the history of recorded weather.

8

The Deans of September

FRANKIE FRISCH'S STOMACH must have looked like a pretzel. Fortunately, no X rays were taken. The Fordham Flash had enough problems handling his unpredictable players, with their antics off the field and their looney base running.

St. Louis opened September with a win over the Cubs to sneak by Chicago into second place. Then the team traveled to Pittsburgh where they lost a Labor Day doubleheader, with the Deans getting the defeats that dropped the Cards back into a tie for second. It was a depressing way to celebrate a holiday and made cold beer taste like warm buttermilk, especially to the tongue of the fiery Frisch who detested the mere thought of defeat.

Sometimes, in a sour mood, manager Frisch turned to coach Gonzalez for comic relief. One morning after a tough loss, he invited the happy-go-lucky Cuban to his room for breakfast. While Frisch was shaving, he listened to Mike Gonzalez order breakfast over the telephone.

"How many time must I tole you what I want!" Gonzalez shouted his order. "OK. I give you wance more. Sakarahak juss. You catch him, OK? Two fry egg. You catch him, OK? Two-three slice hang. You catch him, OK?"

As Gonzalez continued yelling into the phone, Frisch had to cover his mouth to keep from roaring with laughter. "What you say?" The coach bellowed again. "I tole you, *sakarahak* juss! You ask me, I tole you SAKARAHAK juss, SAKARAHAK juss!"

Coach Gonzalez banged down the receiver and waved his arms as manager Frisch entered the room. "Dampool, Frahnk. Mike she tole her sakarahak juss, two, three times but she no understand English." Frisch had to pick up the telephone to order the sauerkraut juice.

After the Labor Day debacle, the Cardinals went to New York to play the Dodgers a four-game series. Dizzy Dean won the opener with a three-hitter for his twenty-fourth win.

The next day, September 6, Tex Carleton won his fifteenth game, 7–5, pitching strongly until the ninth when the Dodgers scored three runs. The final two games of the series were rained out and the Cards moved on to Philadelphia, where they won four out of six at Baker Bowl, with Paul picking up his fifteenth win and Dizzy his twenty-fifth. Walker and Hallahan were the other winning pitchers, although Dizzy had to come in as a relief hurler to save Wild Bill's victory. The Cardinals lost the final game of the series by blunders on the bases.

On September 13, St. Louis faced the Giants in the Polo Grounds with Paul Dean opposing Fred Fitzsimmons. The game went twelve innings before the Cards scored twice as DeLancey and Durocher drove in Medwick and Collins. Paul Dean pitched all the way, allowing only six hits, relying on his blazing fast ball and showing great poise when the Giants put men on base. The victory left St. Louis four and one-half games out of first place, a margin that was widened the next afternoon as Hal Schumacher beat St. Louis 4–1. Experts now predicted that New York had the pennant won. The Giants only had fourteen games left to play; St. Louis sixteen. New York had an 88–51 record; St. Louis 82–56. If the Giants played at a .500 pace, winning seven and losing seven, the Cardinals would have to post a 14–2 record to come out on top by half a game. An unlikely possibility, particularly since the Giants were playing most of their final games at home.

The third game of the series was rained out, setting up a doubleheader for September 16.

The day was damp and dark, but an enormous crowd of nearly 63,000 surged into the Polo Grounds. The fire department locked the gates as 15,000 more fans swarmed around the pillars of the elevated tracks on Eighth Avenue and jammed the crest of Coogan's Bluff.

Leroy "Tarzan" Parmelee faced Jay Hanna "Dizzy" Dean in the first game: two power pitchers working in the dim afternoon light. With the Giants leading 3–0, Parmelee looked unbeatable. Going into the seventh, he had given up only three hits; but with one out the Cardinals took aim. DeLancey and Orsatti singled as did Spud Davis, batting for Durocher, driving in the Cardinal catcher. Now the two managers began to maneuver.

Frisch sent Whitehead to run for Davis, and then summoned a pinch hitter for Dizzy Dean.

"Number eleven," the loudspeaker blared, "Pat Crawford, now batting for Dean."

The Cardinals' best pinch hitter stepped into the on-deck circle, swinging his bat savagely. He was trying to look *real* mean, for this was one of the few times in his career that Crawford wasn't eager to bat. The visibility was poor and Parmelee had a fine fast ball and a good fork ball. *I hope I can get the fast ball,* Crawford thought, taking another vicious swing and shooting an angry look at the mound.

"Time out!" Manager Bill Terry called from his position at first base. Crawford's performance must have impressed Memphis Bill. As the huge crowd buzzed with concern, Terry waved to the bullpen. In came Al Smith, a left-hander.

Frankie Frisch moved to the top of the dugout and called to the umpire. The loudspeaker crackled again. "Number four, batting for Crawford, Chick Fullis."

Pat Crawford heaved a sigh of relief. "I was tickled pink to get out of there," he said later.

Fullis lined out to the shortstop and Terry once more called time to bring in another pitcher. It was Hal

Schumacher, whom he thought could take care of Pepper Martin. Instead he walked Martin *and* Rothrock to force in a run.

The crowd stood and roared as the next batter advanced. It was Frank Francis Frisch, former hero of the Giants, now setting himself at the plate. He looked tired, worn down by the long, hot season and the pressure of playing and managing. "My eyes ached," he recalled. The bat felt heavy in his hands.

Three Cardinals edged off base as Prince Hal Schumacher wound up and threw. Frisch drove the first pitch into right field for a single that put the Cards ahead 4–3. St. Louis scored another run in the ninth and won, 5–3, as Tex Carleton set down the Giants in order in the last three innings.

The second game went eleven innings with King Carl Hubbell and Paul Dean struggling all the way. Led by Pepper Martin, who sliced a homer into the right-field stands, the Cardinals touched up Hubbell for two runs to win the game 3–1. It was the second straight extra-inning victory for young Paul, who threw a six-hitter. His teammates had backed him with key hits under pressure and with superb fielding, particularly by Rothrock and Medwick.

After five hours of tense baseball, the dispirited New York fans stumbled out of the Polo Grounds under the glittering exit lights.

The Cardinals boarded the train for Boston, three and one-half games out of first place; the firm of "Me and Paul" had a total of forty-three wins (Dizzy had twenty-six); and the team was running like a well-greased machine.

The Cardinals were rained out on the 18th and 19th, forcing a doubleheader with Boston on the 20th. They won both games, the first 4–1, on a three-hitter by Tex Carleton, the second 1–0, on a strong game by Bill Walker. Then they moved back into New York to play a makeup doubleheader against Brooklyn. It turned out to be one of the most incredible twin bills ever played in the majors.

The morning of the doubleheader, September 21, Dizzy told a reporter that "Zachary and Benge [the Dodgers' pitchers] will be pitching against one-hit Dean and no-hit Dean today."

In the Cardinals' clubhouse, the team held its customary meeting, with Frisch going over each of the Brooklyn hitters, explaining precisely how he wanted each man pitched. The St. Louis pitchers had all they could do to keep from laughing. For as Frisch ran down the lineup, Dizzy interrupted him after each instruction.

"I want you to throw curves to Tony Cuccinello." Frisch pointed at Dizzy. Dean just shook his head.

"That's crazy, Frank," the pitcher said. "I ain't never give him a curve and he's still trying to hit a foul ball off me."

As Frisch's face grew red with rage, the players bit their lips to keep from laughing out loud. Finally, Dizzy stopped the whole proceeding.

"This is silly, Frank. I've already won twenty-six games and it don't look right for an infielder like you to be telling a star like me how I should pitch."

Manager Frisch exploded. "Yes, sir," Tex Carleton told a writer. "Old Frank *really* told Diz he could pitch any way he damn well pleased even if he got his ears knocked back." Carleton laughed. "Diz was going to pitch his own game anyhow, no matter what Frankie said. He'd throw his rising fast ball inside to right-hand hitters and he'd throw it outside to left-handers."

Before the first game, Dizzy teased the Dodgers in their dugout. "You ought to get a pitcher like me and develop a team around him," he advised Casey Stengel.

Dizzy shut out the Dodgers on three hits to win the opener 13–0, not giving up a hit until two were out in the eighth inning. Paul Dean shut out Brooklyn 3–0, and nearly pitched a perfect game. The only man to reach first base was Len Koenecke, who drew a walk in the first inning. Nobody else reached base and Paul Dean became the first major-league rookie to throw a no-hit game in his first year. "If I'd of knowed Paul was going to pitch a no-hitter," Dizzy said later, "I'd of pitched one, too."

He might have done it, for his predictions usually were right. Between the two Deans, they now had won the forty-five games as Dizzy said they would in the spring. Dizzy had twenty-seven and Paul had eighteen wins. The Cardinals had won three straight doubleheaders and had cut the Giants' lead to three games. Their next stop was Cincinnati for a two-game series with the Reds.

They split the series and moved to Chicago for a single game. Bill Walker pitched a seven-hitter and, backed up by outstanding fielding, beat the Cubs 3–1.

When the Cardinals returned to St. Louis for the final week of the season, they were two games behind the Giants. They had six games left, two with Pittsburgh and four with Cincinnati. The Giants had four games remaining, two with the Phillies and two with the Dodgers. For the Cards to become champions, they had to keep winning, and the Giants had to play losing baseball. Since September 14, St. Louis had won ten and lost one, while the Giants were winning five and losing the same number.

On September 25, the Cards topped the Pirates, 3–2, as Dizzy Dean pitched a six-hitter for his twenty-eighth win. In New York, Curt Davis of the Phillies shut out the Giants 4–0, allowing only four singles. The Cardinals now were only a single game out of first place with a record of 91 wins and 57 losses; New York had 93 wins and 57 losses. The stage was set for a wild finish to one of the most exciting pennant races in the history of the National League.

September had been a dramatic month for headline writers. The *Morro Castle*, a luxury liner, caught fire off the coast of New Jersey. One hundred and thirty-five people lost their lives in the burning ship. Two hundred thousand textile workers walked off their jobs in a nationwide strike. Bruno Richard Hauptmann was arrested by the police and accused of the kidnapping and killing of the nineteen-month-old son of Charles A. Lindbergh. And the Assembly of the League of Nations in Geneva admitted Soviet Russia to membership.

In St. Louis on the morning of September 26, Leo Ernest Durocher and Grace Dozier were married at the Municipal Court Building. It was the second marriage for each. Center-fielder Ernie Orsatti served as best man—and juggled the box containing the wedding ring, which amused the guests and members of the wedding party.

On any other team but the Cardinals, the wedding of a key player during the last week of a pennant race would have been considered an act of insanity. With a pennant at stake and only five games remaining, no rational baseball executive would want the team's captain distracted by a bride—except Branch Rickey. He knew that Durocher was wildly in love with Grace Dozier and felt that the best possible thing would be for the two to marry immediately. Rickey knew Grace Dozier and intervened on behalf of Durocher. She was smitten with Leo but wasn't sure that it was the most appropriate time for their marriage. However, Rickey persuaded her to marry Leo right away so that the shortstop would be free to concentrate on hitting and fielding.

Frankie Frisch merely groaned when he heard about the decision. "What a time for a wedding!" he snorted. That very afternoon the Cardinals were shut out 3–0 by Waite Hoyt of Pittsburgh, as Paul Dean lost his eleventh game of the season.

The defeat brought tears to the eyes of Grace Durocher and a snarl to the lips of manager Frisch. But back in New York, the Phillies routed Schumacher, Hubbell and old Dolph Luque to beat the Giants 5–4.

The Giants were to be idle for the next two days, so manager Bill Terry suggested the boys take in a movie and forget about baseball. After all, there was plenty of good entertainment in the Big Apple that week: *Caravan,* starring Charles Boyer, Loretta Young and Jean Parker, was having a world premiere at Radio City Music Hall. At the Rivoli, Robert Donat could be seen in the opening of the third screen version of *The Count of Monte Cristo.* And, at Loew's, the lovely Claudette Colbert starred in Cecil B. DeMille's *Cleopatra.*

Back in St. Louis, the lovely, talented *and* prosperous Grace Dozier Durocher was spending most of her morning writing checks. Her husband Leo had piled up a number of debts and Mrs. Durocher, who owned a dress manufacturing company, decided to wipe the slate clean. That this cultured, beautiful and intelligent woman could be in love with Leo Durocher astonished many people. However, Branch Rickey knew Durocher could "charm your eye out of its socket, but back him into a corner and he's still that kid from West Springfield with the butt of a pool cue in his hand." Rickey felt that Grace Dozier would have a civilizing, perhaps inspirational effect on the peppery shortstop.

That afternoon, September 27, the Cardinals beat the Reds 8–5, and Captain Leo Durocher played a leading role in the contest. He had two hits, a single and a double, and drove in two runs. The next afternoon, Dizzy Dean took the mound for the first game of a four-game series with Cincinnati. Dizzy shut out the Reds 4–0, scattering seven hits for his twenty-ninth win and sixth shutout of the season. Ducky Medwick and "Slug" Durocher led the hitting attack, each driving in two runs. The win put the Cardinals in a tie with the Giants.

Saturday, September 29. The St. Louis Cardinals and the New York Giants were tied for first place in the National League with ninety-three wins and fifty-eight losses each. Throughout the nation, baseball fans devoured their daily newspapers and huddled around their radios for tidbits about the coming games.

In St. Louis, Dizzy Dean had attended a benefit rodeo

show for Christian Brothers College and was invited to try his hand at roping a calf, an invitation he declined over the PA system.

"I just can't do it, folks," Dean said. "We gotta win that National League title and that's more serious now than roping a calf, don't you think so?" The crowd roared its agreement. "But I could've done it," Dizzy whispered to a friend.

"Is Brooklyn still in the league?" Bill Terry's quip was being tossed back at him.

In *The New York Times*, John Kieran penned some ominous verse, chiding the Giants' manager for tempting the Gods of Chance and the Demons of the Gowanus. His opening stanza:

BALLAD OF BITTER WORDS

Why, Mister Terry, oh! why did you ever
Chortle the query that made Brooklyn hot?
Just for the crack that you thought was so clever,
Now you stand teetering right on the spot!
Vain was your hope they forgave or forgot;
Now that you're weary and bowed with fatigue,
Here is the drama and this is the plot:
Brooklyn, dear fellows, is still in the league.

That afternoon the Dodgers stormed into the Polo Grounds led by the sharp-tongued Casey Stengel and followed by their wild-eyed fans who longed to see Bill Terry and his boys soundly thrashed. It was a gray, rainy day and the game was delayed twenty-one minutes to get the field ready. Finally, at 2:10 P.M., the contest began. On the mound for New York was Tarzan Parmelee. His opponent: Van Lingle Mungo, a broad-shouldered fireballer.

Heavy, threatening mists hovered over the field, making the fast balls of Parmelee and Mungo look as small as aspirin tablets. The teams went scoreless for four innings, but in the fifth the Dodgers broke through when Mungo singled and moved to second on a passed ball by Gus Mancuso.

Lonny Frey then singled home the big Brooklyn pitcher for the first run. The Dodgers scored another run in the sixth when Mungo came up with two out and lined a single over first-baseman Terry's head. The Dodgers scored a single in the seventh and two in the ninth, while the best the Giants could do was one run in the seventh. Van Lingle Mungo poured fire on the head of the Giants, striking out the side in the ninth to win a five-hitter, 5–1.

In St. Louis, Paul Dean was on the mound looking for his nineteenth win. Facing him was Big Paul Derringer, a Cardinal castoff who would dearly have loved to beat St. Louis. Although the Reds collected eleven hits off Dean, they managed to score only once, on a homer by another ex-Card, Jim Bottomley. St. Louis got twelve hits off Derringer and played brilliant defensive baseball. The final score was 6–1, and the Cardinals were in first place by a single game. They had not led the league since June 1.

The clubhouse was strangely quiet after the game, with the players merely shaking Paul's hand and saying, "Nice work, Paul." Sitting at his locker, old Pop Haines muttered to himself, "Whatta nine, whatta nine." Pepper Martin didn't say anything, but a huge smile lit up his country-boy face. Dizzy Dean also grinned and patted brother Paul on the back while guaranteeing his teammates that if they gave him a "couple of runs there ain't going to be any play-off."

The only chance the Giants then had was to win on Sunday, September 30, against the Dodgers, and for St. Louis to lose, that same afternoon against Cincinnati, forcing a play-off.

In New York, 45,000 fans charged into the Polo Grounds, swarming across the river from Brooklyn and literally fighting each other to squeeze through the turnstiles. The Dodger rooters filled the stands with a continuous din, blowing horns and whistles and ringing cowbells, shouting, jeering and hooting.

The Giants tore into the Dodgers in the first inning, scoring four runs off Brooklyn's Ray Benge. The Dodgers bounced back with single runs in the second, fourth and sixth and two runs in the eighth. But the Giants had also scored a run in the fourth and the game was tied 5–5 after nine innings. In the tenth, Hal Schumacher was on the mound, having replaced Fred Fitzsimmons in the eighth. Sam Leslie of Brooklyn singled to open the tenth and when Tony Cuccinello followed with a double, manager Terry replaced Schumacher with Carl Hubbell. Hubbell couldn't stop Brooklyn from scoring. The Dodgers won 8–5, as young Johnny Babich held the Giants scoreless in their last inning at bat.

For dethroning the Giants, manager Casey Stengel was named a Kentucky Colonel by that state's governor, Ruby Laffon. Casey joined a distinguished brigade, which included film star Mae West. It was a most appropriate appointment, Stengel said. "I've been a leading patron of Kentucky whiskey for years."

Meanwhile in St. Louis, Sportsman's Park was also bulging with customers. (Now the Cardinals might finish in the black ink instead of the red, for the final day's attendance brought the year's total to 327,000.) The fans were about to watch two games, one on the field against the Reds and the other on the scoreboard between Brooklyn and New York. They roared when the batteries went up for the Giant game, and then shifted their attention to the field when the Cardinal Boys Band marched out for the flag-raising ceremony. At home plate, the Deans and Frankie Frisch were presented with diamond rings and Paul Dean received a silver statue in honor of his no-hit game against Brooklyn.

Some of the fans groaned when the first-inning score of the New York game was posted. But the Cards also began with a rush, scoring two in the first. Although Dizzy Dean was pitching with only one day's rest, the Reds failed to score in the first eight innings. Dizzy was after his seventh straight win, his seventh shutout of the season and his thirtieth victory.

In the ninth inning, the scoreboard flashed the news that

Part I: The Gashouse Gang

Branch Rickey (left) loved "hungry" players, and Pepper Martin was the hungriest of all. (*St. Louis Post-Dispatch*)

Frankie Frisch (left) with Sam Breadon, president of the St. Louis Cardinals. The Fordham Flash was Sam's favorite player. (*St. Louis Post-Dispatch*)

Warming up in Bradenton, Florida: (left to right) Tex Carleton, Jesse Haines, Dizzy Dean, Bill Hallahan and Bill Walker. (*St. Louis Post-Dispatch*)

Right First baseman Rip Collins led the 1934 Cardinals in home runs and runs batted in, and supervised most of their pranks. (*Courtesy Baseball Hall of Fame*)

Below Mike Gonzalez was a colorful coach who could steal an opponent's sign without batting an eye. (*Courtesy France Laux*)

Left to right: Utilityman and pinch hitter Pat Crawford, Leo Durocher, Pepper Martin and Frankie Frisch. (*St. Louis Post-Dispatch*)

Bottom left "Showboat" Ernie Orsatti was a dashing fellow and a speedy center fielder. (*Courtesy Baseball Hall of Fame*)

Bottom right Joe Medwick. Called "Ducky" by the fans and "Muscles" by his friends, his temper was as explosive as his bat. (*St. Louis Post-Dispatch*)

Burgess Whitehead played the infield like a gazelle. (*Courtesy Burgess Whitehead*)

Dizzy and Paul Dean. Between them they won 49 games in the 1934 season. (*St. Louis Post-Dispatch*)

Bill Terry. The manager of the Giants was a brilliant strategist, but his wisecrack about Brooklyn may have cost New York the pennant. (*Courtesy Baseball Hall of Fame*)

Manager Casey Stengel led his Dodgers into the Polo Grounds where they proved that Brooklyn was "still in the league." (*Wide World Photos*)

Heading for Detroit and the 1934 World Series were (left) Ernie Orsatti, Frankie Frisch, traveling secretary Clarence Lloyd and Mr. and Mrs. Dizzy Dean. (*St. Louis Post-Dispatch*)

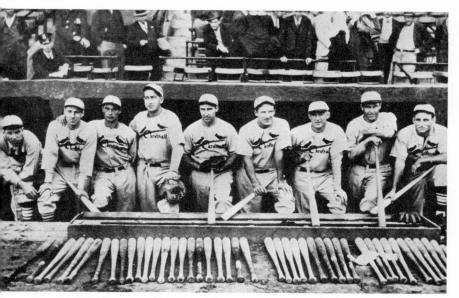

The Cardinals' starting lineup for the first game of the World Series was (from left) Dizzy Dean, Leo Durocher, Ernie Orsatti, Bill DeLancey, Rip Collins, Joe Medwick, Frankie Frisch, Jack Rothrock and Pepper Martin. (*Wide World Photos*)

Jay Hanna "Dizzy" Dean. In 1934, he was the compleat pitcher, winning thirty games in the season and two in the World Series. (*St. Louis Post-Dispatch*)

Starting pitchers for the second game were (left) Bill Hallahan and School-boy Rowe. (*Wide World Photos*)

In the slide that triggered a riot, Joe Medwick barreled into third-baseman Marv Owen. (*St. Louis Post-Dispatch*)

After the seventh game of the 1934 World Series, Detroit police escorted the St. Louis Cardinals back to their hotel. (*St. Louis Post-Dispatch*)

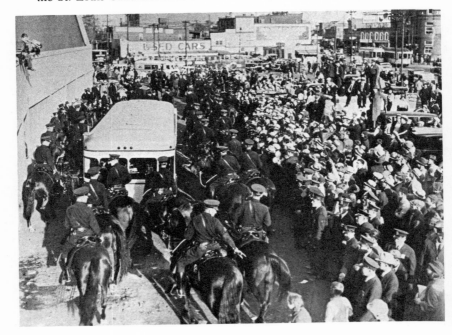

Dizzy Dean holds a toy tiger with knots in its tail as Mrs. Dean and brother Paul grin in triumph. (*St. Louis Post-Dispatch*)

The city of St. Louis staged a wild celebration after the Cardinals won the 1934 World Series. (*St. Louis Post-Dispatch*)

Part II: Some Forty Years Later

Joe Medwick as minor league batting coach of the St. Louis Cardinals.

Jim Mooney at his desk at East Tennessee State University.

Pat Crawford on the veranda of his lovely old home in Kinston, North Carolina.

Jack Rothrock poses with his favorite bat at his home in San Juan Capistrano, California. (*Bill Libby*)

Virgil "Spud" Davis of Birmingham, Alabama.

Tex Carleton at home in Fort Worth, Texas.

Jesse "Pop" Haines, the senior citizen of Clayton, Ohio.

Bill Hallahan (left) chats with the author. (*Eric Hood*)

Burgess "Whitey" Whitehead at home in North Carolina. (*Courtesy Burgess Whitehead*)

Brooklyn had beaten the Giants. The Cardinals had won the pennant.

But at that moment, three Reds were on base with nobody out, threatening Dizzy's shutout. He was not about to let that happen. Dean bowed his back and poured the ball in, striking out the next two men and getting the last out on a pop foul to catcher Bill DeLancey. The fans stormed onto the field and Dizzy raced off surrounded by police.

Rip Collins danced into the clubhouse warbling, "We're in the money." He was followed by a yelling, jubilant gang who rushed to the showers shouting and singing. Coach Buzzy Wares, Pepper Martin and Ducky Medwick formed a barbershop trio with, "I want a girl." Mike Gonzalez was grinning and exclaiming: "Mike, she tole you, we could do."

Frankie Frisch sat on a bench, his head bowed in weariness, suffering from a momentary letdown. But he recovered quickly, and rose to accept the congratulations of Cardinal officials and to go on a nationwide radio hookup. Announced as "The Man of the Hour," Frankie stood before the mike wearing only his underwear and thanked all his players for their great performance and congratulated manager Mickey Cochrane, whose Detroit Tigers would oppose St. Louis in the World Series on Wednesday, October 3.

The city of St. Louis went wild. Grand Boulevard was packed with cars tooting their horns, engines backfiring and people unleashing war whoops. Battered old flivvers and expensive limousines carried signs, "Bring on the Tigers" and "Tell it to Terry." One Model T Ford carried an effigy of Bill Terry. Cars were decorated with banners honoring the names of the Deans and Frisch, Pepper and Ducky and Rip and Leo, and all the rest. Festooning many cars were Depression "ticker tapes," removed from nearby bathrooms. The Cardinals had just won their fifth pennant in nine years. It was time for another World Championship.

That night a small party of Cardinals celebrated at the Grecian Gardens, a restaurant favored by ballplayers. It was owned by Jim Mertikas, a native-born Greek who had received his culinary education at the Planters and Jefferson hotels. A heavy-set, hearty man, he greeted them at the door:

"Congratulations!" He shook hands with Tex and Fanny Carleton, with Mr. and Mrs. Dazzy Vance, Bill Walker and girl friend, and with bachelors Medwick and Hallahan.

"You win the pennant, you deserve the best." The owner bowed them to a table, and snapped his fingers at a waiter.

"No, no!" He waved the man back. "No menus. Bring a bottle of Mestika."

Jim Mertikas poured the resinous liquor into nine glasses, the last one for himself.

"To the victors," he raised the glass in toast.

"Now I must personally take care of your dinner. Leave it to Jim. Eat what he brings. It will be good, you'll see." The owner hurried off to the kitchen.

The Carletons, the Vances, Bill Walker and his girl friend, Medwick and Hallahan had a festive evening, drinking Mestika and dining on egg-lemon soup, lettuce salad with feta cheese, shish kebab and stewed green beans. For dessert, they ate baklava, a luscious pastry of nuts and honey.

Dazzy Vance called the waiter to the table. "Bring me a Dazz-Marie," he said.

When the waiter looked puzzled, Vance got to his feet and went behind the bar. "I'll mix it myself." The big right-hand pitcher began pouring an assortment of liquor into an oversized glass filled with ice cubes. He dumped in a dollop of rye, bourbon and Scotch and one-half shots of gin, sloe gin, vermouth, brandy and Benedictine. Then he ladled in some powdered sugar, stirred the concoction, topped it with a cherry and carried it back to his chair.

"Anybody want some?" Vance offered to share his drink. A shudder went around the table.

"Nobody could drink that." Hallahan said.

Tex Carleton raised his highball in a toast. "Bring on the Tigers," he said.

"We'll turn 'em into pussycats," Dazzy Vance said as he took a large swallow of his Dazz-Marie.

9

Seven Days in October

DETROIT WAS BEDLAM. On the night of October 2, campfires burned along the roads leading to Navin Field where the first game of the World Series would be played. Flames and smoke and the smell of cooking hot dogs filled the evening air as thousands of fans waited to buy bleacher seats the next morning. They had brought camping equipment, blankets, tents, drinking water and enough food to last until the end of the first game. Nearby residents were selling empty fruit crates and boxes for fifty cents each, for use as pillows. Two hundred policemen surrounded the ball park, the fire department stood by with equipment, and city hospitals prepared for casualties with wards of freshly-made beds.

The lucky fans who held reserved seats were whooping it up in downtown bars and cocktail lounges. The hotels were packed to capacity with people who had flocked to town on overcrowded trains, or driven in on highways jammed bumper-to-bumper with cars, trucks and buses. The Book-Cadillac Hotel, which housed the Cardinals, bulged with writers and radio announcers. The business office of the Detroit baseball team sent out 30,000 cards apologizing for its inability to fulfill the demand for tickets. Frank Navin, president of the Tigers, announced that the team would sell 1,500 tickets for standing room only. All the reserved seats at $6.60, $5.50 and $3.50 had been purchased. Scalpers could get $20 each for a choice seat.

126

Throughout the day and night, hawkers sold banners, badges and stickers. Civic groups showered the Tigers with radio, wristwatches, fountain pens, as well as shirts, shoes, suits and overcoats. Manager Mickey Cochrane received an automobile and a refrigerator. Schoolboy Rowe and Charley Gehringer also were given free cars.

Veteran baseball writers declared they had never seen such a feverish atmosphere. Trolley cars ignored their schedules; factory workers deserted their machines; clerks left their desks; salesmen neglected their customers. Baseball filled the Detroit newspapers. Only the column of Arthur Brisbane made page one. Radios were installed in all school auditoriums so students wouldn't miss the action. Many children skipped school entirely. No wonder. Detroit had not had a pennant-winner since 1909, when Ty Cobb and Sam Crawford and pitchers George Mullin, Ed Millet and Ed Summers had led the Tigers into the Series against Honus Wagner and the Pirates.

The heroes of the '34 team were Cochrane, the same "Black Mike" whom Pepper Martin had humbled in 1931; second-baseman Gehringer, a great fielder who batted .356 for the year; and at first base the powerful and handsome slugger, Henry "Hank" Greenberg, who had hit .339 that season and driven in 139 runs. The pitching staff was headed by Lynwood T. "Schoolboy" Rowe, winner of twenty-four games, sixteen of them consecutively. Backing him up were Tommy Bridges, Firpo Marberry and Eldon Auker. Detroit had won 101 games and was considered an outstanding squad, with Billy Rogell at shortstop, Marvin Owen at third, and Goose Goslin, Jo-Jo White and Pete Fox as the regular outfielders.

But the betting odds were on the Cardinals to win the first game and to take the Series. Before the opener, Frankie Frisch seemed undecided as to his starting pitcher. Many of his players were lobbying for Wild Bill Hallahan, a hero of previous Series' games. But Dizzy Dean scoffed at such a notion. He declared that he wanted to pitch the entire Series. "Can you fix it?" Dean asked Grantland Rice, the sportswriter. "Talk to Frisch for me."

"You couldn't win four straight," Rice said.

"No," Dizzy said, "but I sure could win four out of five."

On the morning of October 3, police closed the streets around Navin Field where 10,000 fans fought to gain admittance. Lines extended for blocks into the ticket offices. And one angry group of men formed a flying wedge and attempted to crash to the head of the lines. Twenty-five mounted police galloped up and routed the gate-crashers.

That afternoon during the Cardinals' infield drill, the fans were treated to an unusual exhibition. Frankie Frisch told one of his coaches to hit grounders at him so that he could deliberately let the baseballs bounce off his chest. The old Flash was testing the texture and resiliency of the second-base area, trying to determine how the ball would roll. Then if he played one off his chest in the game he would know how to pounce on it.

Dizzy Dean, in his usual boastful mood, sauntered to the Detroit dugout to needle Hank Greenberg.

"How come you're so white?" Dean taunted. "You're shakin' like a leaf. You afraid ole Diz is going to pin your ears back!" Laughing and swaggering, Dizzy returned to the St. Louis dugout.

Dean did not humble the great slugger, for Greenberg slammed a homer, the only real smash off Dean, who scattered eight hits and gave up three runs. The Cards won 8–3, belting out thirteen hits, four of them by Ducky Medwick. Instead of starting his ace, Schoolboy Rowe, manager Cochrane had opened with General Alvin Crowder, a thirty-five-year-old veteran who had won five and lost one game in the season. Cochrane's strategy was not to waste Rowe against the great Dizzy, a strategy that proved to make good sense but poor psychology. It seemed as though Cochrane were conceding defeat before a ball was thrown.

After his winning effort, Dizzy Dean went on the radio and spoke to Admiral Byrd, via shortwave: "Hello, big Byrd down in Little America. I didn't have a thing out there today on my fast ball or my curve ball. I finally staggered through and won a ball game. I can pitch better than that. I would be tickled to death to pitch tomorrow's game. I think I would have my stuff tomorrow, and probably would shut the Detroit Tigers out."

On October 4, Dizzy and Paul were the guests of Henry Ford. They stayed so long that they had to be rushed by police escort to the park where 43,451 fans were on hand. The Deans arrived in time to see Al Schacht and Joe E. Brown stage a "prizefight" behind home plate. Joe "won" by a KO as referee George Raft counted him out. Raft then took his seat in a box with Father Coughlin. Sharing another box were Will Rogers and Henry Ford.

Dizzy Dean was the star attraction before the game, posing for dozens of pictures and autographing balls, scorecards and scraps of paper. As the players went through their practice, Dizzy joined a brass band playing behind home plate. He picked up a tuba and began blowing in it, oompahing along to the tune of "Wagon Wheels." He sounded all right, too. "Give me a week and I'll have your job," Diz informed the regular tuba player. Then he strutted over to the Detroit dugout and offered an apology. "I sure am sorry I pitched so poorly in that game yesterday," he said. "I'll try to show you my real good stuff the next time out."

The pitching opponents for game two were Schoolboy Rowe ("With the wind behind him," Dizzy declared, "he's almost as fast as Paul") and Wild Bill Hallahan. Dizzy was annoyed at the selection of Hallahan, claiming that Paul deserved the nomination.

As soon as Schoolboy Rowe took the mound, the entire Cardinal team lined up at the dugout. Led by Pat Crawford they began chanting, "How'm I doin', Edna? How'm I doin', Edna?"

Poor Schoolboy had appeared on a radio show and blurted out a tender greeting to his fiancée: "How'm I doing, Edna?" Thereafter, every time he set foot on the field he was greeted with the same chorus.

St. Louis scored single runs in the second and third off Rowe. And Bill Hallahan was breezing along until betrayed by his teammates. In the fourth inning, Bill Rogell hit a routine fly to center field. Ernie Orsatti jogged after it. But a strong wind blew the ball away from the center fielder. Realizing his mistake, Orsatti made a headlong dive, breaking his sunglasses and suffering a cut over his left eye. Rogell reached second and was credited with a double.

Bill Hallahan stook quietly on the mound, rubbing up a new ball. "What can you say?" he recalled afterward. "The guy who costs you a run in the field may bat in two and win the game."

Wild Bill got the next man out, but Pete Fox lined a double inside third to score Rogell. The Cardinal left-hander retired the side and, although wild, put the Tigers down inning after inning. Meanwhile, Rowe was throttling the Cardinals, permitting only one man to reach base the rest of the game. The contest went into the ninth with St. Louis ahead, 2–1. With one out and a man on second, Gerald Walker lifted a puny pop between first and home. Catcher DeLancey looked at the ball and figured it was out of his range. Collins was slow to start in, and the ball dropped safely, rolling foul. Given a new life, Walker slammed a single to center, driving in the tying run and sending Hallahan to the showers.

Bill Walker relieved Wild Bill, and battled Rowe into the twelfth inning, when Detroit pushed over a run to win 3–2. The *Post-Dispatch* reported: "Bill Hallahan was at his best. He pitched so well that a shutout would have been his portion, a shutout for his fourth World Series victory, a total never reached by a left-hander in October championship competition, if the Cardinals had not missed two simple fly balls that high-school boys could have caught."

Frankie Frisch was so furious about the defeat that he chased the newspaper men from the clubhouse. "Get the hell out," he roared. Later, he cooled off and invited the writers back. "It was a tough one to lose," he said. "You can't take anything away from Rowe. He pitched a great game. But I felt sorry for Hallahan." Wild Bill sat in dejection. "Brutal," he said. "But there's nothing you can do about it. It's just baseball, I guess."

October 5. A crowd of 34,073 filed into Sportsman's Park for the third game. The weather was ideal, with fleecy clouds in a blue sky and just enough breeze to flutter the flag in center field. The mood of the fans was cheerful, but not wild. The people of St. Louis obviously felt their Cardinals would handle the Tigers with little trouble. And Paul Dean justified their faith, taming the Tigers and Tommy Bridges 4–1. Paul struck out seven and didn't allow a run until the ninth when Hank Greenberg tripled home Jo-Jo White.

After the defeat, the Tigers were battered and downcast. Manager Cochrane was suffering from bruises he received in a collision at home plate with Joe Medwick. Shortstop Billy Rogell was lame, and Marvin Owen, the third baseman, had been hit in the back by a pitch. There was gloom in the Detroit clubhouse in sharp contrast to the joy and exuberance being displayed by the St. Louis team.

On Saturday, October 6, the Tigers struck back savagely, hammering out thirteen hits and mauling St. Louis 10–4. Hank Greenberg collected four. The Cards committed five errors, three by Pepper Martin. Walker was the loser and Dizzy Dean almost got his brains scrambled.

In the fourth inning, pinch hitter Spud Davis singled and Frisch removed the slow-footed catcher for a runner. Out of the dugout charged Jay Hanna Dean to run for Davis. Dizzy, standing on first base, bowed to the governors of

Oklahoma, Kansas and Missouri, who were ensconced in nearby box seats.

Leo Durocher was on second with Dizzy on first when Pepper Martin slashed a grounder at Charley Gehringer, who flipped the ball to Rogell, the shortstop. As the shortstop pivoted and wheeled the ball toward first, Dean went in high to break up the double play. Rogell's throw hit him smack on the forehead, Dean fell to the ground, and the ball bounced forty feet into the outfield, Durocher scoring on the play. Dizzy was tagged out and carried unconscious from the field. He was rushed to the hospital where X rays were taken of his head. The X rays, one newspaper reported, "showed nothing."

Young Paul reported that his brother "was fine. He wasn't unconscious at all. Why, he talked all the way to the clubhouse."

"What was he saying?" a sportswriter asked.

"He wasn't saying nothin'," Paul said. "He was just talkin'."

After a quiet night at St. John's Hospital, Dizzy Dean turned up at Sportsman's Park on October 7. "Give me the ball," he told Frisch, "and I'll go out and get 'em for you."

There were over 38,000 fans in the stands as Dizzy Dean squared off against Tommy Bridges. The indestructible Dean pitched a solid game, striking out six and allowing only as many hits in eight innings, but lost 3–1. Sloppy play by center-fielder Chick Fullis, who let two ground hits slip past him, set up two of Detroit's runs, the third coming on a homer by Charley Gehringer. St. Louis got seven hits off Bridges, but the tough little Tiger had the Cardinals beating the ball into the ground or popping it up most of the afternoon.

The Tigers now led in the Series, three games to two. As the teams prepared to return to Detroit, a sort of madness set in. Several players were furious at the umpires. Bill De-Lancey had cussed out home-plate umpire Brick Owens, who threatened to fine him. Detroit's Goose Goslin and Bill Klem almost came to blows in a St. Louis hotel.

Aboard the Cardinal express heading for Detroit, Frank Frisch delivered an old-fashioned pep talk, walking up and down the aisle, using his fist like an exclamation point. "We'll pull this thing out. We've been down before, this year, and we always came back. We're a better team than they are."

"To hell with Schoolboy Rowe," Pepper Martin growled.

"We'll tie a knot in his neck," Rip Collins chipped in.

"We'll knock 'em off the way we did the Yankees in '26," Pop Haines said.

"It's in the bag," Dizzy said. "Paul'll fog it by them tomorrow and I'll settle their hash the next game."

The Series was turning into a rough-and-tumble, spikes-slashing war. The Cardinals needled Cochrane so sharply he threatened to punch Pat Crawford, who invited him to step into the Cardinal dugout. Cochrane had been knocked flat at home plate by Medwick in the second game and a Detroit caption labeled the manager "OUR STRICKEN LEADER." It was the kind of phrase bench jockeys love.

October 8. When the two teams arrived in the Motor City early in the day, the waiting crowd filled the railroad station and surged into the streets. Fans stood on parked trucks, on rooftops, and some even hung out of windows. Bands blared and an American Legion Post in brass helmets paraded to the Book-Cadillac, where a sound truck was blasting forth with "Hold *Them*, Tigers!"

That afternoon, the largest crowd of the Series, 44,551, swarmed into Navin Field and watched a duel between Rowe and Paul Dean. Leo Durocher, who had been in a batting slump, led the Cardinals to a 4–3 victory, with three hits, including a double. After Durocher's double in the seventh inning, Paul Dean singled in the winning run.

The sixth game had been a rough one. Jo-Jo White had stolen second and knocked Frankie Frisch flat, racing to third when the ball rolled free. Manager Cochrane was spiked on the knee, the same leg Medwick had crunched in an earlier game.

The night before the last game of the Series, Detroit fans kept their sound truck circling the Book-Cadillac Hotel. They chanted, "Hold *Them*, Tigers. Hold *Them*, Tigers," hoping to keep the Cardinal players awake all night. The Cardinals threw wastebaskets and bags of water at the circling truck in an attempt to stop the monotonous din.

The weather for the final game on October 9 was clear and 40,902 fans were expecting an explosive game. As Goose Goslin said: "Everybody seems to be mad at everybody else in this Series, with all hands sore at the umpiring, which has been terrible. So watch out for fireworks today."

Tempers were short and tongues were sarcastic. As Eldon Auker warmed up to start the seventh game, Dizzy Dean shouted at manager Cochrane: "He jes' won't do, Mickey."

What Dizzy meant was that Auker just wouldn't last in a head-to-head clash with ole Diz himself. The Cardinals knocked Auker out of the box in the third. Cochrane brought in Rowe and St. Louis bombed him. Elon Chester "Chief" Hogsett, a slim left-hander, was the next victim. The Cards nicked him for two runs, one of which was driven in by Dizzy Dean's second hit of the inning. Tommy Bridges finally put out the fire, but the Cardinals had scored seven runs and led, 7–0.

With Dizzy Dean on the mound, everything should have been an anticlimax after the third inning, but the sixth brought another eruption. Ducky Medwick lined a ball off the center-field wall and, sliding hard into third, triggered a riot.

"As I rounded second," Medwick later recalled, "Coach Gonzalez gave me the stand-up sign. But Marv Owen, the Detroit third baseman, made a phantom tag at me."

Owen didn't have the ball, but not knowing this, Medwick slid hard into third. Owen raised his foot to get out of the way, brought it down on Ducky's leg, and then fell on him. In the melee, Medwick retaliated with a kick of his spiked shoe and they rolled around in the dirt, swinging and swearing at each other. After umpire Bill Klem separated them, Medwick grinned at Owen and apologized, offering to shake hands. Owen refused the friendly gesture, called Ducky another choice name and waved him off with his hands. The Detroit fans misunderstood the scene. Thinking that Medwick wanted more combat, they gave him a going-over from the stands.

When he took his position in left field, the fans showered him with bananas, tomatoes, oranges, rolled-up newspapers, bottles and pieces of metal. At first he used the apples to play catch with Ernie Orsatti and Pepper Martin. The fans grew uglier. The Tigers were losing by a lopsided score in the final game of the Series and their rooters boiled with frustration. Attendants had to clear the field three times, as Medwick advanced and retreated from the bombardment.

Leo Durocher came out, grinning. "Aw, it's nothing, Joe," he said. "Don't let it bother you."

"Nothing, hell," Medwick snapped. "If you think that, you play left field and I'll play shortstop."

Now, Ducky Joe was in an ugly mood. He stood in left field, hands on hips, jaw thrust forward and glaring at the fans. Left field was carpeted with vegetables, papers and empty bottles.

The Commissioner of Baseball, Judge Kenesaw Mountain Landis, was stationed in a box along the third-base line. He summoned Medwick, Owen, Frisch and the umpires to his seat. After holding court, Commissioner Landis removed Medwick from the game, to avoid having the Series end in a forfeit. Medwick resented it. If he had to be removed, why not Owen, too?

"Putting me out," he declared, "made it look as though it was all my fault." It also deprived him of another turn at bat and a chance to tie the World Series record for total hits. He had eleven when he left the game and his replacement,

Chick Fullis, got a hit when he came to bat. It annoyed Medwick that he would never know what might have happened had he stayed in the game.

"It's a good thing Joe didn't have a bat in his hands," Frisch said. "He would have killed some of those fans!"

The Cardinals went on to crush the Tigers 11–0, smashing seventeen hits. Dizzy Dean pitched a six-hitter and taunted the Detroit batters as they came to the plate. The Tigers had two men on in the ninth with two out and Hank Greenberg at bat. Dean fired two strikes past the big slugger. Then he reared back and threw his ultimate fireball, turning his back before the ball reached the plate. Greenberg struck out. The 1934 Series was over. The Cardinals were champions of the world.

The police escorted the winners to the Book-Cadillac. In the elevator together, Medwick and Hallahan noticed two tough-looking men—who followed when they got off. Later, there was a knock on their door. When Medwick opened it, there stood the two tough guys, one of whom asked:

"Which of you is Joe Medwick?"

"He is." Ducky pointed at Wild Bill.

"I am *not!*" Hallahan exclaimed. "*He* is!"

The men were plainclothes detectives assigned to guard Medwick until he left town. They wouldn't even permit him to go out to dinner with his teammates. One of the stars of the Series, Joe Medwick celebrated the Cardinals' victory in his hotel room.

The Deans became the darlings of the nation and the delight of St. Louis. They had done everything Dizzy had predicted, winning forty-nine games during the season and two games each in the Series, victories that brought each Cardinal $5,389.57 in cash. Gehrig and Ruth, Simmons and Foxx? St. Louis preferred the brothers Dean. Thousands of fans greeted them at Union Station the day after the great triumph. Yelling and waving, the crowd called for their favorite hero and Jay Hanna stepped onto the platform. He was wearing a white pith helmet and carrying a toy rubber tiger. It was about sixteen inches long and looked emaciated, as though only half full of air. Dizzy pointed to its long tail. In it were four knots, symbolizing the four defeats suffered by Detroit. Holding the tiger aloft, Dizzy choked it by the throat as the crowd shrieked its approval.

The city celebrated all that day and most of the night. A motor parade started the festivities, with the Deans riding in a car behind the mayor, Mr. and Mrs. Breadon and Mr. and Mrs. Frisch. Each and every Cardinal received a roar of tribute, particularly Ducky Joe Medwick. "Have a banana, Joe!" a youngster yelled at Medwick, joshing him about the fruit barrage in Detroit. Downtown bars were clogged with customers. In a dance hall a band played "Hold That Tiger" over and over. From a hotel room a radio blasted forth: "Don't Let Your Mind Go Ga-Ga."

St. Louis *was* ga-ga over the Gashouse Gang—a team that looked like a winner for years to come. Sam Breadon was a happy man. The long exciting Series had put his team in the black. Frankie Frisch was jubilant, having won a championship in his first year as a manager. And Branch Rickey looked to the future, for down in the minors he had more stars ready to step into the spotlight.

PART THREE

WINDING UP WITH THE GANG

10

Exit Dynasty, Enter Legend

AFTER THE GRAND TRIUMPH OF 1934, Sam Breadon and
Branch Rickey had every right to expect more championships. But what had looked like a dynasty crumbled in 1935
when the Cardinals lost the pennant in the last week of the
season.

Chicago arrived in St. Louis needing two victories to win
the pennant. Waiting for them were the Deans, who again
were pitching superbly; Ducky Medwick, now an acknowl-
edged star; and Rip Collins, having another productive year.
The two lefties, Hallahan and Walker, were performing
well, as were Durocher, Martin, Whitehead, DeLancey and
Rothrock. And Frankie Frisch, although no longer a fielding
flash, could still hit the ball. Out of action was a gifted young
center fielder named Terry Moore, who had broken his leg
earlier in the month.

Lon Warneke beat Paul Dean 1–0, in the first game of the
series. Sitting in the visitors' dugout and enjoying himself
immensely was Tex Carleton, whom the Cardinals had
traded the previous winter. The tall right-hander had gone
to Chicago in exchange for pitchers Bud Tinning and Dick
Ward, and cash estimated at $10–15,000. He won eleven
games for the Cubs in 1935. The *combined* record of Tinning
and Ward at St. Louis was 0–0! It was a bad trade for the
Cardinals, who wound up with some cash and two hurlers

141

who never again played in the majors. Tex Carleton had several more good years at Chicago.

Forty years later, Carleton recalled that September series. The day after beating Paul Dean, the Cubs faced the Cards in a doubleheader. Bill Lee was scheduled for the opener and Carleton the second game. It was a wild afternoon in which the Texan deliberately picked a fight with Dizzy Dean.

"I'd got a good workout before the game," Carleton recalled. "I went into the clubhouse, showered, changed uniforms and came back to the bench. The game was underway. Billy Herman was the hitter. The whole Cub bench was on Diz, riding him hard. Evidently he'd knocked down Stan Hack. I hollered:

" 'Hey, you illiterate bastard!' Diz thought I said, *illegitimate* bastard. He charged off the mound to fight me. Hell! That was just what I wanted. I'd get him out of the game."

Dizzy and Tex scuffled in front of the dugout, taking a few wild swings before being separated.

"And Goddamn!" Carleton continued. "You know they had a big crowd that day, and they appealed to Charley Grimm to let Diz pitch when he should automatically be out of the game for fighting. Grimm let him continue, but we beat him 6–2." The Cubs won the next game, too, for their twenty-first straight victory.

After nearly winning in 1935, the Cardinals were an also-ran team for the remainder of the decade. Sam Breadon did not get his dynasty until 1942, '43, '44 and '46 when St. Louis won pennants and the fans found new idols in Stan Musial, Marty Marion, Whitey Kurowski, the Cooper brothers, Red Schoendienst and Enos Slaughter.

Throughout the 1930s the Cardinals made headlines with their high jinx and fisticuffs, creating a legendary Gashouse Gang, whose stars might have been conceived by a comic-strip artist. Dizzy and Pepper played the clowns, Rip Collins the sly instigator, Leo became the Lip, Frisch the harried manager, and Medwick the stormy petrel.

The term "Gashouse Gang" is part of the oral history of baseball and its origin is difficult to determine. Warren Brown of the Chicago *Herald and Examiner* claims to have used the expression as early as 1932, when Pepper Martin made his debut as a third baseman. Pepper's unorthodox fielding and grubby appearance reminded sportswriter Brown of a refugee from a gasworks. Possibly Martin's rambunctious play in the 1931 World Series triggered the association.

The Gashouse Gang flourished after the rough-and-tumble 1934 Series. Warren Brown used the phrase in print in July, 1935, after the Cubs played a tough series with the Cardinals. The Chicago team was bedded down in its Pullman berths when Brown sauntered down the aisle.

"What's the matter, boys?" he boomed. "Afraid Pepper Martin is on the train? Better be good or the Gashouse Gang will get you."

Throughout the Depression, St. Louis often played in Chicago or New York looking dirty and greasy, because their heavy wool uniforms could not be quickly dry-cleaned. One afternoon in 1935 several New York writers were chatting with shortstop Durocher at the Polo Grounds.

Frank Graham of the New York *Sun* asked Durocher if he thought St. Louis could win the pennant. Dizzy Dean overheard the question, and quickly answered. "We could win the pennant in either league," he bragged.

Durocher snorted and shook his head. "They wouldn't let us play in the American League. They'd say we were a lot of Gashouse ballplayers."

From 1935 on, the Cardinals were the Gashouse Gang, tough, cocky and colorful.

Pepper Martin was addicted to automobiles and owned a midget racer, "The Martin Special," which took up a lot of his spare time and cost him a good deal of money. His escapades frightened the front office. One summer night, manager Frisch happened by a track, bought a ticket and sat in the stands. Relaxed and ready to enjoy himself, he suddenly sprang to his feet at the sight of two familiar figures. Helping push a midget car onto the track were Pepper and Dizzy. The boys were unwinding, the night before a doubleheader. Frisch, Breadon and Rickey felt that they should be concentrating on baseball.

Eventually, the Cardinal management convinced Martin that he should forget racing, but they couldn't curb his passion for horseplay. One evening Frisch was standing in front of his hotel in Boston when a bag of water exploded at his feet. Frank was drenched and so were some innocent bystanders. The irate manager knew one of his players had thrown the bag from the window. The culprit was Pepper, who sought forgiveness by promising to hit a home run the next day. He was forgiven and he did deliver a homer the following afternoon.

One rainy afternoon, bored but playful, Martin, Dizzy Dean, Bill DeLancey and Rip Collins invaded the ballroom of the Bellevue-Stratford Hotel in Philadelphia. They were wearing coveralls and carried a ladder, buckets of paint and brushes. Three hundred people had just finished an excellent lunch of roast beef and were waiting for a luscious parfait.

"Set the scaffold up over there," Rip Collins directed.

"Don't slosh that paint around," he shouted as Martin shoved his way between the tables of well-dressed guests.

"Go right ahead with your program," Dizzy told the toastmaster. "You won't bother us. "As the pitcher carried a ladder across the dais, somebody recognized him.

"It's Dizzy Dean!"

"And Pepper Martin," a youngster shouted.

The toastmaster's face lit up. "Fellows," he said, "why don't you sit down and have some coffee and dessert?" The gang was happy to comply.

Pepper Martin organized the famous Mudcat Band, which entertained in the clubhouse, in hotel lobbies and, finally, even on radio shows. The sound of the country music made Frankie Frisch snort in contempt. A cultured man, Frisch loved classical music and had a large collection of records at his home in New Rochelle, New York. Pepper's group specialized in such songs as "Buffalo Gal" and "Possum Up a Gum Stump." Martin and Lon Warneke, whom the Cards had acquired from the Cubs in 1936, picked on guitars, Max Lanier played the harmonica and Bill McGee the fiddle. Meanwhile, Frenchy Bordagaray played a washboard with thimbles while Bob Weiland blew on a jug. Of course, Dizzy Dean took a part, warbling his favorite tune, "The Wabash Cannonball."

Dizzy was the heart of the Gang, and his trade to the Cubs in 1938 ended an era. In five full seasons with the Cardinals, from 1932 to 1936, Dean was one of the greatest and most colorful pitchers ever to play baseball. He was an irrepressible competitor who couldn't resist a challenge.

Once while visiting a hospital, a boy asked him to strike out Bill Terry that afternoon. Then another boy shouted, "Yeah, strike out Bill Terry!" Dizzy said he would, although he wished they had picked somebody easier.

Late in the game, with the bases loaded, up came Memphis Bill. Dean threw two blazers past the Giant manager. Then he strolled halfway to home plate. "I'm gonna have to strike you out, Bill," he said, "cause I promised some sick little kids."

He returned to the mound and threw another fast ball down the middle for strike three. Then he laughed. "Old Bill was so surprised he never took his bat offen his shoulder."

Another time he made a bet that he could strike out Vince DiMaggio every time the free-swinger came up. He fanned the outfielder the first three times easily. The fourth time Dean slipped over two strikes, but DiMaggio lifted the next one, a foul behind home. As Bruce Ogrodowski, the young catcher, camped under the ball, Dizzy raced in shouting, "Drop it! Drop it!"

Ogrodowski let the ball fall to the ground. An enraged Frankie Frisch jumped to his feet so savagely he banged his balding head on the dugout roof. "What in hell's going on now," he yelled.

Dizzy whiffed Vince DiMaggio on the next pitch, winning a total of eighty cents.

Diz didn't always prevail in his war with batters. In the Texas League, he knocked down Al Todd, a big, tough catcher. Todd jumped to his feet and shouted, "You do that again and I'll punch you in the mouth." When Dean wheeled in another one at Todd's head, the batter charged the mound.

"I thought we was gonna talk a little," Dizzy recalled. "Hell, every fight I was ever in we'd jaw at each other before punching." But Todd didn't waste any words, flattening the pitcher with a single blow.

Dizzy got up again, his head spinning, and was greeted with a left hook. He was knocked down several times that day and never did get to chat with Al Todd. Years later, Dizzy Dean would tell this story with a chuckle. "I could out-talk that guy anytime, but I never wanted to fight him again."

Dizzy could take a punch or a reprimand, and he was fast with a retort when caught in an embarrassing situation. As a nineteen-year-old, he stayed out beyond curfew one night. He met the president of the team in the lobby. "Well," he drawled, "I guess you and me'll get hell for this, Mr. Ankenman. But I won't say nuthin' if you don't."

Baseball was a lark to Dean, but 1937 proved a troublesome year. After a balk was called on him in a close game, he later made a speech attacking umpire George Barr and Ford Frick, president of the National League. He was suspended and asked to extend an apology. He refused. "I ain't signin' nothin'," he said. And he never did. The suspension was lifted.

At the All-Star break that year, Dizzy had a 12–7 record and was streaking toward another big year. He wanted to skip the game, but his wife, Pat, convinced him that he should play in it. It was sound advice but the outcome was sad. In the third inning, Earl Averill hit a line drive up the middle that rocketed off Dizzy's left foot, breaking his big toe. The toe was put in a splint, but Dizzy just couldn't abide inactivity, especially when the team needed him. He went back to the mound before his toe was healed, changed his pitching motion, and wrecked his great arm.

The Cardinals sold Dizzy Dean to the Cubs after the 1937 season, even though Chicago's Phil Wrigley knew the pitcher's arm had lost its power. Dizzy won seven games and lost one, posted a low ERA of 1.80, and helped the Cubs win the 1938 pennant. He did it with a sore arm, a slow curve—and with courage and savvy. Against New York in the World Series, Dizzy Dean pitched his last dramatic game, holding the powerful Yankees in check for seven innings. New York finally beat him, but his courage and poise added another dimension to the legend of Jay Hanna Dean.

Dizzy acquired more acclaim and wealth after his baseball career.

He went into the broadcasting business where his Okie grammar delighted country folks, but enraged English teachers. "The runner slud into second," Dizzy would announce. A shortstop did not throw to first; he "threwed" it. Runners always returned to their "respectable" bases. When English teachers protested the way he mangled the language, Diz appeared undisturbed.

"Lots of people that don't say 'ain't,' " he retorted, "ain't eatin!"

Radio broadcasts during World War II were not permitted to describe the weather. Dizzy evaded the rule:

"I can't tell you why the game's delayed, folks," he announced. "But if you stick your head out the window, you're gonna get wet."

Later he worked for a midwestern brewery as a successful promoter of beer drinking. He also achieved some notoriety in 1970 when he was searched in his Las Vegas hotel room by police and by the Internal Revenue Service investigating a gambling syndicate. He was not arrested, but later was named as an unindicted co-conspirator. With tears in his eyes he appeared before a grand jury in Detroit and denied the charges, saying he had only been making bets for a friend. Nothing further was made of the case.

The episode did little to tarnish Dizzy's image. He was respected and renowned, ranking among the great names in baseball history. At his induction into baseball's Hall of Fame, Jay Hanna Dean summed up his career with a merry sentence. "I want to thank the good Lord for giving me a good right arm, a strong back and a weak mind."

Dizzy died a millionaire, but Paul never achieved anything like the wealth or acclaim of his big brother. He lived in the shadows and claimed to be content there. "Dizzy was a natural," Paul said, "a front-runner from the time we were kids. I always depended on him. He was bold and I was glad to follow him because I got a kick out of him like everybody else did.

"I'll tell you what kind of fellow Dizzy was," Paul recalled. "He believed in doing a fellow right. He never saw a man he didn't like or respect, and I never saw anyone who didn't respect or like Dizzy."

Although Paul had been labeled, "Daffy," the title was a misnomer. He was quiet and not given to colorful stunts or witty sayings. Early in 1936, Paul hurt his arm. "I threw too hard, too soon in spring training when I wasn't in shape," he recalled.

Now living and working in the small town of Springdale, Arkansas, Paul Dean has had a variety of jobs over the years, including managing in the minors, and as a baseball coach and athletic director for four years at the University of

Plano, Texas. Of his children and grandchildren, he claims he wouldn't want them to be professional baseball players. "I want them to amount to something," he said. His comment seemed jocular but there was an acid note in his voice. Despite the joy of being with Dizzy in the glory years, life in the majors was not an unbroken stretch of happiness. For him, pitching had been nerve-racking. "It was the kind of job," he said over the telephone, "where you sweat before you go onto the playing field."

By 1938, most of the old Gang had left St. Louis. Spud Davis played for Cincinnati and for Philadelphia again. Bill DeLancey was out of baseball. Leo Durocher was playing for Brooklyn. And in September of that year, Mike Gonzalez replaced Frankie Frisch as manager. Jesse Haines had retired. Bill Hallahan was with the Phillies. Ernie Orsatti was working in Hollywood. Jack Rothrock, Jim Mooney and Bill Walker were in the minors. Burgess Whitehead was playing for the Giants. Owner Sam Breadon and general manager Branch Rickey still headed the operation and Buzzy Wares pranced along the sidelines. Although on the roster, Paul Dean appeared in only five games, winning three and losing one. Pat Crawford, Chick Fullis, Fran Healy and Dazzy Vance were finished. Carleton and Collins were with the Cubs. Only Pepper Martin and Medwick remained to stir the fans with their fiery play.

Champions for only a single season, the 1934 St. Louis Cardinals do not rank with the all-time great teams. Yet for color and flair and wit and charm, there never has been another group quite like them. The Gang held its twenty-fifth reunion in 1959, returning to put on Cardinal uniforms, to stage a nostalgic show and to reminisce.

Suiting up for the old-timers game was a struggle for Dizzy Dean, who weighed 275 pounds.

"What have you been doing with yourself?" Frisch asked.

"I been raisin' a couple hundred head of cattle," Dean answered.

"You look like you ate the whole herd," Frisch observed.

Dizzy just smiled, being accustomed to wisecracks about his girth. Once, he had been scolded by President Dwight Eisenhower, during a golf match. "I don't understand, Dizzy," the President said, "how a man who plays golf so well can permit himself to get so overweight."

"Mr. President," Dizzy replied, "I was on a diet for twenty-five years. Now that I've got some money I aim to eat real good to make up for those lean years."

Dizzy needled Frisch, reminding him of his last game as an active player at age thirty-nine. The old Flash was on second with Terry Moore on first when Medwick drilled the ball into the right-field corner. As Frisch chugged around third, the speedy Moore was close behind. Sizing up the predicament, coach Gonzalez shouted:

"Moore come, Frahnk, you go. He come; you go."

As Frisch's spikes hit home plate, young Moore slid hard and upended the manager. "Any time they could run down the old Flash," Frisch recalled, "it was time to quit."

Mike Gonzalez was unable to attend the anniversary celebration, but his colorful presence was felt nonetheless. Everybody had his favorite story about the Cuban. One of the best involved Buzzy Wares, Branch Rickey and Leo Ward, who succeeded Clarence Lloyd as traveling secretary.

Senor Gonzalez and Wares were arguing loudly in their hotel room. "You dumb, Bussy. You dong know what you say. You dong know where you are, you so dumb."

"I know where I was," Wares said. "That's more than you ever know, Mike." Buzzy was beginning to bristle.

"You so smart, Bussy, you dong know the way to Boston. I tole you three, four time now. The way to Boston she be through Springfield, like Mike say."

At this point, Branch Rickey entered the room and was compelled to adjudicate the matter. He listened carefully as Wares explained how Gonzalez insisted that the Cardinals always went through Springfield when traveling from New York to Boston. In an effort at compromise, the general manager drafted the new traveling secretary, Leo Ward. Poor Mr. Ward was caught in the middle of a dispute he remembered to his dying day. Finally, trapped into a statement, Ward admitted that the Cardinals never went through Springfield on the New York to Boston route.

Wares beamed in triumph. But Gonzalez refused to concede defeat. He glared at Buzzy, at Branch Rickey and at Leo Ward. He pointed his finger dramatically at each man.

"I dong care where you fellas go. I, Mike, he always go through Springfield."

Frisch was reminded about two of his outspoken players, Durocher and DeLancey. Early in his managing career, Frankie had suspected Leo of not hustling. After the shortstop made a poor throw that let in a run, the manager confronted Leo in the clubhouse.

"That lousy throw will cost you fifty dollars," he hollered.

"Make it a hundred," Durocher said.

"I'll make it two hundred."

"Make it three hundred," Leo rasped.

"I'll make it a grand," Frisch bellowed.

"Make it two grand," Durocher bellowed back.

Now the clubhouse was rocking as players and coach howled at the spectacle. Suddenly Frisch was laughing, too, and Leo joined in. The manager did not fine the shortstop, but there was no problem with hustle thereafter.

Bill DeLancey, the tough young catcher, was a great prospect and a special project for Frisch. He could insult the manager with impunity, describing him in scornful style.

"Lay off that rising fast ball," Frisch directed one day. "You'll only pop it up."

The next time at bat DeLancey smacked a high fast ball over the roof of Sportsman's Park. He raced into the dugout, chortling: "That's how much you know, you dumb Dutchman."

William Pinkney DeLancey died of tuberculosis at age thirty-five on his birthdate in 1946. Although he had caught only 219 major-league games, Branch Rickey named him one of the three greatest catchers he had ever seen. Mickey Cochrane and Roy Campanella were the other two.

Other faces were missing from the reunion. Chick Fullis also had died in 1946, at age forty-two, having dropped out of baseball due to eye trouble. He opened a tavern in Girardville, Pa., which he ran until his death "of a complication of diseases." Doc Weaver passed on in 1955. And Sam Breadon died shortly before his seventy-third birthday in 1949 after an illness of two years. Breadon had sold the Cardinals after the 1947 season and seemed to deteriorate afterward, losing forty pounds within a year. Complications set in and cancer caused his death.

A little-known story was told about the Cardinal owner. Breadon never went on scouting trips, but once he was in Hawaii and spotted a big, handsome player. He personally signed the muscular young man to a contract, and shipped him to a minor-league team. There the good-looking Hawaiian demonstrated his social skill by catching gonorrhea. Seven months later he was back in the islands, and that was Breadon's first—and last—attempt to sign a superstar.

Joe Medwick recalled an encounter he had with Breadon. Faced with a cut of $2,000 in salary, Ducky had a showdown.

"I'm not going to give you that two thousand dollars, Joe," Breadon declared. "It's a matter of principle. Why, I'd rather throw the money out the window."

"Mr. Breadon," Medwick replied, "if you threw that much money out a window, you'd still be holding on to it."

One story led to another at the 1959 reunion. Pepper Martin needled Frisch about the time the manager gave a pep talk on hustling during spring training. He had called the team together on the sidelines.

"If there's one thing I won't tolerate," he roared, "it's a loafer. I want hustlers on this team. Now, if any of you rookies don't know what I mean, pick out one of the veterans and follow his example."

About fifteen minutes later, Frisch noticed a rookie relaxing in the shade. He was yawning and appeared to be on the verge of sleep. The red-faced manager charged up to the kid and snarled, "I guess you didn't hear a Goddamn word I said. Why didn't you imitate one of the veterans?"

The rookie gave the manager an innocent look. "Why, Mr. Frisch," he said. "You're the model I picked."

Another spring training story concerned a famous fight in which Ducky Medwick rushed to the defense of Dizzy Dean.

The action took place in the Tampa Terrace Hotel. A New York newspaperman braced Dizzy in the lobby, accusing him of being more showman than pitcher. He had been criticizing Diz in print, but when the reporter confronted the pitcher in public, Dean boiled with anger. One insult led to another and soon the lobby was a battleground.

Chairs and vases were smashed, potted palms overturned, ashtrays and other loose objects flew through the air. Hotel guests, bellboys, even manager Frisch scurried for cover. Then Irv Kupcinet, a Chicago writer, moved into the middle of the melee. A good Samaritan, he tried to stop the brawl, forgetting that only fools and small children try to separate angry athletes.

Peacemaker Kupcinet was rewarded with a hard right to the face by Muscles Medwick. Down went the writer, proof that the paw was mightier than the pen.

Fighting with umpires was another trademark of the Gashouse Gang. Pity the poor man in blue who had to face the blistering tongues of Frisch, Durocher, Dean, Collins and DeLancey all at the same time. But off the field, Frisch was friendly with several umpires, especially with Beans Reardon.

Frisch and Gonzalez were enjoying a cold beer in a favorite spot, the "Coal Hole," a dark taproom in the Hotel Coronado. A familiar nasal voice interrupted their conversation.

"Happy, my boy, how ya doing?" It was Beans Reardon, who still called Frisch "Happy," even though he had thrown the manager out of a game only a few hours earlier. Before "Happy" could open his mouth to bark at the umpire, Reardon raised his hand in a gesture of peace.

"The ball game is over, pal. We're still friends, right?"

"All right, you bastard." Frisch scowled. "Give him a drink," he directed the bartender.

"Frankie, my boy," Reardon smiled as he sipped his beer. "That's a beautiful new Packard you got. How about lending it to me for the night?"

"Well, I'll be Goddamned!" Frisch swung around on his stool. "You really like that car, huh?"

"It's the best, Frankie, the very best."

The manager put down his drink, walked to a nearby telephone, and ordered the hotel garage to get the car ready. He and Gonzalez were on their third beer when the phone rang. It was Reardon.

"Whatta ya want now, Beansie?" Frisch asked.

"There's hardly any gas in this car, Frankie. Will you have them fill it up for me?"

"Why, you son of a bitch, you!" Frisch exploded into the phone. But he had an attendant fill up the tank of his Packard.

At the twenty-fifth anniversary banquet, several of the old gang gave peppy little talks. But the principal speaker was Branch Rickey, who described Durocher as having "the most fertile talent in the world for making a bad situation infinitely worse." The old general manager then praised the '34 team for its skills and fighting spirit.

"Why," Rickey said, "they loved the game so much—by Judas Priest!—I believe these boys would have played for nothing."

At this point the speech was interrupted by Pepper Martin's loud whisper: "By John Brown, Mr. Rickey, we *almost* did."

11

Jim and Jack and Spud

WITH HIS GRAY HAIR and horn-rimmed glasses, Jim Irving
Mooney could easily pass for a professor of economics. He
possesses a bachelor's degree and a master's, but he treats
them as lightly as he once did a runner leading off first base.
A Cardinal relief pitcher in 1934, Mooney was a left-hander
with a classy delivery.

In the minors he came into a game with one out and
men on first and third. He picked the man off first, and the
man on third, breaking for home, was thrown out. Mooney
retired the side without throwing to the plate—a performance
that made Ripley's column, "Believe It or Not."

When I visited Mooney he was working as a VA advisor
at East Tennessee State University in Johnson City. He
occupied a modest office in the department of admissions
and records. There was nothing officious about the old left-
hander. He reminisced in a good-old-boy style, chuckling
and chopping up his participles as he gave his impressions
of the Gashouse Gang.

"Shoot!" he exclaimed. "Of course, there was no one like
Dizzy Dean. He was a smart fella out there on the hill. He'd
pitch just as hard as he had to. If we made a lot of runs,
Diz would just coast and clown. But if he had a tough ball
game, he'd really bear down. You think Pepper Martin
was the greatest competitor of them all? Naw. Diz was the

greatest. He could do it all and he'd tell you he could."
Mooney chuckled as he recalled how Dean would raise hell
if he lost a game.

"He'd charge into the clubhouse when we were all taking a shower and be a-gripin' about somebody not getting a
base hit at the right time or something. And Rip Collins
and Pepper would jump all over him. I've seen them beat
him up many a time." Mooney threw back his head and
laughed. "Never really hurt him, but they'd get on him.

"Ole Diz was a character." Mooney chuckled. "I once
asked him where he was living."

" 'I live in Bond, Mississippi,' he replied.

" 'Where in tarnation is that?' I asked.

" 'Why,' Diz said, 'it's just across the street from Wig-
gins.' "

Mooney had roomed with Collins. "Rip had nightmares,
you know. I'd wait until he was snoring before I tried to
get some sleep. I once chased him down the hall of a New
York hotel. He was gettin' ready to go on the elevator in his
pajamas. Walking in his sleep. I don't know why he'd do
those things. Didn't seem to be a worrier. But he'd get up
in the middle of the night and start lookin' under the bed."

Born in Mooresburg, Tennessee, in 1906, Jim Mooney
moved to Johnson City in 1924 and attended East Tennessee
State, playing there in the spring, and semipro ball in the
summer to finance his education. He started his professional
career with Chattanooga in the Class A Southern League.
There he was scouted by John McGraw, who brought him
up to the Giants in 1931. Mooney had a live fast ball and
that incredible pick-off move taught him by manager Mc-
Graw. "Folks used to come to the park just to watch me pick
fellows off first," Mooney drawled.

The left-hander had been a starting pitcher with the
Giants from 1931 to 1933, and it was a disappointment to
him when the Cards turned him into a reliefer.

"The Cardinals were trying to build up Paul Dean,"

Mooney recalled. "They kept starting him and he'd get his ears beat back. But they went on until he finally got his feet on the ground. He had a good year, but for my money he couldn't carry Dizzy's glove. He was just a thrower."

The disappointment at not pitching regularly was dampened by the joy of being with the Cards. "They were so different from the Giants, under McGraw and Bill Terry. You had to be a gentleman on the Giants. Dress properly. The Cardinals? It didn't make any difference what you wore."

Mooney's eyes sparkled as he described Pepper Martin's attire.

"Pepper always wore his Texas boots, ten-gallon hat, and a suit of clothes. It wouldn't be twenty minutes until that suit was dirty. We started out one time from St. Louis to New York. He came down into the lobby with a brand-new suit on. Looked real nice. Had his pockets full of cowboy magazines. Time we got to New York you'd think he'd slept in it. Baseball uniform—the same way. Pepper'd put on a clean one and the first thing he'd do would be go out and roll in the dirt and get tobacco juice all over it. He was a great player, though, and I enjoyed watching him, playing ground balls off his chest and sliding headfirst into the bases."

"What about Joe Medwick, my hero?" I asked.

"Medwick was moody," Jim said. "If he was hittin', gettin' his base hits—everything was fine. But if he went into a slump, just leave Joe alone. He'd sit off in a corner by himself." Mooney shook his head.

"I used to hit fungoes to Medwick all the time. And shoot! You had to hit 'em right in his hands. He wouldn't even run to catch 'em. Medwick had a funny attitude. I never could figure him out."

When asked about Leo Durocher, an unpleasant look appeared on Mooney's face.

"Nobody liked him. When he put on his street clothes, nobody associated with him. He was a prima donna. Carried a couple of trunks of clothes on road trips. Everytime you saw him he was dressed differently."

Jim Mooney had spent four years in the U. S. Navy in World War II. As skipper of an LST in the Pacific, he had taken part in numerous invasions and returned home a lieutenant commander. Intelligent and decisive, accustomed to leadership, he would have made an excellent manager. *I thought.* He snorted at my notion. After the war, he had played part-time for Johnson City, pitching home games and sometimes at towns nearby. Once he had filled in briefly for the manager and, in the process, learned a lesson. He was told to pitch a certain youngster, even though he felt the boy wasn't ready. The order came down directly from Branch Rickey in St. Louis. Not wanting to be a yes-man, Jim Mooney gave up managing as quickly and gracefully as possible.

"I didn't like somebody in St. Louis telling me what to do in Squeedunk," he stated. "That's the way Rickey ran things." He smiled. "Branch Rickey could make salt taste like sugar in your mouth. He had a tongue that wouldn't quit."

Mooney turned in his chair and began reminiscing about Frankie Frisch.

"Always out there giving his best. Liked to play around a little, have fun and argue with the umpires. Frisch and Klem. One time I was pitchin' and there was a commotion behind me at second base. It was Frisch and Klem going at it. Another time, at home plate, Klem drew a line and dared Frankie to cross it, saying, 'If you cross that line you're out of the game.' Frankie got down on his hands and knees and rubbed out the line and then walked right over it."

Mooney laughed long and hard at the thought of Frisch and Klem, but a sad look appeared on his face when I mentioned the names of Bill DeLancey and Chick Fullis, both of whom died young.

In January 1974, when I interviewed Jim Mooney, thirteen of the 1934 Cardinals were still living. Tex Carleton, Pat Crawford, Dizzy Dean, Paul Dean, Spud Davis, Leo Durocher, Jesse Haines, Bill Hallahan, Francis Healy, Joe Medwick, Mooney, Burgess Whitehead and Jack Rothrock.

Heart attacks had claimed Dazzy Vance (1961), Pepper Martin (1965), Ernie Orsatti (1968) and Rip Collins (1970). Vance was sixty-nine and living in Homosassa Springs, Florida, where he had a fishing camp. Martin had been living on his ranch near Blocker, Oklahoma. After his retirement as an active player in 1944, Pepper had been a minor-league manager. Orsatti, a successful Hollywood agent, had died four days before his sixty-fourth birthday. Collins passed away at age sixty-five in the small town of Haven, New York. At the time he was a scout for the Cardinals, after working for the Cubs as a coach and as an executive for a sporting goods company in the 1960s.

Lefty Bill Walker was a victim of cancer in 1966. Coach Buzzy Wares had died in 1964 of infirmities at seventy-eight. Death came to Frankie Frisch in 1973 after injuries suffered in an automobile accident. The great Branch Rickey, one of the true pioneers in baseball history, died in December 1965, shortly before his eighty-fourth birthday.

Jack Rothrock, right field. Few fans remember his name or his position, yet he was the only Cardinal to play in every inning of every game in the 1934 season. He batted a solid .284 and his steadiness and stamina won him the praise of manager Frankie Frisch, and the admiration of teammates such as Tex Carleton.

"Jack was a winning ballplayer." Tex said. "He was always in the big rally."

Rothrock lives in a mobile park in San Juan Capistrano, California, about sixty miles north of San Diego. His home overlooks lovely rolling hills, not far from the Pacific Ocean. The trailer park is a middle-class retirement community.

Rothrock enjoys talking about the old times, particularly

when he was a member of the Gashouse Gang. Gray-haired, a little overweight, but vigorous at the age of sixty-nine, he puffed on cigarettes during the interview. His second wife, Aretha, an articulate woman, sat by. The only visible symbol of his baseball past was a large Cardinal poster containing head-and-shoulders photos of the 1934 team.

"I remember the last game of that season," Rothrock began. "We're going into the ninth inning leading. All of a sudden, factory whistles were blowing and horns were tooting. Then we knew for sure that the Giants got beat.

"The '34 team was one big family," Rothrock recalled, "even though we had arguments and fights in the clubhouse. It was a very competitive, rough ball club. All around—mentally, physically, competitively—it was as good a team as you'll see." He grinned as he recalled a Dizzy Dean-Pepper Martin story.

"I remember one day Diz and Pepper were wrestling, playfully, and Diz stepped aside as Pepper charged in. Pepper went into one of those steel lockers and cut his face. Doc Weaver, the trainer, put on some flesh tape to stop the bleeding, but didn't get it all stopped. So the blood was running from Pepper's face when the game started. Rickey saw Martin from the other side of the field, so he comes to the dugout at third base and says:

" 'Frankie, what's the matter with Pepper?'

" 'I don't know!' Frankie says, and hollers, 'Hey, Pep, look at me!'

"Pepper says, 'Whadda-ya want,' out of the corner of his mouth. He wouldn't turn to show the blood running down his face." Rothrock chuckled.

"Pepper was superstitious. He never changed his underwear. Not until he came home from a road trip. Then his wife wouldn't let him in the house until he did."

Rothrock admired Frankie Frisch, but pointed out one of his shortcomings as a player.

"Frankie couldn't go back after a ball. He'd just turn

around and say, 'Come on, Jack!' . . . Rest his soul! But he knew how to handle men. You say one of the teammates said: 'Durocher was the brains of the Gashouse Gang?' No way! I think Leo must be the one who said that. Frank was in a peculiar position. He didn't have the ordinary run of ballplayers, not with players like Martin and Dean."

One of Rothrock's favorite characters was Harrison J. "Doc" Weaver, the club trainer. An osteopath by profession, Doc Weaver was a psychiatrist without portfolio, father-confessor and cheerleader for the Cardinals for twenty-eight years. Called "Bucko" by the players, Doc Weaver plucked on a mandolin as the Cards rolled around the nation on road trips. Weaver died of a heart attack at sixty-nine in 1955, and sportswriter Bob Broeg wrote the necrology for *The Sporting News,* recalling:

"He was quite a character himself, a garish dresser addicted to floppy-brimmed, gay-colored Nassau straw hats and loud neck scarves." He also was a man of some dignity, and Jack Rothrock remembered an incident where Weaver's feelings were hurt by a practical joke.

"Coming up from spring training," Rothrock recalled, "Doc had his trunk in the baggage compartment. He had it all packed nice, getting ready for the season to open. We took it and put it in the men's room. All his medicines and stuff. The next time the train stopped—Doc was upset about this—he was a sincere man, you know, and we loved him no end. Well, Doc got off the train, saying, 'I quit.' The train went on, Doc changed his mind, but he didn't have any money to buy a ticket on another train. But he had a bunch of stamps and the railroad accepted them in exchange for a ticket."

Jack Rothrock enjoyed his life in baseball and misses the camaraderie of the old-time players. "They were a different breed, those old-timers. I don't know about today's kids, they don't seem to be as friendly to one another as we were. During spring training we'd all go out to dinner after exhibition games. We'd get acquainted with players from the opposite league. It was a good life."

Rothrock knew hard times growing up in what he called "Hogan's Alley," in Long Beach, California, and at age fifteen went to work as a stevedore in San Pedro. He was an outstanding athlete who could run the 100-yard dash in ten seconds in a baseball uniform. He was signed to a pro contract after a scout saw him in a softball game, sliding home on a *concrete* field.

Rothrock ended his playing career in 1944 as a player-manager in the California State League. After World War II, he was a successful minor-league manager until his retirement from baseball in 1950. Then he took a job as a supervisor of the street department in San Bernardino, and retired from that job in 1970, moving to San Juan Capistrano in 1971.

He and his handsome wife are an affectionate, contented couple who live a comfortable life, fishing, playing golf and visiting old friends. Between them, they have three grandchildren and one great-grandchild.

Looking back on his baseball career, Rothrock doesn't feel neglected. "I feel well-remembered," he said. "But I'm glad I got out when I did."

How good were the 1934 Cardinals? Of all the members of the old guard, Virgil "Spud" Davis gave the most positive answer. Sitting in a hotel room in Birmingham, Alabama, the big, burly catcher didn't hesitate.

"Bob," he said, "I was in the big leagues for thirty years as a player and a coach and I never saw any team that could do everything any better than they could. They played to beat you—and they'd do *anything* to beat you."

Davis had left baseball in 1953 to run a service station, which he continued to do until 1958 when he retired.

Birmingham, where he was born and raised, is the home

of such celebrated athletes as Harry and Dixie Walker; Ben Chapman and Virgil Trucks; Luman Harris and Alex Grammas; and Sammy Byrd, who starred in baseball and as a professional golfer.

"I haven't done anything since 1958 except have fun," Spud Davis said. He fishes, hunts and plays golf. He has been an avid golfer since the late 1920s when he was with the Philadelphia Phillies. Then his teammates on the links were Chuck Klein, Pinkey Whitney, Burt Shotton and Lefty O'Doul.

O'Doul was a great batter, superb golfer and a witty man. Somebody asked him in 1960 what he thought Ty Cobb would hit if he played that year. "Only three forty," O'Doul replied, "although you have to take into consideration that he's seventy-three years old."

When Spud and Lefty were with the Phils, they got in a lot of golf. At that time, the team didn't play on Sundays in Pennsylvania because of blue laws. "Lefty was a real good golfer," Spud recalled. "But they finally put a stop to our playing. O'Doul was playing *every* morning before the ball games."

Baseball people felt the golf swing would ruin a batting stroke. It did not hurt the average of Lefty O'Doul, though. He hit .398 and .383 at Philadelphia.

"Hell," Davis snorted, "playing golf didn't hurt you. If it had," he said, "it would have wrecked a lot of good hitters."

Golf did not even dent the average of Virgil Davis, who is still swinging away at age seventy. He is bright-eyed, alert and looks fit enough to play an inning or two.

"I feel as good as I did ten years ago," he said knocking on the wooden arm of the chair. He was the huskiest member (six feet one, 200 pounds) of the 1934 Cardinals. As a catcher, he has two rare achievements. He once made an unassisted double play; and as a full-time backstop he had a lifetime average of .308. You can count on the fingers of his battered hands the number of catchers who hit .300 or better as full-time receivers.

Catching is so arduous that few manage to hit for high averages. The constant squatting, the endless moving up and down and sideways, the heavy equipment, the bruises and bumps and broken bones suffered from hard-sliding runners and sailing fast balls, the sheer pressure of handling every pitch—all this wears a man down. The key to hitting is in the hands, where a catcher is most vulnerable to injury. A catcher with a bruised hand is like a base runner with a sprained ankle. He might as well stay in the clubhouse. Yet it wasn't unusual for backstops to play while hurt during the Depression and before. Players did not want to sit out a game for fear of losing their jobs.

"Things were different," Davis recalled. "I don't understand today's players. We played with broken fingers and toes. Now, they get a scratch and they go to the hospital." The mere thought of such a notion made the powerful old catcher scoff. "When I came up if you couldn't take it, you didn't last. Pitchers would knock you down and then laugh at you. Why, I've seen Burleigh Grimes throw at Frisch four times in a row. Frank would get up and try to drag a bunt so he could cut up Grimes. Spike him."

Manager Frisch did not pass out Purple Hearts to bench warmers. "He was a hard loser," Davis said. "He simply couldn't stand it." Spud, who played and coached for Frisch for fifteen years, liked and respected him, while pinpointing his shortcomings as a manager.

"He was demanding. He couldn't stand mistakes. He was so perfect himself. He could steal a base anytime he got ready. Everything he did was so natural, he thought everybody could do the same. This was bad because they couldn't. He was tough to play for. He couldn't handle men, but he always treated me all right."

Davis drummed his fingers on the arm of the chair. "Frisch was the best money player I ever saw. But if he had been with a tail-end team, he wouldn't have been worth a quarter."

Then the burly catcher smiled. "We all had a lot of fun —Rip and Pepper and Diz. Up until the game started, we used to run Frisch crazy."

There was humor and affection in the voice of Virgil Davis as he told a story about Pepper Martin. The Cards had lost a crucial game against the Giants. "Pepper made several wild throws that let in a lot of runs," Davis recalled. "Afterwards in the clubhouse, he just sat and cried. He thought he had ruined our chances for the pennant."

Davis played with three of the greatest right-hand hitters, Hornsby, Medwick and Hafey.

"The greatest I ever saw was Chick Hafey," he declared. "And he was one of the greatest all-around players, too. He could do everything. Run the bases. And he had that arm! He could stand against the fence in left field in St. Louis and throw strikes to the plate all day long. The ball came in light as a feather. If his eyes had been good, there's no telling what he could have done."

Hafey had been one of Rickey's projects. Sitting in the stands during a workout, chatting with an associate, Mr. Rickey looked up at the smash of bat against ball.

"Judas Priest!" he exclaimed. "Who hit that?" The ball had landed in the distant stands.

"A kid named Hafey," he was told. "He's a pitcher."

"He *was* a pitcher," Rickey declared. "From now on he's an outfielder."

"Mr. Rickey was a great baseball man," Davis said. "He was the best judge of ballplayers I ever saw. He could look at a player and tell whether or not he was a prospect."

Bennie Borgmann, a former Cardinal scout and minor-league manager, remembers the time the general manager visited him in a southern league. He came into the clubhouse and pointed his cigar. "I want you to play that boy at shortstop tomorrow," Rickey said.

"There were two kids standing where he pointed," Borgmann recalled. "One of them was well-built and strong looking. The other was skinny and frail. I thought Mr. Rickey meant the husky one."

The next afternoon, Borgmann had the well-built boy playing shortstop when Branch Rickey walked rapidly onto the infield.

"I told you to play *that* fellow at shortstop," he said sternly.

"I had picked the wrong guy," Borgmann said. "Mr. Rickey wanted the tall, skinny kid." His name was Martin Marion, who became one of the greatest of all shortstops.

Spud Davis saw a lot of good pitchers in his career. He caught Pete Alexander. He handled Paul Derringer and Claude Passeau, Ray Benge and Rip Sewell and Kirby Higbe. He batted against Hubbell and Warneke and Charley Root and Hall Schumacher, against Bucky Walters and Bill Lee and Fred Fitzsimmons. And he caught the blazing fast balls of the Deans.

"Paul threw a heavy fast ball," Davis said. "It was like catching a ton of bricks. Dizzy threw a rising fast ball. He was a natural. Diz could do everything. He had a wonderful fast ball, a good curve and a change-up. He was a pretty good hitter and he could run the bases. But," Davis hesitated, "I couldn't rank him with the greatest pitchers. He didn't play long enough."

Davis paused, thinking about all the great ones he had caught over the years. Then he said: "If I was a manager and needed one ball game—for a pennant or a World Series—I'd rather have Bill Hallahan than anybody."

12

Binghamton's Wild Bill

WILLIAM ANTHONY HALLAHAN is a soft-spoken man who lives in a middle-class neighborhood in Binghamton, the "parlor" city of New York. At seventy-two, he has a full head of silvery hair and is in reasonably good health, having survived two severe attacks of bronchial infection, which have cut down on his physical activity. Of average height—about five feet ten, and 170 pounds—there is nothing athletic or powerful in his appearance. With his dark-rimmed glasses, he could pass for a retired banker or schoolteacher. The kids on the block didn't even know he had been a pitching star until they saw him on television in 1973, when he and Lefty Grove were honored at the fortieth anniversary of the all-star games. The two old adversaries had been the starting pitchers in the first all-star contest in 1933.

"One of the kids across the street came over the next day," Hallahan said. The boy chided him. "Why didn't you tell me you were a baseball player?"

Although Bill Hallahan makes no secret of his baseball success, neither does he flaunt his achievements. During his career in the National League, he won 102 games and lost 94, appeared in four World Series, winning three games and losing one and compiling a low earned-run average of 1.36. A left-hander with a classic overhand delivery, he had three strong pitching weapons: a blazing fast ball, a curve that broke down like a coin rolling off a table—and a tendency now and then to throw the ball against the backstop. This tendency earned him the title of "Wild Bill," although his teammates called him "Moon," because of the shape of his face.

"Nobody was up there digging in against me," Hallahan said. "Because—what the hell!—they didn't know whether the first ball was going to knock them down. They were glad to get out of there. Other pitchers would come close to a guy and there'd be a fight. The batter figured he was being thrown at deliberately, because the pitcher had good control. With me nothing was said. Never got put out of a game or nothing. They never told me to knock anybody down. No manager. The manager always said, 'What the hell's the use of telling you to knock anybody down. They aren't going to stand up there anyway.' "

Hallahan smiled when he remembered the effect he had on hitters. "I was fast," he said. "Wally Berger used to say: 'Jesus, I don't know what to do against you. I used to start swinging when you started winding up—and I'd be swinging that way all during the game.'

"I didn't have a bit of trouble with Wally," Hallahan said. "I used to throw him rising fast balls up and in tight, right on his fists. There's nothing like a fast ball. Nobody hits a really good fast ball thrown in the right place. A ball doesn't have to move much to fool a batter. A fast ball doesn't hop—not the way some people think it does. It takes off, when thrown well and with rhythm. When a pitcher has his rhythm and he's coming back nice and easy and letting the ball go smoothly —there is a pattern there. The ball seems to be thrown without effort."

As the old fast-baller talked, you could almost see him leaning back on the mound, rocking into motion, the ball leaving his hand like a streak. I confess I shuddered a little thinking back and remembering a certain wild left-hander who once had scared me spitless. *He had been a big, wild kid on the staff of the Binghamton Triplets when I tried out there one year and the manager was watching me in the batting cage and I could feel my hands sweating and my left foot wanting to dance down the foul line. I ground my teeth to keep my feet planted and I could feel my tail twitching . . .* Even now, relaxing in the Hallahans' living room, I could taste the old fear on my tongue as the ball came in like a rocket. God! How I hated the Goddamn manager that day. Sonofabitch. Buddy Hassett, wherever you are . . .

Here I was in the middle of Hallahan's career, trying to pull a story out of his past, and my own past was intruding like an unwanted relative on a weekend. Binghamton, New York—ah, yes, I knew it well, having spent four years of my life there, going to college in nearby Endicott. Binghamton, Endicott, Johnson City—the Triple Cities of the southern tier of the state—the heart of the industrial empire of IBM and the Endicott–Johnson Shoe Company. I had played industrial-league baseball not far from Hallahan's home, at Recreation Park. Played there on mild spring days and during the heat of the summer, shading my eyes against the sun, backed up against the center-field fence, a high screen fence that separated the diamond from the tennis courts, watching helplessly as the towering fly ball flew overhead and then took a kangaroo bounce on the cement of the court . . .

Recreation Park. Hallahan strolled often to this park on summer days to watch kids play baseball, the game he often had dominated with a fast ball and a sharp curve.

Studying Wild Bill in his comfortable home, I was puzzled by the paradox of a gentle, average-sized man who could throw a baseball at a speed of ninety miles an hour or better. This ability had nothing to do with weight or height or muscular strength. Major-league players had explained the nature of the gift of speed to me; it had to do with *leverage, rhythm, coordination, with long, loose back muscles, rubbery arms and supple wrists.* Maybe so. But still, for a batter it is like looking into the muzzle of a high-powered hunting rifle. Like all weak hitters I hate and fear pitchers, deep down in my chicken heart. But Bill Hallahan was not someone you could hate—at least not in a living room. Still. In his day, this self-effacing man could terrify the strongest batters in baseball—brutes such as Jimmy Foxx and Al Simmons of the Philadelphia Athletics, and Wally Berger, the strong boy of the Boston Braves.

Imagining Foxx, Simmons and Berger twitching and sweating at the plate—especially old *Double* X Foxx—made me feel a little better. Fear, the old common denominator, I thought. It also made me admire the exploits of Wild Bill Hallahan as he intimidated the sluggers of baseball, sending them back to the bench.

Born in 1902, in Binghamton, Bill Hallahan was one of seven children, three boys and four girls. His father was a railroad man. One of his brothers was a captain in the fire company. The other worked in the city water department. Bill and one sister are the only members of the family still living.

Hallahan played baseball for Binghamton Central High School, leaving there in 1920 to play semipro baseball in Croton, New York. He pitched for the Corona Typewriter Company until he joined the Cardinals in training in the spring of 1924, weighing in at about 135 pounds. He spent three years in the minors, but played on the pennant-winning Cardinal team of 1926. Then he was farmed out again for two more years, coming back to the big time to stay in 1929. In 1930, he had his first outstanding year in the majors; he was the top pitcher on the team, with a record of fifteen wins and nine losses.

Perhaps the finest game Hallahan ever pitched—and certainly the most dramatic game—took place in September 1930, in Ebbets Field, Brooklyn. His opponent was another fastball pitcher, Arthur C. (Dazzy) Vance, who would become a teammate on the Gashouse Gang. It was a key game as the Cardinals, Dodgers, Giants and Cubs were fighting for the pennant. Bill Hallahan started the game in pain with two fingers of his right hand in splints and sticking outside his glove. He had been up most of the night with the hand packed in ice.

"Ray Blades and I and another player went downtown to a movie that night," he recalled. "Afterward, at about eleven o'clock, I got into a cab and was going to move over to let the last guy in. Well, he slammed the door. *Jeez!* He caught the fingers of my right hand. Probably broke one of them. Hell, you didn't go to the hospital in those days. I was up nearly all night with Doc Weaver, the trainer, working on it. Branch Rickey came in.

" 'Do you think you'll be able to pitch tomorrow?' he said. 'You probably won't be able to pitch.'

"I said, 'Well, it's on my right hand and I pitch left-handed.' "

The next afternoon 30,000 fans streamed into Ebbets Field to watch Wild Bill challenge the powerful Dazzy Vance. Hallahan set down the first twenty Dodgers who came to the plate, and didn't allow a hit until the eighth inning. The game went scoreless until the tenth when the Cardinals drove in a single run. In the last of the tenth, the Dodgers threatened with the bases loaded and one out. But Wild Bill Hallahan got the next batter to ground into a game-ending double play, the Cardinals won 1–0, and went on to take the pennant.

It was one of the most bizarre weeks in the history of the National League, because of the antics of Hallahan's roommate, Charles F. (Flint) Rhem. Now Rhem (also called "Shad" Rhem) was one of baseball's most delightful characters, and could easily qualify for any all-time, all-tippler team.

He sometimes showed up at the ball park in an unsteady condition. A former teammate tells the story of Rhem trying to repair the pitching mound in Cincinnati. He was staggering around with a pick in his hands, slashing away at the hard dirt when the manager led him off to the showers *before* the start of the game.

(There really ought to be a special wing in the Hall of Fame for characters like Flint Rhem, who couldn't keep his mouth shut in the presence of whiskey. The wing would have to include the pitcher, Bugs Raymond, who demonstrated his curve ball one night by throwing a beer glass into a mirror in a saloon. And relief pitcher Ellis Kinder, who once slid into second base and broke the pint of rye in his hip pocket. And it wouldn't be complete without Rabbit Maranville, a little shortstop with a huge thirst. "He was a *very* adept base runner," Casey Stengel fondly recalls. "He could slide into a base and *never* break a bottle of booze." Maranville, a five-foot five-inch imp, would be my shortstop on any all-time, all-drunk team. He once scared his roommate to death by walking in the rain on a hotel windowsill twenty stories above the street. He sometimes appeared on the stage as a professional storyteller. In one appearance, he demonstrated his base-stealing skill, sliding over the footlights into the pit, where he tore a hole in the bass drum. According to Gene Karst, author of *Who's Who in Professional Baseball*, Rabbit Maranville reformed in 1927. As Karst tells it, Rabbit took to the wagon saying, "From now on my hobby is staying sober.")

A drinking crony of Grover Cleveland Alexander, Flint Rhem was a droll chap who was enchanted by bright lights and whiskey. Once after a night on the town, he told his manager that he had got drunk merely to protect his pal, the great Alexander. "I knew how important it was to keep Alex in shape," he said. "So I went along and drank real fast and more than my share so that Alex wouldn't get too much."

Anybody who can offer such a delicious alibi is capable of boundless fantasy, as Rhem proved in mid-September 1930. Scheduled to pitch a key game in the series against the Dodgers, he disappeared for a day or so. When at last he returned, wobbling and weaving into the hotel, he told this story to manager Charles E. (Gabby) Street.

He had been kidnapped by gangsters. They had held a gun on him, forced him into a car, and driven to a roadhouse.

There, they had poured large quantities of whiskey down his throat. Then the gangsters drove the drunken right-hander back to the hotel, warning him not to pitch against Brookyn. "I had to go with them," he told manager Street.

Bill Hallahan chuckled when he remembered the incident. "Flint said he was kidnapped, but he didn't know what the hell else to say!"

Hallahan specialized in winning crucial games, "hanging tough" as they say in baseball. "The tougher the going, the better he pitched," recalled Tex Carleton, his friend and teammate. In the 1930 Series with the Cardinals down two games to the powerful Philadelphia team, Wild Bill shut out the As in the third game, 5–0. He was the losing pitcher in the sixth and final game, but his World Series performance was strong and set the stage for his finest year in the majors and for brilliance in the 1931 Series.

The Cardinals won the pennant easily in 1931, led by the pitching of Hallahan, Paul Derringer, Burleigh Grimes and Jesse Haines. Hallahan won nineteen games to head the staff. It was to be his best year in the majors. In the World Series, the Cardinals again faced the Athletics, one of the great teams in baseball history. Philadelphia had won the American League pennant by thirteen and a half games. Their pitching staff was led by Robert Moses (Lefty) Grove, whose fantastic year (thirty-one wins, four losses) included sixteen consecutive victories. Backing him up were George Earnshaw, Rube Walberg, Roy Mahaffey and Waite Hoyt. It was a team of superior hitters—Al Simmons, Jimmy Foxx, Mickey Cochrane, Bing Miller, Mule Haas and Jimmy Dykes. Their leadoff batter was Max Bishop, who "set the table" for the big sluggers by collecting 112 walks during the season. It was said of Bishop that he never swung at a bad pitch. His radar-like vision enabled him to collect a walk per game throughout his major-league career. As a second baseman he was a marvel who set records for fielding averages and once went fifty-three straight games without an error.

The Philadelphia As had won two straight World Championships and they wanted a third, which would have been a record at that time. Their manager was Cornelius Alexander McGillicuddy (Connie Mack), a tall, lean patriarch whom players called "Mr. Mack." Many baseball people considered him worthy of sanctification; skeptics called him a skinflint. At any rate, he was a fine manager and he had great players in Grove, Cochrane, Foxx, Simmons and the rest. The Athletics were favored to win the World Series of 1931.

"We were underdogs," Hallahan said, shaking his head as he thought about that fall so long ago. "God—that Simmons!" There was a look of awe on his face as he conjured up the image of the slugging left fielder. As Bill Hallahan paused to reflect, I thought about the story told me by Wally Moses, a fine outfielder with the As in the 1930s and now baseball's finest batting coach.

"I was in Mr. Mack's office one day," Moses said. "There was a big picture of Al Simmons on the wall. Goddamn! My curiosity got the better of me and I asked: 'Mr. Mack? With all those great players you had, how come Simmons is the only player you've got a picture of?'

"He looked straight at me," Moses recalled, "and said: 'Wallace, with the winning run on base and Simmons at bat in the last inning—the game was ours!' "

Bill Hallahan told a story about Simmons. "I was talking to Lefty Grove last year," Hallahan said. "You know, one year he won sixteen straight games and then he lost the seventeenth. Simmons had gone home that day and didn't play. Grove came into the clubhouse and began throwing things around. He wasn't mad at the players. He was furious at Simmons." With Al in the lineup, Grove might have won several more games in a row. Forty-two years later, Lefty Grove was *still* mad at Simmons. Hallahan threw his head back and burst out laughing. "He was pretty mad."

Pretty mad for Grove could mean the destruction of

furniture or the battering of a sloppy infielder. Pitching for Boston one year, he had lost a close game when manager Joe Cronin let an easy ground ball go through his legs. Cronin raced to the clubhouse and locked himself in his private office, while an enraged Grove tried to break down the door. Unable to gain entrance, the left-hander pushed a table close to the wall, climbed upon it and shouted curses through the grill above the door.

Lefty Grove had been a fiery competitor and Al Simmons one of the greatest of all clutch hitters, but Hallahan had bested them.

"Simmons was a *big* gun," I said.

"Oh—you better believe it!" Hallahan exclaimed. "He was a guy they didn't try to change much either, with his foot in the bucket stance. *Cripes.* You wouldn't think he could hit a ball away from him." Hallahan gestured to indicate the outside corner of the plate. "But that was his power. He could—*boom!* Right field, over the fence . . . And that Foxx could wind up—*pow!*"

Wild Bill Hallahan paused, recalling that exciting World Series of '31, when Pepper Martin became a national hero with his wild base running and hard hitting. Martin's heroics overshadowed Hallahan's superb pitching; a pity, for the left-hander deserved more attention than he ever got. He won two games and saved a third, allowing one run for a brilliant ERA of 0.49. He shut out the Athletics 2–0, to win the second game, which had ended with a weird scene that embarrassed catcher Jimmy Wilson and could have turned him into a goat if Hallahan hadn't been so cool under pressure.

In the ninth inning, with the Cards leading 2–0, Hallahan had walked Jimmy Foxx. He got Bing Miller out, but walked Jimmy Dykes, and then struck out shortstop Dib Williams. With pitcher George Earnshaw scheduled to bat, Connie Mack sent up a pinch hitter named Jim Moore. With two strikes on Moore, Jimmy Foxx broke for third, Moore swung at a curve and missed, and catcher Wilson got the ball on one hop. He should have thrown the ball to first or tagged the batter, as required by the rules. Instead, without thinking he threw to third-baseman Jake Flowers, who scrambled to tag Foxx. The third-base umpire ruled Foxx safe. Meanwhile, the Cardinal players were yelling at Flowers to throw the ball to first base, but Bottomley had wandered off the bag thinking the game was over. Pinch-hitter Moore, who had sauntered away from the plate toward the bench, finally reached first safely. The bases now were loaded with two out as catcher Wilson conferred with Hallahan on the mound.

"What did you say to Jimmy Wilson," I asked Hallahan, "when he came out to the mound?"

"Oh, I didn't say *anything*," Hallahan said, "although I *wished* he had thrown to first base."

"Do you recall saying to him, about the next batter, Max Bishop: 'Don't worry. This guy couldn't hit me with six bats'?"

"Jeez! I wouldn't say that about anybody, especially Bishop. They used to call him 'Camera Eyes,' you know. He used to average a hundred walks a year. Besides that, in our short park in St. Louis, it didn't take much for a left-hander to hit against the screen or over in right field. Ah, Jeez, no, I wouldn't say *that* about him."

Hallahan went to work on Max Bishop, getting him to pop a foul to Bottomley to end the game. "The not so funny part," Hallahan continued, "was that third-baseman Jake Flowers pretty near tossed the ball into the stands after Wilson threw it to him. He told me later he thought the game was over. Christ! That would have been something. That would have scored everybody."

On such a narrow thread does the hero hang. Hallahan went on to win the fifth game 5–1, and then came back in the ninth inning of the seventh game to relieve Burleigh Grimes. Two were out and two were on base. Again his opponent was old "Camera Eyes," Max Bishop. Hallahan ran the count to three balls and two strikes before getting Bishop to line out to center-fielder Pepper Martin. The 1931 Series was over.

In the 1934 World Series, Bill Hallahan had pitched a strong game, but miscues by his teammates cost him a victory.

Wild Bill had one more good year for the Cardinals, winning fifteen games in 1935, but slipped badly the next year. In 1936, he was traded to Cincinnati and from there to Philadelphia, where he finished his big-league career in 1938. He pitched for Minneapolis in 1939, and then retired from baseball, returning to Binghamton where he has lived ever since, except for brief service in the U. S. Army in World War II. He was married in 1946 to Marion Forbes, and they have one child, Mary Alice Cunningham. Hallahan now is retired, having worked as a warehouse supervisor for Ozalid (now GAF) for twenty years, beginning in 1942. He used to be involved with little-league baseball, when it first started in Johnson City. Of late, though, he has confined himself to the role of spectator, strolling to nearby Recreation Park to watch the kids in action.

Walking away from Hallahan's home on a sunny day in late fall, I thought about this fine old left-hander, an easy man to talk to with a slight Irish lilt in his voice and a quiet sense of humor. "A hanging curve is a base hit *before* it leaves a pitcher's hand," he had declared. Bill Hallahan was intelligent in his awareness of life's absurdities. Although satisfied with his records, he felt he had more ability than he showed. Wildness hurt him.

"Of course, you have to be satisfied," he had chuckled, "because you don't get a chance to do it over."

13

A Visit with Pop

AT AGE EIGHTY, Jesse Haines has the look of an ancient eagle. His hair is thin and white, but strong features overpower the thinning crown above the heavy, curving nose, firm mouth, and the sharp, almost ferocious eyes. Looking into those eyes I was reminded of what his teammates thought of him.

"He had an awful bad temper on the mound and on the bench," Tex Carleton had said. "Off the field, he was kind and considerate, one of the grandest characters of all time, and a tremendous influence on me." And tough-guy Joe Medwick called him "the finest person I ever knew. A real gentleman. But when his eyes grew wide," Medwick said, "we all got out of the way. We knew he was really mad."

A hard loser, especially when his fielders didn't back him up, Haines once stalked off the mound in a game against the New York Giants, returning to the bench supposedly to give way to a relief pitcher. Instead he gave his teammates a tongue-lashing, shouting at the fielders: "If you fellows can't win this game for me, I'll do it myself." He charged back to the mound and began mowing down the Giants with a fast ball, grinding his teeth and going on to win the game.

In his first year with the Cardinals, he was pitching a shutout when his catcher, Pickles Dillhoefer, made a wild throw that let in the only run of the game. Poor Pickles escaped with his skin when his teammates managed to subdue the raging Haines. His will to win didn't cool with advancing years, either. As late as 1935, after a tough loss in Cincinnati, Jesse Haines tore up the furniture in the clubhouse.

Sitting in his living room in Phillipsburg, Ohio, looking into the old man's eyes, I thought I saw both glory and death in equal measure. Fanciful thoughts came easy that rainy April morning as Jesse Haines reflected on a baseball career that covered twenty-five years of minor- and major-league pitching, most of them with the St. Louis Cardinals. There had been enough success for several pitchers: 210 major-league wins, two no-hit games (one in the majors), participation in four different World Series, highlighted by the dramatic seventh game of the 1926 Series against the New York Yankees. A distinguished career, marked by fierce determination never to yield nor to quit, had won him a niche in the baseball Hall of Fame.

The son of a carpenter, Jesse Joseph "Pop" Haines was born in Clayton, Ohio, not far from the city of Dayton. He was remarkably clear in his recollection of his boyhood, remembering when the Haines family moved to Phillipsburg a few miles up the road. There he began playing town ball traveling throughout Montgomery County; and in 1913, at the end of the season, he pitched a game for Dayton in the Central League. In 1914, the year World War I began, he hurled his first full season of professional ball for Fort Wayne in the Central League and for Saginaw in the South Michigan League, where he won seventeen games. His salary was $135 a month.

During the next six years, he moved about the minors from Saginaw to Springfield to Topeka to Hutchinson to Tulsa and Kansas City. He served a long apprenticeship, interrupted only by some brief bench-warming with Detroit and Cincinnati. Baseball officials didn't think he could make the majors, even though he eventually would win ninety-seven games in the minors. But each time a big-league club released Haines, he went back to the minors and pitched harder. Finally, his talent could not be ignored. In 1919, he had a brilliant season for Kansas City, winning twenty-one and losing only five (with an ERA of 2.11). This performance caught the attention of Branch Rickey who, after watching him actually pitch for only two innings, hurried to the office of the team's owner and offered to buy the big right-hander for $10,000.

He didn't have the money, but Rickey made the deal anyway. On the train back to St. Louis he worried about raising the cash. The Cardinals were a shoestring operation, with a lot of small stockholders to back him, and a dozen or so of them signed a bank note to get a loan to buy Haines from Kansas City.

"Rickey told me all about it one day in a smoking car. I reminded him," Haines recalled, "of the day he had called me to his office at the ball park. 'I thought you was going to leave me go,' I says."

Rickey had puffed on his cigar and peered through the smoke at Haines. "Remember what I said? Don't get scared," Rickey said. "I'm not goin' to fire you. I'm just gonna give you a five hundred dollar raise."

The $10,000 purchase price and the tiny raise were a bargain for a workhorse like Haines, who won thirteen games his first year in St. Louis. By the end of the 1926 season he had won ninety-six games for an average of sixteen wins a season. That year, he was a key member of the first Cardinal team to win a pennant. He shut out the Yankees in the third game of the Series, and started the seventh game, the one everybody cites when listing thrilling moments in baseball history.

"How they do dramatize that doggone game," Haines said, almost with a sigh. But for a moment there was a flicker of excitement in the rheumy old eyes. It *was* a great game. He knew that, but he was tired of being reminded of it. Yet

I sensed he would have been disappointed if we had neglected that game, even though we were plowing an old field. Manager Rogers Hornsby had called it "the peak of my whole baseball career," and Grover Cleveland Alexander named it his "greatest day in baseball." There are as many versions of the famous game, especially of the seventh inning, as there were people in Yankee Stadium that afternoon.

The World Series was tied at three games each as Jesse Haines faced Yankee starter Waite Hoyt. The Yankees scored a run in the first inning, the Cardinals got three in the fourth, and the Yankees got another in the sixth inning, setting the stage for the famous seventh. The score was 3–2 Cardinals when Haines grew wild, walking three men to load the bases with two out.

"I'd worn the skin off my finger from throwing the knuckle ball," Haines said. "And I kept looking at the knuckles on my hand." Unlike most knuckle-ball pitchers, who gripped the ball with their fingertips, Haines held it with his knuckles. I had brought a baseball for him to autograph, and now he demonstrated his grip, managing to do so with some effort, because his fingers had stiffened with age. He held the ball in his long fingers while he talked.

"I kept a-lookin' at my finger and it had a big blister and was bleeding. Hornsby came over from second base to the mound.

" 'What's the matter?' he says.

" 'I got a blister,' I says.

" 'Let me see,' he says, looking at it. 'You can't pitch with that thing,' he says."

Hornsby waved to the bullpen to bring Alexander in to face Tony Lazzeri. Now Alexander was notorious for sneaking strikes across the plate before a batter was ready to swing. But Lazzeri was ready and swung at the first pitch, missing a curve. The next pitch was a fast ball and Lazzeri lined it foul, just inside the left-field pole. How far did the ball go foul? For Yankee fans it was a matter of inches. For manager Hornsby it was about two feet. For pitcher Alexander it was "eight or ten feet" foul. Alexander threw another curve, striking out Lazzeri, then pitched another two innings to hold the lead for a Cardinal World Series championship.

"They said Alex was drunk when he came to the mound," Haines said. "I don't think he was. I don't know, though, because I didn't stay there. I went into the clubhouse. He couldn't have been drunk, not the way he pitched those two and a third innings." Now Haines shook his head in disgust. "They never gave the old fellow the credit he deserved."

Haines went on. "There never was a pitcher like Alex. The manager would bring the lineup before the game and say: 'There you are, Alex. Go over the batting order and tell the team where you want them to play.'

"I never saw a machine like him. Every pitch he threw was the same. Low outside. To every hitter. The only thing he adjusted was the position of his infield and outfield. He'd shift the fielders around. He didn't care who the batter was. He'd pitch him low outside. Throw him that fading fast ball. Or curve him. I saw a lot of pitchers in my time, but I never saw a machine that worked any better than he did." Jesse Haines sat in bemused wonder at the recollection of Alexander's pitching perfection.

Alex. The greatest pitcher of them all. Winner of 373 games. How many would he have won if he hadn't been such a dedicated drinker? How many games were lost by hangovers, or literally went down the drain when Alexander went to the mound weak and bleary-eyed?

And what of Dizzy Dean, his teammate on the old Gashouse Gang?

"Dizzy was the kind of pitcher who wanted to pitch every day," Haines said. "He'd pitch today, and tomorrow he'd go to the bullpen—'If you need me, I'll be ready,' he'd say. I'd tell him, 'Look, Diz, this is your bread and butter. You can't do that.'

" 'Ah, yes, you can,' he'd say. 'She's rubber,' he'd say, pointing at his right arm.

" 'All right,' I'd say. 'Your rubber's gonna snap one of these days.' And she did.

"After the All-Star game in '37 when Averill hit him in the foot with that line drive, we rode back from Washington together on the train," Haines recalled. "Diz's berth was right across the aisle from me. He says to me, 'Pop, you know my toe's sorer than thunder. It hurts.'

"I said, 'Put 'er up here once and let's take a look at her.' So he puts his foot on my berth and I took ahold of his toe and worked it until I heard a grit. Then I said to him, 'That toe's broke.'

" 'Naw,' he says.

" 'It is,' I said. 'When you get back to St. Louis go out and see Doc Hyland.'

"Well, he did and the toe was broke. Doc, he splinted it, but Diz wouldn't pay any attention to the splints. After a week or so he told Doc to take them off. 'I'm gonna pitch.' he says. He started a-pitchin' and he hurt his arm. Didn't throw natural. He would have been a great pitcher if he'd of listened and laid off for three or four more weeks. He was a character, though." Haines flashed a rare smile.

"In '34, we're in a tight game and needed a run. We've got men on first and second. Frisch calls Diz to the side and says: 'Get those men over. Bunt 'em over.'

" 'All right, Frankie,' Diz said.

"Well, at the plate Diz changes his mind when he sees the infielders running in. He taps the ball right over the third baseman's head. It hits the dirt behind the bag, spinning and rolling in fair ground into left field. Everybody was a-running and two runs scored, and they tried to make a play on Diz at second. They didn't get him, so he jumped up and ran to third, sliding in. My! How the dust just flew! Diz got up—this was at St. Louis—brushed himself off, looked over to the bench, and smiled. Nobody said a word. Some-

body hit a fly ball or a base hit—I forget which—and Diz
scored. When he sat down on the bench, everybody was just
as quiet as could be. Pretty soon Frisch said. 'Diz?'

" 'What Frankie?'

" 'Come here,' Frisch said.

"Diz walked over to Frisch, who said: 'I thought I told
you to bunt.'

" 'What the hell's the use to bunt,' Diz said, 'when you
can do that?'

"Boy," Haines said, "if he'd of hit into a double play it
would have been just too bad! But those Gashouse boys were
great boys, they were," Haines said. "That Medwick was my
kind of ballplayer. Hit the ball to any field. Hit the ball to
right field like a rifle."

What about Leo Durocher? Jesse Haines laughed out
loud at the mention of Leo Durocher. "It'd take an automobile to keep up with him," he said. As a shortstop, Haines
said, Durocher was somewhat like Tommy Thevenow, who
played with the Cardinals' pennant winner of 1926. "Thevenow was a good fielder and quick thrower," Haines recalled.
"His style was a little bit different than Leo's. He'd field
the ball and get it away from him quick."

"Didn't Leo have a very quick release as a shortstop?" I
asked.

"He could if he wanted to. He loafed," Haines said. Then
he laughed a little wheeze of a laugh, an old man's laugh.

But didn't Frisch loaf, too, when it didn't matter?

"Well, Frisch was the type ballplayer who wanted to
play on a winner," Haines said. "I wanted to be on a winner,
too. I didn't wanna be on a bottom club. By God, I couldn't
play on that San Diego club today. No, sir. Loafers, that's all
they are. I couldn't manage today. I remember the time I
went down to Cincinnati when Hornsby was managing. He
was sitting back in the dugout and he calls to me. 'Hey, come
here. Sit down.' Then he said: 'God, this is terrible. These
humpty-dumpty ballplayers. Why they've got their grips

packed all the time. If you say anything to them, they're ready to go home.' "

Like Hornsby, Jesse Haines has little use for the modern player. After all, it had taken Haines seven years to get to the majors, he was twenty-six when he arrived, and he pitched eighteen years for the Cardinals. "Arm trouble? Yes, I had some arm trouble. But a lot of arm trouble is in the head." Now the old eagle eyes did seem to widen, the warning sign of anger.

"Why, I could sit right here in this room watching TV and tell you when that young right-hander over in Cincinnati was going to quit," Haines snorted. "What was his name? Anyway, just watching him I could tell when he was going to quit. He'd start feeling his arm, and I'd say to my wife: 'He'll be out of there in the next inning.' Sure enough, he was out . . . I'll tell you, I was this kind of pitcher: I didn't want to relieve. I wanted to start a game and finish it. And I didn't want anybody to come in from that bullpen and help me out. Today they think if they finish six or seven innings, that's enough. I could see myself out there on that mound pitching that ball—and these humpty-dumpties today out there throwing four or five or six innings and making seventy-five thousand dollars to do it."

Jesse Haines took home $12,500 one year, his best "payday." He used his first World Series checks to build his house in Phillipsburg, where he has lived ever since. He has one daughter and two grandsons, one of whom is an outstanding baseball prospect. Haines retired from baseball in 1938, after serving as a coach for Burleigh Grimes in Brooklyn.

"One day," he recalled, "early in the spring of '38, there was a couple of fellows come to this front door. Said they wanted me to run for public office.

" 'Go-wan,' I said. 'Get away from here!'

" 'No,' they said. 'Listen. We want you to run. You can be elected. You're a Republican and this is a Democrat county, but you can be elected.'

"I said, 'Let me talk it over with my wife, and I'll come downtown and leave you know.' "

Haines decided to take a shot at politics and run for county auditor. "If I was licked," he said, "I figured I still could go back to baseball." That fall, after his coaching stint under Grimes, he returned to Phillipsburg to do some electioneering around the county.

"Now this is a pretty good-sized county—Montgomery County," he said. "But I was elected by ten thousand votes in 1938. Four years later I ran again and was elected by twenty-five thousand votes."

Haines was elected as county auditor to seven straight four-year terms, the last time with a victory of more than 30,000 votes. He retired on January 1, 1966. There is a county baseball program named in his honor, and he used to watch the kids play. "I can't anymore," he said, with the trace of a smile on his face. "I'm washed up myself."

14

The Pinch Hitter

CLIFFORD RANKIN "PAT" CRAWFORD lives on a wide, tree-lined street in Kinston, North Carolina, a city of 30,000 people in the eastern part of the state. His gracious old home with its wide veranda and stately columns is an instant reminder of the antebellum South. The Cardinals' top pinch hitter in 1934, Crawford looks like a Southern aristocrat, but his hazel eyes still have the hard intensity of a batter under pressure.

Crawford possessed a courtliness that quickly put a stranger at ease. He picked me up at the airport on a rainy January evening and drove me to the motel where he had made my reservation. It was the day after his seventy-second birthday. He limped, but managed to look erect as he escorted me to his car. He insisted on carrying my bag and, after placing it in the trunk, ushered me to the front seat.

Strange. This Southern gentleman was the man Leo Durocher ranked with the great all-time pinch hitters, the Dusty Rhodes of the Depression. And this was the player who led the bench jockeying in the '34 Series. Independent and strong-willed, Pat Crawford was somewhat the maverick during his career.

He had once put John McGraw into shock. The Giants manager had wired him to come to Charlotte, N. C., where New York was playing an exhibition game. Crawford went to McGraw's hotel room where they discussed how playing major-league baseball would help Crawford as a college coach. McGraw's arguments were cogent, but Crawford was reluctant to leave his job as director of athletics at Guilford College, a small Quaker school in North Carolina. He said he wouldn't be interested "unless I had a substantial salary for two years."

McGraw roared, "You mean you want me to give you a two-year contract!"

"That's exactly what I want," Crawford said. McGraw looked as though he were going to have a stroke.

"Crawford!" McGraw said, "we don't even give our star players two-year contracts. I have only seen you play two games of Class B ball and here you are asking me to give you a two-year contract." McGraw pointed out that should Crawford have an exceptional year with the Giants, his salary could be much more at that time. Crawford preferred a two-year contract at $3,500 a year. And he got it.

He had begun his professional career in 1924 when baseball wasn't considered a "proper profession" for an educated man. "I had a college education," he said, "and I didn't give a damn whether I played or not. Frankly, I felt it was beneath me and I resented having to play baseball in order to earn a living."

Sitting in the den of his lovely old home, Pat Crawford chuckled over his debut in 1924.

"The veterans on the Charlotte team resented me *terribly*. After my first game, I took a shower. Walking back to my locker I had to pass by the cubbyhole where the players were sitting—and they spit tobacco juice on my legs. Tobacco juice ran down my thighs, and I had to take three showers before they let up on me. I just kept my mouth shut, because I expected some hazing. Taking the place of one of their buddies, you know—they resented that. Then there was a feeling of animosity toward college boys. I think I was the only college graduate on the team."

Crawford finished the season at Charlotte with a .303 batting average, playing both first and third base. He could handle these positions, but his arm, injured in a boyhood accident, never would be strong enough for a major-league shortstop, catcher or outfielder. And he wasn't very fast. But he could swing that "good bat," as baseball men say. In the winter of 1924, he was drafted by the Class A Chattanooga team. A reluctant pro, Crawford refused to report.

"By teaching and coaching for nine months," he said, "and playing semipro baseball in the summer, I was earning more than I could earn just playing for Chattanooga." Then, too, he had a large Sunday School class and did not feel that it would be right to play on the Sabbath.

When Chattanooga didn't respond to his letter, Crawford figured they had written him off, and agreed to play semipro ball for Union, South Carolina. He got through one game before the telephone rang. It was the manager of Greenville in the South Atlantic League. Cease and desist playing for Union or you will jeopardize the careers of all your teammates and all the players you compete against. There was no choice. If Pat Crawford wanted to play it had to be professionally. At Greenville, he was offered the managership, because of his intelligence, poise and experience as a college coach. He refused. Only twenty-three years old, how could he handle players older than himself? The owners insisted. Crawford agreed, reluctantly, and led the team to a fifth-place finish, the same position it had occupied when he assumed command. Shortly after Crawford became manager, Wilcy Moore was hit on the wrist by a pitched ball, which broke a bone and sent him home for the rest of the season. But Moore was back in 1926, along with Pat Crawford, who was replaced as manager by Charles Franklin "Frank" Walker. Walker had bought a share of the club and appointed himself skipper.

"We had a fine club," Crawford said "and easily won the pennant. Wilcy Moore won thirty and lost only four games."

Wilcy's record caught the eye of the New York Yankees, who bought his contract even though the right-hander was nearly thirty years old. Moore won nineteen games for the great Yankee team of 1927, and became one of baseball's top relief pitchers.

The Greenville team won again in 1927 and Crawford was voted its most valuable player. During the summer, manager McGraw of the Giants made a scouting trip through the South Atlantic League. He asked Crawford to come to New York during that winter. The young player met with McGraw and with the president of the Giants, informing them that he intended to coach baseball at Guilford College. They wanted him to report for spring training in Augusta, Georgia. He insisted on living up to his agreement with the college, and left New York not knowing if he'd ever play pro ball again.

In the spring of 1928 he was coaching a college game in Concord, N. C., which is about twenty miles from Charlotte, where Greenville was playing that day. Frank Walker, the Greenville manager-owner, visited the young coach and urged him to take a shot at the majors. "If you will report to the Giants after the close of the college season, I'll give you five hundred dollars. And if you remain with the Giants until June fifteenth, I will give you a thousand dollars!" Crawford said he'd think it over, and returned to Guilford. The next morning he received a wire from Walker doubling the offer. "That was too much of a temptation," Crawford recalled. "So I wired him that I would accept his offer if I could work out a satisfactory arrangement with the Giants."

Crawford then negotiated the two-year contract that almost gave McGraw apoplexy, and he reported to the Giants in May 1928. He worked out for ten days and then was shipped to Toledo to learn the McGraw style of play under the tutelage of Casey Stengel. He hustled hard in the field and at bat, winning the respect of Stengel, who reported that Crawford was major-league caliber. Shortly afterward, he received a check for $2,000 from Frank Walker.

After the close of the American Association season, the Giants wanted Crawford with them for the last two weeks of National League play. He told them it was impossible. He was going to Springfield College to work on his master's degree. En route he stopped at Lake Junaluska, N. C., to present his fiancée, Sarah Edwards, with an engagement ring. They were married in December 1928, in the house they still occupy in Kinston.

Crawford joined the New York Giants in the spring of 1929. After three weeks of practice in San Antonio, Texas, John McGraw called him into his hotel room and asked him to manage the Giants' second team on the way north. Crawford was delighted at the prospect of managing and playing instead of sitting on the bench.

In those days major-league teams played their way north with an itinerary that sounded like a railroad timetable: Waco, Galveston, Wichita Falls, Monroe, Jackson, Greenville, Columbus, Durham, Norfolk, Baltimore, West Point (not to mention Johnson City, Bluefield and Bramwell). After the game in Norfolk, the Giants' B squad boarded the Old Dominion Boat Line and steamed up to Baltimore.

At Baltimore Crawford hit three home runs, two with the bases loaded and the third with one man on. He singled and scored a run, accounting for all the Giants' runs in their 10–6 win over Baltimore. Columnist Ed Sullivan called Crawford "one of the greatest natural left-handed hitters who has ever come up to the big leagues, although as yet he hasn't played a single game of big-league baseball."

In 1929, Crawford appeared in sixty-five games, batting .298, with three pinch-hit homers, one of which still makes his face light up: It was struck with the bases loaded in a game against Boston, played before 50,000 fans in the Polo Grounds. He went to the plate and fouled off several balls before hitting a hanging curve into the right-field seats.

In the spring of 1930 Crawford again managed the Giants' B team. On the way north his second baseman was sent to join the regulars. Crawford put himself in at that position where, much to his surprise, he found he could make the plays with no trouble. Except the double play, which requires a good deal of experience. Given time, he might have become a top second baseman, but manager McGraw needed a polished infielder immediately. On May 27, 1930, he traded Crawford and pitcher Lawrence Benton to Cincinnati for second-baseman Hughie Critz, pitcher Pete Donahue and outfielder Ethan Allen.

At Cincinnati, Crawford batted .290, mostly as a second baseman. At age twenty-eight, he figured to have at least six or seven more good years in the majors. But luck was against him. He was in the wrong city at the wrong time. The Reds had a young, strong second baseman at their farm team in Columbus. His name was Anthony Francis Cuccinello and he was ready for the majors.

After the 1930 season, the Cincinnati Reds sold Pat Crawford to Hollywood in the Pacific Coast League. He refused to report. The Crawfords expected a baby in the fall. "I didn't want to take an infant on that long trip to California," he said. "I wanted to finish my work on my master's degree and get a position in a college."

Crawford went back to Springfield College, while Sarah and daughter Patricia, born in November, remained in Kinston. During the spring quarter, he got a telephone call from a dynamic baseball executive, Larry MacPhail, the president and general manager of Columbus. The St. Louis Cardinals had bought the Columbus franchise from Cincinnati and since Pat wouldn't report to Hollywood, MacPhail said he now belonged to Columbus. He wanted Crawford to play for him. Crawford said: no, thanks. He only cared about continuing his education. MacPhail wanted to talk the matter over in person. No good, Crawford said.

Now Larry MacPhail was not the kind of man to take no for an answer. "The next day he called me again and said that he had talked with a member of the Ohio State University physical education department and had discussed an attractive proposition. He suggested I come down to Columbus at his expense the next weekend. I told him that I would talk over the matter with a member of the Ohio State faculty and call him on the coming Saturday. He had already worked out a schedule that would enable me to make the trip to Columbus and back to Springfield without missing any classes."

Pat Crawford met a professor at Ohio State and worked out an arrangement whereby he could get his master's in three quarters at the university. Meanwhile, he could play ball for Columbus. Crawford had an outstanding season in 1931, leading the league in batting, home runs, runs batted in and in total assists for a first baseman. The spring of 1932 saw Pat Crawford in a St. Louis Cardinal uniform. He was back where he belonged. However, something was going on behind the scenes.

Larry MacPhail wanted desperately to win a pennant for Columbus fans, for himself and for the owners of the St. Louis Cardinals. He needed an experienced first baseman, someone who could hit, field and help pull the team together. Didn't they have such a man right there with the big team in Bradenton? After all, Pat Crawford could be spared, since the Cardinals already had a young, switch-hitting first baseman named Rip Collins.

"Toward the end of spring training," Crawford remembered, "Mr. Rickey asked me to come to his room at the hotel. I can see him to this day. He was sitting in bed surrounded by papers—letters, telegrams, scorecards, envelopes with notes scrawled on them. He was smoking a big cigar and a cloud of smoke hung over his head. He began discussing the situation at Columbus—the city was ripe for a winner. Its brand-new stadium would be ready for opening day. The fans would support a winner. Still, I deserved another shot at the majors on the basis of my fine 1931 season. He stopped talking and looked at me straight in the eye.

" 'Pat,' he began. 'I'm going to ask you to go back to Columbus. We'll pay you a major-league salary. Furthermore, I'll guarantee you'll be back in St. Louis next year.' "

Crawford agreed to return to Columbus, even though with his credentials he should have been with some big-league team. He had another great year and was voted most valuable player in the American Association in 1932.

Branch Rickey kept his word and brought Crawford back to the Cardinals in 1933, which he spent as a utility man and pinch hitter. The stage was set for Pat to become the pinch hitter of the Gashouse Gang.

Most of Crawford's hits in 1934 came in moments of pressure.

"One time I really impressed Leo Durocher," Pat chuckled. "We were in Philadelphia and we had a winning streak going. There was a man on third and one out and Frisch and Durocher were in one of their huddles in the dugout. You know, Leo gave Frankie a lot of help that year, made suggestions in key situations, although Frank had the final decision. Anyway, Frankie called me to go up and hit, and I said to him, 'Do you want a base hit, or do you just want that runner in?' I figured I could hit a long fly ball. I wasn't going to try to hit a line drive. It might go straight at somebody. Durocher was astonished.

" 'Good night!' he exclaimed. 'Just go up and hit the ball!' "

Crawford went up swinging. "I was just looking for a waist-high fast ball, something you rarely get. They either jam you or pitch you high outside. This particular time in Philadelphia, Phil Collins was pitching, a right-hander. They called him 'Fidgety Phil.' While he was out there fidgetin', I was relaxed and waiting. Just looking to hit the pitch. Well, I guess Phil had been told by his manager, Jimmy Wilson, not to give me a fast ball. His first pitch was a high outside curve ball. I was ready for it.

"In came that hanging curve, the easiest pitch in the

world to hit. I drove the center fielder against the scoreboard to catch it. I often wondered why I didn't pull it a
little more and knock it over that short fence in right field.
Anyway, the runner scored easily."

While Pat was on the road, helping in the pennant fight,
Sarah Crawford, a petite charmer, stayed in St. Louis with
three-year-old Patricia. They lived in an apartment behind
the old Fairgrounds Hotel, not far from Sportsman's Park.

"It was a very hot summer even for St. Louis," Mrs.
Crawford recalled. "I remember going down to the railroad
station early one morning to meet Pat coming in from a
road trip. It was six A.M. and people were lying in the yards
sleeping. We lived in a two-story house. We had the down-
stairs. The house was in a small park. I remember getting
up very early every morning and closing the windows and
pulling down the shades to keep it cool."

There was little social life for a ballplayer's wife, particularly a young woman confined to an apartment with a three-
year-old. Occasionally, Sarah Crawford got together with
other wives when the team was on the road, to play some
bridge or attend a movie. And, like some wives, she attended
home games, leaving her daughter with a sitter. Still it was
a dramatic year for the Crawfords, wild, happy, fun-filled
and a prelude to tragedy. Pat was a member of one of the
most colorful teams in baseball history, involved in a pre-
posterous pennant fight and rough World Series. And it was
to be his last year in professional baseball and, sadder still, his
last year as an athlete.

During the '34 season, he had suffered from bleeding
hemorrhoids, which weakened him. He decided to have
surgery before the next season, and entered the hospital
in early January, expecting to be home in a few days. Instead, he wound up with blood poisoning and was lucky to
come out alive. To save his life, it was necessary to ankylose
his left hip joint, which left him with a stiff hip and ended
his athletic career. As he fought for his life, his only link

with baseball was his correspondence with Burgess Whitehead, who had been his road roommate in 1934.

The St. Louis Cardinals finished second in 1935, and
voted Pat Crawford a full share of their second-place money,
even though he wasn't a member of the team. This enabled
Pat and Sarah to go to Florida to strengthen his leg by
wading in the warm waters of the Gulf. The sun, the wind,
the warmth did wonders for Crawford. He was bitterly disappointed, though, knowing the frustration a first-rate athlete
feels when there is no longer hope for physical achievement.
But he was a strong man, mentally and morally, and he had
good friends and a good education.

Shortly after Crawford had gone into the hospital, the
St. Louis Cardinals had appointed him manager of Rochester
in the International League, but during his illness the news
was kept from him. Sarah was afraid if he learned he was no
longer a player with the Cardinals, it would delay his recovery. His long period of recuperation and his trouble
walking prevented him from taking the job.

Then, in the fall of 1935, Branch Rickey offered Crawford the position of secretary on the Columbus Red Birds of
the American Association. Crawford accepted and spent
most of the season with Columbus as a bookkeeper, but got
out of the office on scouting trips and to organize try-out
camps in the South. During one such junket, he was getting
shaved in a small-town barbershop. (Rickey felt that was a
good place to pick up baseball information.) He asked the
barber if they were any prospects around.

"He walked around in front of me with his razor in his
hand," Crawford remembered.

" 'You're not one of those fellows who'd like to break up
our local team, are you?' he asked.

" 'No,' I said. 'I just want to contact boys who might
make the majors someday.'

" 'Well,' he said, 'there was a young pitcher who lived
down the road a piece. He could really throw the ball.'

Where did he live? Well, he lived 'over the hill and around the bend and then you go over the bridge around the curve.' "

Pat Crawford drove into the country in search of the pitcher. After several inquiries, he spotted a young man wearing a baseball cap, motioned him to his car, told him he was a St. Louis scout and asked him to throw a few. Was there anyone in the neighborhood who could catch him. No, the young man said, but his younger brother could hold him until he started throwing real fast.

"While he was warming up in the yard with his brother," Crawford recalled, "I drew a rectangle about the size of the strike zone on a clay embankment at the side of the road. Then I explained that I wanted him to stand across the road on level ground and throw into the rectangle. I opened the trunk of my car and dug out several new baseballs.

" 'I'll break the threads,' he said.

" 'Don't worry,' I said. 'I have plenty of balls.'

"He threw several at moderate speed and then began to cut loose with some dandy fast balls. The dust flew. I thought I had found another Dizzy Dean."

The youngster was Rae Scarborough, whom Crawford recommended to the Cardinals. He did not try to sign the boy, for Rae's father wanted his son to go to college first. Rae Scarborough eventually made the majors with the Washington Senators, and pitched in the American League for ten years. Crawford also discovered Ernie White, a fine left-handed pitcher who shut out the New York Yankees in the 1942 World Series.

The summer of 1937 was the final baseball year for Clifford Rankin Crawford. That winter he built a sailing camp which he opened in 1938 and ran until his retirement in 1959.

Before I left Kinston, Pat Crawford dug out an old brown bat from the closet of his den. It was covered with the autographs of the Gang. Frankie and Ducky, Rip and Pepper and Dizzy. Crawford hefted it in his strong old fingers and, almost unconsciously, fell into a batting stance, feet close together, hands back—a fine hitting position. It was only a second that seemed to stretch back into time and I wondered what he was thinking, but not wanting to break the spell, I did not ask.

15

Almost There

HE WAS A MAN OF MEANS and fame and achievement, who retired gracefully from his profession, returned to the country of his childhood, started a new career—and lost nearly all his wealth. Although he now lives with a benign sense of regret, this is muted by good humor. Like Satchel Paige, James Otto Carleton never looks back—well, *hardly ever.*

Nicknamed "Tex" by a sportswriter with nothing to do on a rainy day, Carleton was a major-league pitcher for eight years, playing on three World Series teams, including the Gashouse Gang. If you analyzed the careers of the several thousand pitchers who have played major-league baseball, you would note that his record is well above average. The average playing career is less than five years, and few players get into a single World Series, let alone three. Only a small percentage of pitchers win 100 major-league games; Carleton won 100 and lost 76. Although he is not unhappy about his career, still, he feels, "I should have had a better record."

He should have been a twenty-game winner. "But I wasn't. I was allergic to the sun, and during the hot months of July and August I used to weaken about the sixth or seventh inning. Then I had to come out of the game." Today, when relief pitchers take over as soon as a pitcher breathes heavily, he would win twenty games a year easily, for he was a first-rate pitcher for six innings. Still, he did not live up to his own expectations. The Cardinals kept him in the minors too long, seven grueling seasons. In 1929, he led the International League in pitching, but St. Louis didn't bring him up. "The Cardinals turned down a lot of money for me, from both the Yankees and the Giants. They wouldn't deal for me."

Tall and slender—about six feet two, and 180 pounds in his playing days—Tex Carleton was too intense to be a great player. "I was always worried about losing the game," he said. "I didn't want to be the losing pitcher."

This fear of losing intensified the pressure in the long, hot pennant races of the 1930s. He helped a team most in the cool months of spring and fall, making valuable contributions to three pennant winners, the '34 Cards, the '35 Cubs and the '38 Cubs. He worked quietly and steadily, always in the shadow of the Dean brothers, of Big Bill Lee and Lon Warneke, of Charlie Root and Larry French. When the New York Giants edged out the Cubs for the 1937 pennant, Carleton was the best pitcher on the Chicago team, with a 16–8 record. A side-armer with a deceptive delivery, his money pitch was a low sinking fast ball that was hard to hit solidly. It puzzled right-hand hitters, because it seemed to be heading right at them, only to break down and in at their knees. It made batters long for the shade of the dugout.

Even such deadly left-handers as Bill Terry fell before his sinking fast ball. "One day in the Polo Grounds," he recalled, "I threw Terry a slow curve ball and he hit it over the right center-field fence up against the *upper* facade. He was an opposite field hitter. And you can't throw an opposite field hitter off-speed pitches, because he's waiting until the ball's on top of him. Then he jumps on it."

"So I started pitching Terry mediocre fast balls, with a nice easy motion—not putting everything I had on the ball, but not throwing a change of pace either. An ordinary sinking fast ball, low, over the *middle* of the plate, not low *outside,* nor low *inside,* but over the middle of the plate knee-high. And he would hit the Goddamnedest shots at the short-stop on one hop you ever saw. It would be an easy out. That was all he could do with the pitch, bounce it to short. He couldn't lift it in the air. Day after day, he'd ground out to the shortstop off me. He got a lot of hits that he couldn't quite get around on, grounding them just to the shortstop's right. Or he'd drill some back through the box. He got his base hits, but I doubt if he batted anywhere near three hundred when he was hitting four hundred against the rest of the league."

Born in Comanche, Texas, in 1906, James Otto Carleton moved to Fort Worth at age eleven. His father was a railroad man. He had two brothers, who died in infancy. His younger brother Virgil, who lives in the Fort Worth area, also played pro ball for three years as a minor-league catcher.

Tex was the star of the family, one of the most outstanding pitchers in the state. He played high school baseball and went to Texas Christian University where, he said, he majored in "baseball." He chuckled, "I quit in my sophomore year."

He signed his first contract with Texarkana in the East Texas League in 1925. He played there about three months, but when the club wanted to cut his $275 monthly salary, he refused to accept it and was released. He spent the remainder of the year as a semipro ballplayer, traveling all over Arkansas, Louisiana, Mississippi and into Missouri, where a Cardinal scout signed him to a contract. His last year of minor-league apprenticeship was 1931 with Houston, where he won twenty games, lost seven and had a fine 1.89 earned-run average. On the same team was Dizzy Dean.

In 1932, Carleton became a starting pitcher for St. Louis, enabling Branch Rickey to trade pitcher Paul Derringer to Cincinnati for shortstop Leo Durocher.

Tex Carleton relishes life. He loves to talk about baseball, and enjoys a good yarn. He came to my hotel room in Fort Worth, knocked on the door in midmorning, hung up his topcoat and sporty-looking hat, sat back in a chair—and talked for nearly four hours. He talked easily, about his career and life after baseball, chuckling as he recalled a good day, shaking his head ruefully at a bad memory. He spoke about the Cardinals and Cubs and Dodgers, evoking the pennant races, colorful personalities and great games. In a swirl of words, bat hit ball, Herman went to right with the pitch; Jurges flashed across the bag to get two; Hartnett gunned down a base-runner; Berger struck out; Lombardi grounded to Reese; Dressen mocked a pitcher and Durocher punched a fan; the Cubs conquered the Cards. He analyzed players, hitting and fielding styles; teams, their strengths and weaknesses—and he did it honestly. Relaxing and puffing on one cigarette after another, he rolled through the '30s, recalling the weary train rides from St. Louis to Boston, from Chicago to New York to Philadelphia when there was no air-conditioning.

"You sat in the station, waiting to get on the Pullman. They had great big old units that blew cool air into the Pullman. But the minute the car started—there was no refrigeration—and it got hot again, you just had to open up the window—and work your way out of the cinders the next morning. We had long trips of ten to sixteen and eighteen hours, all overnight trips. We used to play cards and fool around before going to bed."

Usually they had lower berths, although sometimes the Cardinals, hard-pressed for cash, had to sleep in upper berths. They traveled in three Pullmans—players, managers, coaches and trainer, and newspaper men. Looking back, it was a folksy kind of caravan and the players were together much more than today's teams who travel by jet. Train rides gave them more chance to talk baseball and to learn about each other, to iron out personal differences.

Carleton chuckled as he recalled the 1933 season when he lost so much weight the club worried about his health. Dr. Hyland, the Cardinals' physician, couldn't find anything wrong with him. "He recommended two or three highballs before dinner each night, to stimulate my appetite. I used to get prescription whiskey—it still being Prohibition—and carry it with me on the road. I'd have a couple of highballs and go around blowing my breath in the other guys' faces."

They had a lot of fun playing the game of baseball then. "You couldn't wait to get out there," Tex said. "They beat you today? Let me at 'em tomorrow."

No quarter was expected. And nobody was surprised when none was given. "If you wanted to knock a batter down, you'd holler: 'Look out!' As though the pitch had slipped out of your hand."

When the Cardinals went to spring training in 1934, Carleton said, "we had hopes of winning the pennant. I had won seventeen ball games in '33 and Diz had won twenty. Hallahan was still a good pitcher and we'd got Bill Walker from the Giants. Haines was getting old but still could pitch good ball. Jim Mooney was a prospect."

Paul Dean had come up from Columbus, or rather was pushed up in a way he wouldn't have been if his name had been Smith or Jones. At least Carleton is convinced of that, as are some of his old teammates.

"Rickey wanted somebody to pair off with Dizzy, who was so colorful. It was to the club's advantage to have a brother act. Not to take anything away from him, but Paul was nowhere near the pitcher Dizzy was," Carleton said. The younger Dean was strictly a fast-ball pitcher, and he got by very well for a couple of years. "By the grace of God and a fast outfield and a lot of luck, he won nineteen games in 1934," Carleton said.

Dizzy was another story. He was as fast or faster than anybody in the National League—Van Lingle Mungo threw harder, but not faster—and he had a pretty good curve. His thirty-game season is a plateau not reached since in the league, and I declared: "He was the greatest pitcher in baseball at that time."

"He was like hell!" Carleton sat up in his chair and his Texan drawl straightened out into an exclamation point. "Carl Hubbell was. If my life depended on a ball game, I'd rather have Hub pitch it than Diz. Diz could have a bad day occasionally, or he could have a great one. Hubbell had a good day every time he walked out there. If you beat him 5–2 or 5–3, that was a high-scoring game."

Even a foolish writer wouldn't challenge an old pitcher on his home grounds, particularly when he had an ace like Hubbell working for him. It was Hubbell who in the 1934 All-Star game struck out Ruth, Gehrig, Foxx, Simmons and Joe Cronin. He holds the major-league record for most consecutive games won, twenty-four. Tex Carleton was involved in one of Hubbell's most remarkable games, on July 2, 1933. Hubbell pitched eighteen innings to beat the Cardinals 1–0 —and he didn't walk a single batter. Carleton was the opposing pitcher. "I only went sixteen innings," he grinned. He was relieved by Jesse "Pop" Haines, and the Giants got a run off him, Tex recalled, "on a little butterfly hit by Hughie Critz."

That was only the first game of the doubleheader. In the second game, Ray Parmelee and Dizzy Dean squared off, and the final score was Giants one, Cardinals zero. Tex shook his head. "Diz and I and Pop allowed two runs in that little ole Polo Grounds and lost a doubleheader."

On the road, Carleton roomed with pitcher Bill Walker, whom he described as somewhat of a "night-life Charley," one of Tex's favorite phrases.

"Bill liked the better things of life. He was a little bit of a playboy, a lot like Durocher in that respect. He liked night life and entertainers. We used to go around to nightclubs in some of the cities. I'll never forget, though, Frisch would try to catch Bill and me out after hours In New York, we went to the Hollywood or one of the clubs with a good friend of Bill's who'd made a mint of money in the stock market. We'd have drinks and dinner. Well, Bill and I would always leave by cab just in time to get within a block of the hotel ten or fifteen minutes before midnight, which was the curfew for the team. We'd stand around the corner until four or five minutes until twelve. Then we'd walk in. Frisch would be hiding somewhere in the lobby, with coach Buzzy Wares stationed at one entrance and Mike Gonzalez at the other, trying to catch us. But he never did."

Once at an old-timer's game, Carleton reminded Frankie of his attempts to trap the two pitchers.

"You and that Goddamn Walker," Frisch growled.

"What *about* Walker and me?" Carleton said. "We were always in shape to play, weren't we?"

"Yeah, but Goddamn. I—I," he sputtered. "You were always out after hours."

"You didn't catch us, did you?"

"No, but I would have."

"Frank," Carleton said, "you weren't about to catch us. We used to take a cab ahead of time and stand across the street watching you guys. We waited till the last minute—just to keep you upset."

"You bastards, you," Frankie exploded.

The sarcastic Frisch and the caustic Carleton must have had some stormy sessions, even though Carleton insists they got along all right.

"Frankie was a New Yorker," Carleton said, "who thought everything west of the Hudson was camping out." Tex says bluntly that "Frisch was one of the worst managers I ever played for. He was very set. He wanted to be a McGraw, but he wasn't a McGraw." Carleton and Frisch had opposite philosophies of pitching. Frisch believed in pitching to a batter's weakness. If he was weak on the curve ball, throw him curves. If he couldn't hit a high fast ball, throw him high fast balls.

Carleton, on the other hand, believed in using his best pitch, the low, sinking fast ball, pitting his strength against the batter's strength. "I didn't care whether a guy was a low-ball hitter or not, because I challenged him. I figured my pitch, my strength, was better than his strength. If I raised the ball up, I lost a lot of effectiveness."

Manager Frisch, adhering to the McGraw school, believed you could get most hitters out with curves. Carleton started the fourth game of the 1934 World Series, Frisch calling the pitches from second base. "He put his fist in the glove for a curve, and his hand outside for a fast ball," Carleton recalled. "The Tigers got me out in the third inning when I threw *seventeen* consecutive curves and slow curves.

"Everybody on the field knew what pitch was coming. Just like everybody in the National League knew all year long. It's pretty hard to pitch out there when they know what's coming," Carleton said. Carleton respected Frisch's great ability as a player. "He was a tremendous hitter, bunter and base runner. But he was prone to loaf. And that was one thing about that ball club, by God, if the manager or anybody else loafed—they'd jump down your throat. That was one of the secrets of our success. We gave it all we had—and you'd better *give* it or you're going to have a bunch of guys on your back."

Joining the Cubs in 1935 was a break for Carleton, for Chicago was an outstanding team, better even than the Gashouse Gang, winning two pennants and finishing second twice in the next four years. Although the Cubs didn't have a pitcher as great as Dizzy Dean, they had a superior staff in Bill Lee, Lon Warneke, Larry French, Charlie Root and Tex Carleton. And Carleton's eyes light up when he talks about the infield of Cavarretta, Herman, Jurges and Hack.

"It was damn near an all-star infield in the league. Billy Herman was a great second baseman, and Billy Jurges was the greatest shortstop I ever saw. He and Herman were the best combination in baseball. Each knew exactly what the other was going to do. Both of them had tremendous throwing arms. Herman was the best hit-and-run man I ever saw. You could not keep him from hitting the ball where he wanted to, regardless of how you pitched him. A tremendous glove man. Unorthodox. Hell, they give Lou Boudreau credit for the infield shift against hitters. Herman's the first guy that ever shifted around. Ernie Lombardi and Wally Berger—he used to play them in short center field, directly behind second base. Against slow left-hand hitters, he'd be playing assistant right fielder, and he could throw them out, too. He and Jurges teamed up with Gabby Hartnett to cut down base runners. Hartnett had the greatest arm I ever saw. Johnny Bench's arm is as strong as Gabby's but Hartnett could throw the ball as hard as Bench and much more accurately. And you could catch the throw barehanded, it was so light." Carleton paused to light another cigarette, and shook his head in admiration.

"We'd put on a pick-off play, and Hartnett would call for a pitch-out or a knock-down. Jurges and Herman would both move to second like they'd futzed up the signals. While one was tagging you out, the other would be stumbling and stepping on you, like he'd got all fouled up. They were both rough ballplayers, but Herman was a little more slick."

Carleton looks back on his Chicago days with fondness and with respect for the players and for P. K. Wrigley, their owner, whom he calls "the finest thing that happened to baseball over the years. He had a lot of innovations. He was the first man to give players expense money for spring training. We never tipped on the Cubs. The management did that. Mr. Wrigley put in a deal where every man on the ball club—as soon as he signed his contract—got a check for two hundred and fifty dollars. So the kids would have a little spending money right away. The veterans got five hundred dollars when they signed. We also had a laundry allowance. And there was no eating limit on the Cubs."

In the spring of 1936, the Cubs returned to Los Angeles from practice at Catalina, where they went every year, to begin the exhibition season.

"I remember," he said, "we were in the clubhouse and

Bob Lewis, the traveling secretary, came in and said, 'Fellows, we're having a team meeting upstairs in the suite. Please be there by six o'clock.'

"Naturally, we wondered what it was all about, because we knew it was Mr. Wrigley's suite. When we got there Mr. Wrigley had a bar set up, and he was bartender. He was a temperate man, but he didn't mind the guys having a couple of drinks. After we loosened up a little, Mr. Wrigley asked our attention.

" 'I guess you're wondering what this is all about. A few days ago I got a report from our auditors on last year's operation. We made more money than we thought we had. You're the fellows who did it. Now I'm going to pass out checks to all of you who had a hand in this last year. They vary in size as to how we evaluated your contributions. I wish you wouldn't divulge what you received. Your opinion may be different from ours, but we did it as fairly and generously as we could.' Under Wrigley, if you had a hitting streak or pitched a couple of good games, even if you didn't win them, there'd be a couple hundred extra dollars in your next semi-monthly paycheck. Handing out of bonuses or incentive pay was frowned on by the establishment, but to the players it was a delightful treat.

"Well," Tex drawled. "We got from five hundred dollars —for the guy who had the worst season—up to five thousand each for fellows like Stan Hack and Frank Demaree and Billy Herman."

For those days, Carleton did well financially, making over $20,000 in 1938, paying only $1,700 income tax at a time when, as he said, "you couldn't carry ten dollars in groceries home in your arms."

1938. It was another exciting year in the National League. Chicago bought Dizzy Dean, sore arm and all, from the Cardinals for $185,000, and old Diz won seven games, lost only one and posted a low earned-run average of 1.80. Young Johnny Vander Meer pitched two consecutive no-hit games for Cincinnati. And the pennant race went down to the final series of the season, with the Cubs squaring off against the Pittsburgh Pirates in Wrigley Field.

The Cubs were finishing dramatically after trailing throughout the season. When the two teams met on September 27 for a three-game set, Chicago was a game and a half behind Pittsburgh. The Cubs won the opening game 2–1, with Dizzy Dean lasting until two were out in the ninth inning, which was a pleasant surprise to the Cubs and a severe shock to the Pirates. The second game was a melodrama.

On September 28, another huge crowd of 42,000 jammed the stadium to watch the tense struggle. With two outs in the last of the ninth, up came manager Gabby Hartnett, called "Old Tomato Face" because he laughed so hard it made his face grow scarlet. It was growing dark. Wrigley Field had no lighting system then, and still doesn't. The visibility was so poor the fans could hardly follow the ball as Mace Brown, Pittsburgh's fine relief pitcher, delivered it. Hartnett hadn't had a hit all afternoon, and Brown quickly shot two strikes by him. The next one was belt-high and Hartnett drove it into the left-field stands to win the game. He circled the bases, grinning from ear to ear, shaking the hands of the hysterical Cub fans who poured out of the stands.

Nineteen thirty-eight was Tex Carleton's last winning year in the majors. He won ten games and lost nine, but his earned-run average was a very high 5.41 per game. Worse still, he gave up 213 hits in 168 innings. When a pitcher permits a lot more hits than total innings pitched, he had better consider early retirement. Carleton's arm was bad in 1938, and by 1939 was truly weary from fourteen years of professional pitching. The Cubs sent him to Milwaukee in the American Association where he pitched very little in 1939, but did have a good strike-out record. His arm was recovering. This record was spotted by the Brooklyn Dodgers who, the year before, had had good luck in picking up another sore-armed Milwaukee pitcher, Whitlow Wyatt. He was brought to Brooklyn in 1939, and won eight games. (This was the same Wyatt who would help the Dodgers win the pennant in 1941.) If Wyatt could do it, why not Tex Carleton, whose major-league credentials were much better than those of the journeyman Wyatt?

The Dodgers took a chance and bought Carleton from Milwaukee, even though he no longer had a first-rate fast ball.

"I pulled something back in the shoulder," Tex said. He rubbed the spot to show me where it hurt, wincing as he did. "Larry MacPhail called me in the winter when he made the deal and I said to him, 'Aw, Larry, I don't think I can do you any good.' I hadn't been pitching well and told him I wanted to quit."

MacPhail convinced Carleton that he could help Brooklyn, and Tex pitched for the Dodgers in 1940, winning six games and losing six. It was the first time he had ever won less than ten games. The Dodgers finished second to the Cincinnati Reds. Carleton worked very hard and in the early part of the year was pitching better ball than anybody on the Brooklyn team.

On April 30, 1940, he hurled his last memorable game, against the Reds in Crosley Field, Cincinnati. The Dodgers were on an eight-game winning streak and Tex Carleton made it nine straight, pitching a no-hitter, a 3–0 victory.

Meeting with catcher Herman Franks before the game, Carleton still remembers telling Franks how he intended pitching to big Ernie Lombardi. "I'm going to waste the curve ball outside to Lom," he'd said. "Just show it to him. Let him know I still have a curve. But the pitch he's going to hit is a fast ball right on his fists.

"Well, the first time Lombardi came up he hit one over the laundry behind the left-field fence. It was a fast ball about a foot inside. *Good God,* he hit it hard. But it was foul by thirty feet or more. Franks came running out to the mound.

" 'Goddamn,' he says. 'Don't get the ball in there.'

"So I says, 'It was foul, wasn't it? Just a strike.'

" 'Yeah, I know,' he says, 'but what if he straightens it out?'

" 'He *can't* hit it hard and hit it fair,' I says. 'If he doesn't get around, it'll handcuff him.'

"So I pitched Ernie like that all day, and every time he'd hit a couple of foul balls—*bang!*—into the left-field bleachers. Foul. Then he'd hit one on the handle of the bat, break a bat, and the ball would roll down to Reese at short or to the second baseman, Pete Coscarart."

In 1941, Carleton trained with the Dodgers in Havana. On the day the team was to return to the States he received a telephone call. His wife, Fanny, had been operated on and peritonitis had set in. She was so dangerously ill that a priest had given her last rites. Tex flew immediately to New Orleans to be at her bedside, staying with her for two weeks until she recovered. While in New Orleans, he tried working out with the Cleveland club, but couldn't get his heart into training. The Dodgers picked him up as they swung through town, and on the way north he and Fred Fitzsimmons split pitching assignments. And he pitched fairly well, working every fifth or sixth day. But his major-league career ended on a bitter note in New York, where the Dodgers were playing a three-game series with the Yankees. It was cold, with snow shoveled under the stands, the kind of day to tighten up a pitcher's shoulder. When Carleton loosened up, though, he could throw. When he cooled off, the shoulder tightened up again.

"Durocher was in court," Carleton recalled, "over an incident with a fan. Dressen was running the club until Leo got there around game time. I went to Chuck and pointed out I was behind in my pitching schedule, and asked, 'What are your pitching plans?'

" 'I don't have any for you in the next few days,' Dressen said.

"I said, 'I'd sure like to pitch batting practice.' That way I could get a lot of pitching in.

" 'That's fine,' Dressen said.

"I pitched for twenty minutes until I was about to fall on my face. Then I went in and washed up, changed my sweatshirt and stuff and came back to sit on the bench. Fitzsimmons was supposed to finish up the ball game, go in along about the seventh inning, and he was warming up in the bullpen. One of the coaches came up to the bench and said, 'Fred's arm is hurting.'

"Leo turned to me and said, 'How about you going in, Tex?'

"Well, I looked at Dressen: *and he never said a Goddamn word*. He hated my guts anyway from that time over at Cincinnati where he and I had a little altercation. He just grinned. He had me then, and I'm not going to say, 'Hell, Leo, Chuck had me pitching batting practice.' It was up to Chuck to speak up. I went down to the bullpen and tried to throw. Then I came in and pitched the last three innings, but I didn't pitch very well. Leo figured I was through, and it hurt him to let me go, because he and I were friends. But I'll always hold that against Chuck, because he was just getting back at me."

Carleton paused, seemed to ponder a second, and then laughed as though to take the sting out of the bitter memory.

"Who was it, Bob—a sportswriter in Detroit, I believe —who said: 'Dressen always finished ten games ahead of his team!' That was a great quote, wasn't it?"

Tex Carleton completed his professional baseball career at Montreal in 1941 as a player-coach. Then he returned to Fort Worth, where he worked for General Dynamics, supervising workers who made spare parts for aircraft. In 1946 he moved to Midland, Texas. A town of 22,000 people, Midland had experienced an oil boom after World War II. It was a pleasant community and Tex knew everybody, from the unassuming merchant to the wheeler-dealer oil man. Carleton had walked out of baseball with about $100,000 in assets—at the time a large sum of money—and he invested it in a sporting goods store. Soon it was a small corporation (he was the major stockholder), with branches in two other towns.

In 1953, he sold out his interests in the stores and started an insurance business, which he ran until 1962, moving back to Fort Worth, where he had begun his trip to athletic achievement. "It was a gold mine and I should have made a big bundle," he admits now, but lack of self-discipline, a carefree attitude, inflation, living too high—all the human failings and foibles conspired to wipe out most of his baseball nest egg. "I should have been very successful in the insurance business with my name and the people I knew. But putting off until tomorrow, playing too much golf—I just didn't work hard enough. I didn't like it that much. It was my own fault, so I sold the insurance business."

In Fort Worth, from 1963 to 1973, he worked in a men's clothing store. In the first year his sales were over $100,000, and for the next nine years they ranged from $125,000 to $150,000 every year. Then in 1974 a "youth movement" forced him into retirement at age sixty-eight. Now he works part-time as a wholesale salesman for the Mid-Continent Chemical Company, managing to live simply with his wife, moonlighting as a salesman to supplement his social security benefits.

"There is no shortage of steaks," Carleton says, but he does live well below the standard he might have maintained with better management. His big regret is the way he handled his finances. "I'd do everything I did over again, with the exception of working a little harder and being a little more conservative," he said. Then he laughed. "Don't look back, as old Satchel Paige said—'Somebody might be gaining on you.'"

16

Muscles and Me

The name Medwick comes from the Hungarian
word *medve,* which means "bear."

A LIGHT WIND BLEW, the temperature was near 80, and the
cloudless sky was blue as a tourist's umbrella. It was the
third week in March, the best time to watch baseball at an
ideal site, a minor-league training camp, this one belonging
to the St. Louis Cardinals.

I heard the crack of bat against ball and the cry of "Hat-
a-baby." Through the wire fence I could see about a hundred young Cardinals cavorting on the practice fields.
Interwoven among those huskies—like gray strands in a
brown rope—were portly men standing with hands on hips
and mouths working: managers and coaches, overweight
and overwrought. Walking through the open gate, I stopped
a towering youngster with powerful shoulders.

"Joe Medwick around?" I asked.

He pointed to his left. "Straight ahead, sir."

There stood old Muscles, the name MEDWICK stamped
like an advertisement on his sturdy shoulders. He was talking to a group of outfielders, his voice carrying crisply in
the spring air: "Don't make basket catches, fellows. You're
not Willie Mays. He was a great one, but that's not the way
the Cardinals teach you to catch a fly ball." The players
moved thirty yards away to form a line in front of Medwick.

They began bouncing the ball to him, simulating the throw
made from the outfield to home plate. "Throw overhand,
boys," Medwick instructed. "You can control it better that
way." Now and then the ball skipped off-line a few feet,
forcing Medwick to move to his left or right. Then he'd
holler: "Take it easy, fellows. Remember I'm an old-timer."
He limped after the ball, favoring his right leg which had
been operated on twice.

He doesn't look too big, I thought, edging closer. A compact man (playing weight 180 pounds; five feet ten inches
tall). The nearer I got the larger he looked, which made me
wonder if he were built like Mickey Mantle who, it was
said, grew bigger with each layer of clothes he removed. A
careful look canceled out the analogy: Medwick was sturdy
and muscular, but not massive like Mantle. He looked fit,
though, and I remembered the first time I ever saw him,
when he was playing for the Brooklyn Dodgers.

It was in 1942 at Ebbets Field during one of those crucial series that Brooklyn seemed forever to be having against
the Cardinals. I had worked on a summer construction job,
breaking rocks with a sledgehammer for fifty cents an hour
to earn money to make a weekend trip to see the hero in
action. I was sixteen years old, and made the trip with a
"guardian," an old friend of my father's named George
McDonald. A feisty little Irishman, who had been a prizefighter, he occasionally squared off against me to demonstrate his left jab. He was quick-witted and always took an
adversary stance on whatever I said. "Medwick's the best
right-hand hitter in the National League," I said, as we took
our seats in the grandstand.

"He's washed up, Bobby," he said. "Why he's thirty-five
years old."

"He's only thirty!"

"Have it your way, kid—but he's an *old* thirty."

Hearing that remark, a Brooklyn fan with a cigar stuck
in his mouth turned in his seat.

"You can say that again, buddy. The bum couldn't carry Musial's glove. He ain't even going to play today—thank God for small favors. The bum. Not with Mort Cooper pitchin'!"

Not play today. I was devastated. Yet when the lineups were announced, there it was: "Playing left field for the Dodgers, Augie Galan, number . .."

The Brooklyn fan turned when he heard the sound of anguish. "Ah, don't let it get ya, kid. Galan's a bigger bum than Ducky. Anyway, Medwick'll play tomorrow when the left-handers pitch. The bum!"

Medwick played in the Sunday doubleheader, getting three hits in eight bats against southpaws Max Lanier and Ernie White. Again we sat behind the man with the big cigar and he turned around when Medwick was announced. ("Number seven, playing left field . . .")

"I told ya, kid. There's your bum." He winked at George McDonald, who laughed out loud. Medwick came up in the second inning with nobody on and hit the first pitch off the center-field fence for a double. I shook the shoulders of the cigar smoker, yelling, "See. *See!*"

"Ah," he said. "He was lucky. Musial would've had a triple easy."

That weekend at Ebbets Field had been a long time ago, early in World War II, and I smiled, thinking about it. Now, on this sunny March day at the training camp in St. Petersburg under a domed blue sky, I finally closed in on Muscles and introduced myself.

"I heard you were coming," he said. "I know what you're trying to do." He looked me straight in the eyes. "I'm not going to talk to you about the Gashouse Gang."

I have the world's worst poker face. It starts falling inside me, right behind the eyes, slides to the heart, then the liver, finally, plummeting so that my chin strikes my knees. It must be a God-awful sight to behold; sometimes I look like a man about to have apoplexy. That's the way it must have struck Medwick, for he grasped my arm to steady me.

"I don't mean to be rude," he said. "A book like that makes a lot of money. I might do it myself someday. I'm not going to talk about those days unless I'm paid. I want fifteen hundred dollars or I won't answer questions."

$1,500! $$$$$#*!@SSSS

My face hadn't recovered from its knee-high descent. Now it might never climb back to its proper place. I am empathetic, compassionate, God-fearing, enlightened—BUT GODDAMN IT—$$$$—1,500 *dollars*!

Looking at Medwick, clearly there were dollar signs embossed on his eyeballs. How could he have ever hit all those savage line drives looking through green bills? The beautiful blue sky, the sun, the gentle breeze—all vanished in my mind to be replaced by a terrible blackness.

Standing in the lovely Florida sunlight beneath the postcard sky, I listened to my old hero.

He was chattering about everything but the Gashouse Gang. He talked about modern players, about their huge salaries, even about their meal money (much too high; nobody could eat that much). He discussed his records, his golf game, even the Cardinals' great training camp. Mostly, he talked about the fine art of hitting a baseball. This depressed me. *God,* Joe, I thought—your tips are thirty years too late to help me.

He demonstrated his grip, showing the proper way to hold a bat. His hands caught my attention. I stared at them, not believing my eyes. Those hands that slashed out 2,471 lifetime big-league hits, that established the National League season record for most doubles (sixty-four), that gave him a lifetime batting average of .324, that swung him into the Baseball Hall of Fame—those hands were too small. Mentally, I held up my right hand against his right hand. My hand was small, but his must be smaller. His fingers were short and stubby, reminding me of Casey Stengel's remark about Japanese baseball players: They can't possibly play the game with those little fingers. Yet they did and Medwick led the National League in just about every batting department in 1937. How could he have done that with those stubby fingers?

Medwick finished his lecture on batting and was moving off with a wave of his arm—a friendly wave?—accompanied by several young players. As minor-league batting coach of the Cardinals, he tutored youngsters all spring, every day, hour after hour. Although I wasn't invited, I tagged along behind the imperial Medwick and his entourage, standing in the doorway of the nearby shed which housed two batting machines in parallel lanes. Medwick sat in a chair with his back against the wall, calling out instructions in a clipped voice: "Bunt two and rip away. There's a man on second and nobody out. Get him over to third now, at least. Hit it to right field. Let's see daylight between your arms and body. Don't cock your bat against your head, Number eight."

It must be painful for the old batting champ to watch inept hitting day after day, I thought, feeling sorry for him, but my pity was watered down by the studious way he ignored me. Then there was the barrier between us: 1,500-dollar-bills high, much too high for me to scale without help. I retreated from the lovely field, upon which great writing careers are made or broken, and found my way back to the motel to plan my strategy, but mainly to lick my wounds.

I pondered the problem of Joseph Michael Medwick, the Hammerin' Hungarian with the small hands, both of them outstretched toward me, palms upward. It was not my first experience with money-crazed baseball players. As a writer and editor, I had dealt with a number of them who suffered from a type of lockjaw curable only by a large check. I knew that baseball players, coaches, managers and others were supposed to cooperate free of charge to promote that game we all love. Most of them do cooperate, out of enlightened self-interest if nothing else. Some of them refuse. Usually these are the so-called superstars at the peak of their careers—stars whose names dominate the sports pages. Medwick's name had not been in the news for many years, yet he still felt entitled to big money. He was one of the do-nots and will-nots. His slogan as a young star had been "Base hits and *buckerinos*," and while he made a lot of the former he never seemed to get enough of the latter.

He had been the pride of New Jersey and St. Louis. He had played in two World Series and married a beautiful girl from a fine family. After leaving baseball, he had been in an automobile agency and then in the insurance business. He must have money, I thought. Why *must* he? Maybe most of it slipped through his fingers. After all, it had happened to a lot of famous players who got involved in business without adequate knowledge and without the ability to acquire it. That was it. He actually needed the money, but was too proud to admit it. So the key to his heart was in my wallet. But $1,500!

It was simply a matter of negotiation. The dickering took up the better part of three days. Finally, for $250 Medwick agreed to an interview. In addition, I promised him the free-lance commission I was to receive for a newspaper photo taken during spring training. It turned out to be a lowly $20, which I mailed to him later that year.

One sunny morning I was back at the minor-league field, ready and eager to chat with Joseph Michael Medwick, alias Mickey, Muscles and Ducky-Wucky. We sat in an observation booth on the second floor of a small building that was the hub of the training complex. Below, two St. Louis farm teams were playing a practice game, which we watched while chatting. During that session, and one on the following day, Medwick was cooperative but touchy, sensitive to any suggestion of criticism.

His career had been melodramatic. He was born in November 1911. His parents had been Hungarians who settled in Carteret, New Jersey, and became U. S. citizens. "They were from the old school," Medwick said. "One came from Buda and one came from Pest." Both are dead now, but his two sisters and a brother are still living. As a boy, Medwick was a tremendously gifted athlete—the one-in-a-million kind.

"I participated in every sport," Medwick said. "I was a four-letter man even in my freshman year in high school." He was all-state in football, basketball and baseball, a legend in New Jersey before he ever played professional baseball. In football, he played fullback and then quarterback. He could kick a football fifty-five or sixty yards, and pass an equal distance with ease. He was the team's punter and passer and key runner. "I was a triple-threat man," he said. "You played every minute, too. My parents wanted me to play baseball. But my mother didn't want for me to play football, because she thought I might get injured and not play baseball."

While still in high school, Medwick tried out with the Newark Bears, a farm team of the New York Yankees. Tris Speaker was the manager; Jocko Conlon, the old National League umpire, was the center fielder; Wally Pipp, ex-Yankee, was first baseman. A pitcher named Carl Fischer was throwing batting practice. "He knocked me down," Medwick said. "And Wally Pipp hollered at him: 'Give the kid a chance.' He knocked me down in batting practice. Deliberately."

Medwick's voice rose and his eyes flashed as he remembered the incident. "I got angry and hit a few balls out of the park. Then Fischer really got angry. He wanted to show me up, because I was a good hitter."

Medwick hit a ball out of every part of the park, but after the workout manager Speaker told him he was too young. The finest prospect ever to come out of New Jersey slipped through the fingers of the New York Yankees. Medwick might have been playing on those great Yankee teams of the 1930s, alongside Joe DiMaggio. Instead he went on to become one of the Gashouse Gang. Before settling on a baseball career, Medwick weighed numerous offers for college scholarships, most notably from Notre Dame, which was anxious to add him to its football squad. But the young Medwick lacked one and a half credits for admission, and was reluctant to attend prep school to acquire them.

Shortly after graduating from high school in 1930, he was playing for Scottsdale, Pa., in the Middle Atlantic League. He used the name Mickey King to protect his amateur status in case he changed his mind about a college education. He batted .419 with 100 RBIs in only seventy-five games, an astonishing performance for an eighteen-year-old. This led to his promotion in 1931 to Houston in the Texas League, where he became a big favorite with fans. He led the league in home runs and runs batted in that year and picked up the name "Ducky" when a fan compared his walk to that of a duck. The comparison did not please him, but the creation of a candy bar in his name, the "Ducky-Wucky" candy bar, did, especially since he shared in the proceeds. Medwick played in the city until late August 1932, when the Cardinals called him up to St. Louis. His last game was one of those dramatic performances that had dotted his colorful career.

When he swaggered to the plate for his last at bat of the game, his many fans rose as one to pay him tribute. The noise was thunderous as he tipped his cap and planted himself, his bat cocked and ready. The first pitch was low, but he swung at it and missed. The crowd groaned. The next pitch was a high inside fast ball, a hard pitch to hit. But, according to the Houston *Post,* "Medwick tied into the ball with all the power in his stocky body and the ball sailed over the left-field fence. When the second game was ended, Medwick was surrounded by several hundred kids all anxious to shake his hand."

A glorious way to leave town, a big bouquet for the departing hero? Not exactly. According to Medwick's recollection, there were thorns among the roses. "I was so damn angry," he said. "They used to give you a traveling bag or some damn thing when you leave the city. They didn't give me nothing. And then the fellow who had the candy bars wanted me to leave them there and I said 'Hell, no!' And they had to take all the wrappings off the bars. We had an agreement if I left [Houston] they couldn't sell them."

The comical picture of all those "Ducky-Wucky" bars without wrappings made me want to laugh out loud, but I knew better than to test the Medwick temper. A resentment that smoulders for more than forty years is too deadly to challenge.

After each burst of anger Medwick recalled another dramatic triumph followed by a blister of resentment followed by triumph, each canceling out the other. The Houston experience is typical. Over a decade and a half after he left all those naked candy bars, he returned, an aging veteran on the brink of retirement, to help Houston manager Johnny Keane get into the playoffs.

In August 1948, Joe Medwick led off the second inning, his first time at bat since leaving sixteen years before. The fans began shrieking, "Hit it over the wall, Joe. Hit it over the wall." Ken Sterling, the opposing pitcher, ran the count to Medwick to three balls and one strike. Then Medwick lashed the ball high and far toward left field. "It's a home run!" the crowd yelled. The ball was hit in the same spot as the one he hit in his last at bat in 1932.

"I was on my way out in 1948," Medwick recalled. "And they said I was going to get the Houston ball club to manage. So I went down there, but they changed their mind and I didn't get it."

When Joe Medwick joined the Cardinals in September 1932, he was only twenty years of age, and had played less than three full seasons of professional baseball. But he was ready. He was a major-league hitter, who swung at anything and hit it hard. Pitches at his feet. Over his head. Pitches off the bill of his cap. He attacked them all furiously, batting .349 in the last month of the season.

"He was one of the finest right-hand hitters I saw in my day," Tex Carleton said. "He could hit the ball to all fields and hit it hard. It was murder to throw him a change of pace. It looked like you would get him with his stance and stride—the way he jumped at that ball. But he would recock the bat and restep and hit the ball to right or right center for extra bases, even home runs. He was the only man I ever saw who could hit the change of pace for extra bases. *Hard!* I saw some good change-of-pace hitters, but they all would just lay it out there with their hands and arms. Their body was gone from the swing. But Medwick would do a double shuffle up there, recock, and hit the ball against or over the fence."

Carleton considered himself a benefactor of the young slugger from Carteret. The tall Texan had played with him at Houston and knew what a great prospect he was and how much he could help a ball club. "It wasn't easy to come up to the majors in those days," Carleton said. Older players didn't lay out welcome mats for rookies. As Carleton put it, "You kind of had to fight your way in."

In 1933, several of the players thought Medwick was too pushy. "They gave him a hard time," teammate Pat Crawford remembered. "The veterans rode him viciously. They wanted him put in his place, not to be too much of a take-charge guy. Right from the start, Joe wanted to be a big star. If he wasn't getting that publicity, he'd gripe about it."

In those days, Crawford pointed out, rookies were "to be seen and not heard." Medwick was treated roughly in '33, too roughly, some of the Cardinals felt. The savage riding might break his spirit. Tex Carleton took his part. "I almost had a fight defending him," he recalled.

By 1934, the hazing was over. Medwick was a proven player, having hit .306 and batted in ninety-eight runs the year before, the kind of performance veterans respected. Men such as Frankie Frisch and Pepper Martin, who had been in World Series and appreciated money and glory and prestige, saw that Jersey Joe could help the team to a pennant. Achievement was Medwick's passport to acceptance.

Forty years later, sitting in the spring sunlight in St. Petersburg, Medwick played down his hard times as a rookie and his later reputation as a tough guy. It was just part of the game.

"They used to haze a rookie. They were jealous of a young fellow. A young fellow had to learn how to protect himself. If he didn't, they'd run you out of the batter's box."

Nobody ever ran Medwick out of a batting box, although in 1934 his old friend, Tex Carleton, tried to. Medwick loved to get as much batting practice as possible to sharpen his skills. "Tex was one of the guys who tried to stop me one day. Did he tell you that story?" Medwick asked me.

"Tell it again," I asked.

"I had gone to Frisch and said: 'Frank, I wanna go out and hit.' This was fifteen minutes before the pitchers hit. So I started to go into the batting cage, and Carleton said: 'Where are you going?'

"I said, 'I'm going in the batting cage.'

" 'I don't think so,' Carleton said.

" 'I think so,' I said. And I hit him, right there, that was it. They never stopped me again."

Medwick's version of the famous fight doesn't square with that of Carleton's. Carleton had said: "The pitchers always hit first on a team, and Medwick was always trying to bust in there. This day he did and we had some words and he called me a name and I whacked him and he whacked me around a little bit. But—hell!—it wasn't serious. We became friends within fifteen minutes and remain friends to this day."

Both of these versions are dramatic and violent but, according to Paul Dean, neither is accurate. "There was no fight," he told me on the telephone. "No punches were thrown."

Bill Hallahan has *another* version of the episode. "What actually happened," Hallahan recalled, "was that Medwick was scheduled to pose for photographs and to be paid for this by a national magazine. We all knew about it, except Tex Carleton. When Joe jumped into the cage, Tex said, 'Where the hell do you think you're going?' Medwick hit Tex with a right cross on *top* of his head. Not on his jaw or face. On the top of his head. This stunned Tex."

Later, Carleton exclaimed, "Damn, why didn't you guys tell me Joe had arranged a special deal."

This episode marked the beginning of Medwick's fighting career. "After that," Hallahan said, "Joe was quick with his fists."

His renown as a one-punch artist stems partially from Dizzy Dean's comment: "Durndest man I ever seen. Before you even get to do enough talking and get mad enough to fight, Joe whops you and the fight's over."

One of Joe's victims was a pitcher named Ed Heusser, who was nicknamed "The Wild Elk of the Wasatch." The big pitcher accused Medwick of loafing on a fly ball and permitting a run to score. Muscles knocked the Wild Elk unconscious with one punch, right on the steps of the dugout in the Polo Grounds. Frisch had to rush in a pitcher from the bullpen.

Dizzy Dean and Ducky feuded on and off during the '30s. Once in Pittsburgh, three runs scored on a drive to left field that Dean thought Medwick should have handled, and told him so in the dugout. When Diz and brother Paul made a threatening move toward the left-fielder, Muscles picked up a bat.

"Come on," he snarled. "I'll break up this brother act here and now."

Later in the game, Medwick came to bat with three Cardinals on base, and hit one far over the left-field wall. Returning to the dugout, he filled his mouth with water, walked over to Diz—and spit on his shoes. "There's your three runs and one to spare," he snapped. "Now, let's see if you can hold the lead."

Another of Medwick's adversaries was Rip Collins, with whom he had exchanged punches in 1934. Two years later, Muscles wanted to take Rip apart, limb by limb.

"I had tied the National League record with ten straight hits in ten times up," Medwick recalled. "I was going for a new record. When I wasn't looking, Collins borrowed my favorite bat and broke it in practice."

There was murder in Medwick's voice as he recounted the incident. "He didn't have to do that. He had his own bats. When I found out about it, I was going to kill him. But Frisch stopped me."

If he had committed murder, no jury would have convicted the fiery left-fielder. I wondered if Joe knew that Collins had a fence made of broken bats at his home in upstate New York. I was afraid to ask him *that*.

As a young major-leaguer, Medwick had been a clean-living, well-conditioned athlete. He did not drink or smoke and there was a strong strain of Puritanism in him. He admired Jesse "Pop" Haines.

"If you ever saw a perfect man it was Jesse. I think the only two perfect men I ever saw in my life were Freddy Fitzsimmons and him. Hedy Lamarr could be sitting right there bare-assed"—Medwick slapped the table hard—"and it wouldn't make no difference. I never heard him cuss. I never saw him smoke. I never saw him drink. Freddy Fitzsimmons was the same way."

He respected Frankie Frisch, whom he considered a "good man, very fair. He liked to play. He liked to fool around, but when that bell rang, he was all business. He expected you to play baseball. I liked Frank. To me, he was one of the greatest managers in baseball."

"One of the Gashouse Gang told me Leo Durocher was the brains behind that team," I said.

"That wasn't true," Medwick said. "Frankie Frisch was. Leo had knowledge and he went on to become a pretty good manager. Frankie was a great manager. He never gave up. He was a good teacher. He never bothered you. When you made a mistake, he'd take you aside and talk to you. He never showed you up, which was a great thing. And the way I always felt was: When I made a mistake I wanted the manager to tell me, not the other players. A player's got enough to take care of his own position and his own job. And I would *not* allow anybody to tell me," Medwick's voice rose, "that *I* had made a mistake. Frankie Frisch, my manager, would tell me."

In our interviews Joe Medwick tried to follow the old-fashioned rule: If you don't have anything good to say about somebody, don't say anything at all.

"Any playboys on the '34 team?" I asked.

"I don't like to go into that," he said.

"I won't put it on the tape recorder," I said.

"I'm not *even* going to say it," he snapped. "I don't think it's fair. When we're talking about me, fine. But about anybody else's personal life, I don't want to get into it."

One of his favorite Gashouse stories *is* critical of Dizzy Dean.

"We're playing the World Series," he recalled, "and Hank Greenberg is up. Bill DeLancey is giving the sign, and Diz refused to take it. Finally, Frisch called time.

" 'What's the matter?' he asked Diz at the mound. 'You won't take the sign, Diz? What's Greenberg's power? Don't give him anything up high.' Frisch motioned.

"Diz went back to the mound, Frisch went back to second and DeLancey behind the plate. He kept giving the sign and Diz wouldn't take it. So DeLancey says, 'You throw it and I'll catch it.'

"Greenberg hit one up on top the roof in Sportsman's

Park. As he's running around the bases, Diz is right with him. 'I'm going to strike you out three times after this,' he says. And he did it," Medwick said with an annoyed look on his face. "Here in 1934 if we don't win—shit!—I'm in the red, you know, because we only got about $5,400 at that time. But it was a lot of money. Here we're playing our hearts out and he's screwing around out there. Of course, he and Paul, they win all the four games. Diz wins two and Paul wins two."

Before the World Series, the Cardinals were holding a meeting. "Diz gets up," Medwick went on, "and says:

" 'Frank, what are you having a meeting for? I'm going to pitch the first game and if I get in trouble, Paul will help me. Tomorrow Paul will start. If he gets in trouble, I'll help him. We don't need the rest of these bums!'

"And they win the four," Medwick said. "At that time, Diz could throw the ball, you know. He was a great pitcher, no question. But he got a lot of runs, too. For example, he'd get eight or nine runs. Hallahan would get nothing, Jesse Haines would get nothing."

The 1930s, America's dark decade, were bright and shiny for Ducky Medwick. He married the beautiful Isabelle Heutel in 1936. He was named most valuable player in the league in 1937, when he won the Triple Crown, leading the National League in homers, runs batted in, batting averages and in nine other batting departments. He considered the Triple Crown a wedding-anniversary present for his wife. He led the league in runs batted in for three consecutive years ('36, '37 and '38), tying a major-league record. He established the National League season record for most doubles in 1936. From 1932 through 1939, his batting average was a brilliant .337.

He was a celebrity in St. Louis, a hero to the knothole gang but a hard man to get along with. He used to hit line drives back through the pitcher's box in practice, deliberately trying to knock down a young Cardinal employee named Bing Devine. Now general manager of St. Louis, at that time Devine was a very junior executive in the public-relations department. He dreamed of a career as a major-league player.

"One day," Devine recalled, many years later, "I was heading for the field when Medwick grabbed me by the arm."

" 'Well, whadda you know,' Joe said. 'We've got the God-damn college boy for batting practice again today.' "

Devine was on the spot. Directly challenged by Medwick, the young man felt he couldn't back down, yet he knew Muscles could knock him cold. Young Devine might also get fired for brawling with the star.

"I didn't know what to do," he said. Fortunately, center fielder Terry Moore came by and shoved Joe toward the field.

"Come on, Muscles," Moore said. "You're holding up the parade."

The Cardinal center fielder winked at Bing Devine as he passed by. (Thirty years later, the same Bing Devine hired Medwick as his minor-league batting coach.)

By 1940, Medwick's popularity was declining in St. Louis. He argued with fans at Sportsman's Park. They booed him. Then, in June of that year, in one of the biggest trades of that era, Medwick was sent to Brooklyn to play for his old pal, Leo Durocher. It was a deal that nearly ended his career.

On June 19, 1940, the Dodgers faced the St. Louis Cardinals in the second game of a series at Ebbets Field. There was special tension in the air. The world was exploding. The Nazis were cutting deeply into France and charging through Holland and Belgium. The British were retreating to a dark rendezvous at Dunkirk. And in Brooklyn, the Dodgers had just dropped four straight games and the fans were furious. The Cardinals had won the day before, holding their ex-teammate hitless, and knocking Brooklyn out of first place. They also had needled Ducky Joe sharply.

I remember the game to this day. My father and I were huddled around the Philco, listening to Red Barber, and we were ecstatic when Walker, Lavagetto and Vosmik hit safely in the first inning. Bob Bowman, the Cardinal pitcher, was in the middle of a torn-up pea patch and Ducky Medwick was in the catbird seat. But not for long. Bowman's first pitch sailed high and tight and Medwick was hit behind the ear. He fell to the ground as though shot in the head. Thirty-four years later, on that balmy Florida day, I asked him what had happened.

"What did you do, lose the ball?"

"No," he said. "He threw the ball behind me. I couldn't get out of the way."

"He threw the ball *behind* you?"

"That's the way you hit a batter. If they want to hit you, they throw behind you: Your natural reaction is to fall backwards."

"Fall right into it?"

"That's right," Medwick said.

The beaning of old Muscles caused a riot on the field, charges and countercharges off the field, even an investigation by William O'Dwyer, then district attorney in Brooklyn. Bowman was absolved of all charges, but the incident did accelerate the development of the batting helmet.

After the beaning, while he was lying in a hospital bed, Medwick received the kind of telephone call you could only get in Brooklyn. Medwick remembered it this way:

"Do you want his arm?" the guy asked.

"No, it was just one of those things," said Medwick.

Then the guy said, "I'll get Bowman's arm for you and send it to you."

Now Medwick shook his head in wonder. "That was Brooklyn. They were rough then."

Although suffering from a concussion, earaches and blurred vision, Medwick had returned to the lineup in a few days and battled his way through the season. Baseball people felt he was plate-shy after the beaning and that he didn't attack the baseball with his former fury. Whatever the cause, fear or the failure of reflexes, he never again was the great hitter he had been in St. Louis, although he averaged .300 or better for the next three years.

Traded to the Giants in 1943, he remained with them until 1945, when he was sent to the Boston Braves. Like many fading stars, Medwick was bouncing from team to team. In 1946, he was back with the Dodgers for their stretch against the Cardinals, who won the pennant in a playoff. In the spring of 1947, he went to camp with the New York Yankees, and when they released him, he figured his playing days were over. But one more dramatic appearance was called for.

Sam Breadon phoned him at a golf course where Muscles was about to tee off. The Cardinal owner asked him to rejoin the team, which could use his help as a pinch hitter and part-time player. Medwick rushed back to his home, picked up glove and shoes, and headed for Sportsman's Park. Eddie Dyer, who had been his first manager way back in 1930 at Scottsdale, was managing the Cardinals.

"What are you doing here?" he asked.

"I've just joined the club," Medwick said.

The Cards were playing the Pirates a doubleheader, and Medwick watched the first game from the bench. It was a sunny, beautiful day in May. In the fifth inning of the second game, with St. Louis trailing 2–0, the Cardinals got a man on first and Manager Dyer looked down the bench at Medwick: "You're the hitter," he said.

Medwick broke out in a sweat, feeling fear for perhaps the first time in his life. He went to the bat rack, picked up the first bat that came to hand, and walked out of the dugout. He was wearing number 21 and the fans didn't recognize him, for he had always worn 7 in St. Louis. But when the PA announcer said, "Joe Medwick, now batting for Jim Hearn," the entire stadium rose and cheered. Medwick felt

shivers run down his spine. The old left-hander, Fritz Oster-
mueller, was on the mound for Pittsburgh, and he ran the
count two and one on Ducky. The next pitch was high and
outside, but Medwick reached out and lined the ball toward
the fence in right center field. It hit the number 5 in the
354-foot sign, narrowly missing a home run. Medwick
chugged into second with a double that scored the Cardinals'
only run. When he left the field for a pinch runner, the
crowd gave him an ovation. Tears flowed from his eyes as
he ran into the dugout.

Medwick played out the 1947 season, and then appeared
in a few games in 1948 before going to Houston for his
dramatic farewell in that city. He was a playing manager in
the minors for three seasons and retired from baseball in
1952, returning to St. Louis to live with his wife and son
and daughter. He became a businessman and suburbanite.
He was a first-rate golfer, the champion of his country club;
he dabbled in local politics; he sold cars and insurance; he
coached some baseball at St. Louis University. And he cam-
paigned hard and furiously over the years to make baseball's
Hall of Fame. He button-holed sportswriters, wrote letters,
made telephone calls. Much to the annoyance of the writers
who disliked him in his heyday, Medwick blew his horn,
year after year, until in 1968, perhaps weary of the trumpet-
ing, they voted him in. It was an honor he richly deserved,
as he had been telling the world for many years. The Medwick scowl turned into a grin that lit up St. Louis. He even
made a wisecrack which was widely quoted: "It was the
longest slump I ever had," he said in reference to the twenty
years since he left the majors. "I've been oh-for-twenty, but
not oh-for-twenty years."

1968. It was a triumphant year for Ducky Medwick. In
addition to his induction at Cooperstown, N. Y., he appeared
as a TV commentator during the World Series and was the
featured speaker at the annual meeting of the Illinois Associated Press editors. It was time to take a bow and to play

a mellow, gracious role. According to newspaper reports, he basked in the applause and the spotlight. Such recognition should come to all great players while they are alive to enjoy it. It was good and proper that he celebrate, for pain and suffering lay ahead like a Biblical echo from Ecclesiastes: "To every thing there is a season . . . A time to weep and a time to laugh; a time to mourn and a time to dance."

In April 1969, Joe Medwick entered the Deaconess Hospital in St. Louis, where he stayed for eighteen days. It was his first operation on a hip that had been causing pain and cutting down on his activity. He would require a second operation. It took place in October 1973 at Barnes Hospital, St. Louis, and was performed by Dr. Fred C. Reynolds, a distinguished orthopedic surgeon. Medwick got a complete artificial hip.

"Joe's second surgery was a miracle, just a blessing." Mrs. Medwick told me during a telephone interview. "He hadn't played golf for years, from a year or two before his first surgery. Now he plays golf and is doing just beautifully."

If it weren't for this operation, Medwick could have wound up in a wheelchair and from there, when pain intensified, to a bed flat on his back, a vegetable waiting for the end. A great athlete was spared a hellish ordeal. Of course, instead of par golf he would have to settle for a bogey game, which is a level of golf most people never reach on two healthy legs. To shoot 90 playing on an artificial hip is a splendid achievement, one only a great and stubborn athlete could reach. Several times during our Florida talks Medwick spoke with pride of his new golf game. But never once did he mention any suffering involved in his experiences, and he never discussed the pain connected with his beanings. In fact, he never spoke of any physical pain. Were pain and suffering beneath contempt? Unworthy of a star's acknowledgment? An indication of imperfection? Of human vulnerability?

Joe Medwick certainly wasn't a stoic in other respects. He often felt put upon—by players, management, fans and sportswriters. Every example of his resentment bears in on one point: the failure of others to acknowledge his athletic greatness. He never felt he got his due, whether it was money for an interview or a suitcase as a going-away gift.

Joe Medwick died on March 21, 1975, exactly a year after our meeting. The news reached me in Clearwater, at the minor-league base of the Philadelphia Phillies. It was a beautiful sunny day and several of us had been an audience for batting-coach Wally Moses, one of baseball's most delightful talkers.

"Paul Waner used to bring a bottle of beer back to his room," Moses was saying. "He'd uncap it and let it stand all night. Then he'd drink it in the morning. He swore it was a sure cure for a hangover. Ain't that right, Elmer?"

Wally turned to coach Elmer Valo, his friend and occasional straight man. "That's right, Wally." Valo, a husky man with the head of an old lion, had played twenty years in the majors. He had been a good player, but his claim to uniqueness had been that he was the only big-leaguer born in Czechoslovakia.

"Waner was real loose at the plate," Moses continued. "He kept his bat on his shoulder until he was ready to hit."

"Drunk or sober," Valo chipped in.

"He had this saying," Moses went on, not paying any attention to his pal Elmer. "Waner'd look at the pitcher and say: 'You show me your ass and I'll show you mine.'"

Moses fell into his familiar sit-down batting stance, demonstrating how "Big Poison" used to turn his right hip when the pitcher went into his motion. Just then a long black car drove up and a large man with a leathery tan stepped out.

"You-all hear what happened to Joe Medwick?"

There was total silence around the batting cage.

"He died this morning. Heart attack." Without another word, the man climbed back into his car and drove off.

It had been a massive attack and the sixty-three-year-old slugger had passed away a few hours after the first chest pains.

My instant thought was: *God, I wish I could have given him that $1,500.* Anyway, he didn't linger and suffer, I thought, standing mute as Wally Moses paid tribute to Ducky's batting ferocity.

"Pitches off his shoe tops, pitches over his head. They all looked good to Joe," Wally said. "He hit nothing but frozen ropes."

Muscles was the finest bad-ball hitter of them all, and the meanest, toughest player on the Gashouse Gang, the team that taught me courage when I was a runt growing up in a tough coal town. I'll always see Ducky Joe in my imagination, strutting to the plate as the crowd roars. The public address system blares, "Number seven, now batting for the Cardinals . . ." He stands at the plate with that big brown bat cocked, his muscular arms glowing and a savage look in his eyes. The pitcher winds up, the ball hurtles in, and then—*crash*—a white streak orbits toward the billboards in right center. Runners dash around the bases and, in a cloud of dust, Muscles slides in.

He jumps to his feet, tipping his cap to the ovation of the fans.

The game is over.

BATTING STATISTICS, 1934 ST. LOUIS CARDINALS

	G	AB	R	H	2B	3B	HR	RBI	BB	SO	SB	BA	SA
Rip Collins	154	600	116	200	40	12	35	128	57	50	2	.333	.615
Pat Crawford	61	70	3	19	2	0	0	16	5	3	0	.271	.300
George Davis	16	33	6	10	3	0	1	4	3	1	1	.303	.485
Spud Davis	107	347	45	104	22	4	9	65	34	27	0	.300	.464
Bill DeLancey	93	253	41	80	18	3	13	40	41	37	1	.316	.565
Leo Durocher	146	500	62	130	26	5	3	70	33	40	2	.260	.350
Frank Frisch	140	550	74	168	30	6	3	75	45	10	11	.305	.398
Chick Fullis	69	199	21	52	9	1	0	26	14	11	4	.261	.317
Francis Healy	15	13	1	4	1	0	0	1	0	2	0	.308	.385
Pepper Martin	110	454	76	131	25	11	5	49	32	41	23	.289	.425
Joe Medwick	149	620	110	198	40	18	18	106	21	83	3	.319	.529
Buster Mills	29	72	7	17	4	1	1	8	4	11	0	.236	.361
Gene Moore	9	18	2	5	1	0	0	1	2	2	0	.278	.333
Ernie Orsatti	105	337	39	101	14	4	0	31	27	31	6	.300	.365
Lew Riggs	2	1	0	0	0	0	0	0	0	1	0	.000	.000
Jack Rothrock	154	647	106	184	35	3	11	72	49	56	10	.284	.399
Burgess Whitehead	100	332	55	92	13	5	1	24	12	19	5	.277	.355
Red Worthington	1	1	0	0	0	0	0	0	0	1	0	.000	.000

PITCHING RECORDS, 1934 ST. LOUIS CARDINALS

	W L	PCT	G	GS	CG	IP	H	BB	SO	SHO	ERA
Tex Carleton	16-11	.593	40	31	16	241	260	52	103	0	4.26
Dizzy Dean	30-7	.811	50	33	24	312	288	75	195	7	2.65
Paul Dean	19-11	.633	39	26	16	233	225	52	150	5	3.44
Burleigh Grimes	2-1	.667	4	0	0	8	5	2	1	0	3.38
Jesse Haines	4-4	.500	37	6	0	90	86	19	17	0	3.50
Bill Hallahan	8-12	.400	32	26	10	163	195	66	70	2	4.25
Clarence Heise	0-0	.000	1	0	0	2	3	0	1	0	4.50
Jim Lindsey	0-1	.000	11	0	0	14	21	3	7	0	6.43
Pepper Martin	0-0	.000	1	0	0	2	1	0	7	0	4.50
Jim Mooney	2-4	.333	32	7	1	82	114	49	27	0	5.49
Flint Rhem	1-0	1.000	5	1	0	16	26	7	6	0	4.50
Bill Walker	12-4	.750	24	19	10	153	160	66	76	1	3.12
Jim Winford	0-2	.000	5	1	0	13	17	6	3	0	7.61
Dazzy Vance	1-1	.500	19	4	1	59	62	14	33	0	3.66

Index

THE GASHOUSE GANG
by Robert E. Hood

There has never been a baseball team quite like the St. Louis Cardinals of 1934. Most of the players were superb athletes, but that is not what gives the Gashouse Gang its special luster. Rather, it is the team's spirit, their attitude toward the game and toward life itself, that fills one with the glow of nostalgia.

In retelling the story of that remarkable year and that madcap team, Robert E. Hood has vividly evoked the ambience, events and characters of a bygone era. This is the team that has so far given six of its members to baseball's Hall of Fame: the incomparable Frankie Frisch, dynamic second baseman and switch hitter; Joseph "Ducky" Medwick, the Muscular Magyar of the outfield; three pitchers—the zany Jay Hanna "Dizzy" Dean; Clarence Arthur "Dazzy" Vance, who won his first major-league game at the age of thirty-one; and Jesse "Pop" Haines, who, in eighteen years with the Cardinals, won 210 games—and one of baseball's true pioneers, the brilliant Branch Rickey, who rejuvenated the sport by launching the farm system and by breaking the color line with the signing of Jackie Robinson.

There were other characters, too: Leo Durocher, shortstop; Paul Dee "Daffy" Dean, Dizzy's pitching brother; infielder John "Pepper" Martin; and President Sam Breadon.